Secret History

Secret History

Writing the Rise of Britain's Intelligence Services

SIMON BALL

McGill-Queen's University Press
Montreal & Kingston • London • Chicago

ISBN 978-0-2280-0081-5 (cloth)
ISBN 978-0-2280-0082-2 (paper)
ISBN 978-0-2280-0220-8 (ePDF)
ISBN 978-0-2280-0221-5 (ePUB)

Legal deposit second quarter 2020
Bibliothèque nationale du Québec

Printed in Canada on acid-free paper that is 100% ancient forest free (100% post-consumer recycled), processed chlorine free

Funded by the Government of Canada | Financé par le gouvernement du Canada | Canada | Canada Council for the Arts | Conseil des arts du Canada

We acknowledge the support of the Canada Council for the Arts.

Nous remercions le Conseil des arts du Canada de son soutien.

Library and Archives Canada Cataloguing in Publication

Title: Secret history : writing the rise of Britain's intelligence services / Simon Ball.
Names: Ball, S. J. (Simon J.), author.
Description: Includes bibliographical references and index.
Identifiers: Canadiana (print) 20190235195 | Canadiana (ebook) 20190235225 | ISBN 9780228000822 (paper) | ISBN 9780228000815 (cloth) | ISBN 9780228002208 (ePDF) | ISBN 9780228002215 (ePUB)
Subjects: LCSH: Intelligence service—Great Britain—History—20th century.
Classification: LCC UB251.G7 B35 2020 | DDC 327.1241—dc23

To Helen

Contents

Figures

Acknowledgements

I would like to thank the institutions and people who have made *Secret History* possible.

The research for this book was carried out under United Kingdom Arts and Humanities Research Council (AHRC) Research Grant AH/J000175/1: *Cultures of Intelligence: Military Intelligence Services in Germany, Great Britain, and the USA (Britain, 1918–1947)*. I would like to thank the AHRC, its reviewers, and its officials for this award. *Secret History* exists as a result of *Cultures of Intelligence*.

My biggest debt is owed to Alan MacLeod, the AHRC *Cultures of Intelligence* Research Fellow at the University of Leeds. Alan's work is bound up into every page of *Secret History*. His intellectual influence can be felt particularly strongly in each passage concerning security or signals intelligence.

The AHRC *Cultures of Intelligence* was formally twinned with Gerda Henkel's Stiftung, *Kulturen der Intelligence: Ein Forschungsprojekt zur Geschichte der militärischen Nachrichtendientse in Deutschland, Grossbritannien und der USA, 1900–1947*.

The origin of the twinned research project was a question that Sönke Neitzel, of the University of Potsdam, and I asked each other years ago: Why were the intelligence cultures of Britain and Germany so different in the era of the two world wars? I would like to thank Sönke for being my comrade-in-arms and intellectual interlocutor throughout the gestation and writing of *Secret History*.

I would also like to thank the other leaders of *Kulturen der Intelligence*, Philipp Gassert, of the University of Mannheim, and Andreas Gestrich, of the German Historical Institute, London, for being such gracious and stimulating collaborators. The German Historical Institute, under Andreas's direction, served as our base of operations. The institute was a formal project partner, supporting the *Cultures of Intelligence* joint conference that crystallized *Secret History*. I am particular grateful to Carole Sterckx for being such a wonderful conference organizer.

Many of the concepts that underpin *Secret History* were developed during the discussion of the research of the *Kulturen der Intelligence* project team. It was a pleasure to work with Bernard Sassmann (Mannheim), Frederik Müllers (Potsdam), and Michael Rupp (Potsdam).

Peter Jackson gave the brilliant keynote address that launched the GHIL *Cultures of Intelligence* joint conference. Peter and I were, by then, also running the AHRC International Network, AH/M008711/1: *The Practice of International History in the Twenty-First Century* (*PIH21*), with the Chief Historian, Foreign and Commonwealth Office, Patrick Salmon. Inevitably, *Cultures of Intelligence* and *PIH21* intertwine in my mind. Patrick and, his deputy Richard Smith, were a support throughout. Peter was a fantastic partner, and brought the full weight of his own research to bear on *Secret History*. Peter has heavily influenced *Secret History*, both through discussion and by generously sharing work under development.

At the University of Leeds, I have been fortunate to work with an outstandingly talented cohort of research students investigating intelligence and related fields. My thanks go to Patrick Kiernan, Matthew Lord, Alex Shaw, Luke Daly-Groves, Ben Holt, and Francesca Morphakis for indulging their supervisor's enthusiasms. I am grateful to the White Rose College of Arts and Humanities (WROCAH), the AHRC doctoral training partnership of the Universities of Leeds, Sheffield, and York for awarding full PhD scholarships to Alex, Luke, Ben, and Francesca. I am equally grateful to the School of History, University of Leeds, for awarding full PhD scholarships to Patrick and Matthew.

The final-year undergraduates at the University of Leeds taking my Special Subject, *Secret Service: The World of British Intelligence*, tolerated my working through of ideas and evidence for *Secret History* in their classroom. I had a good time doing so: I hope they benefited from research-based learning in its purest form.

My colleagues at the University of Leeds have been a constant source of ideas and encouragement. Holger Afflerbach was the provider of much useful insight into the role of Walter Nicolai. Michael Brennan walked me through the intelligence contacts of Eric Ambler. I would like to thank particularly Simon Hall and Will Gould for their support when they were Head of the School of History and its Director of Research, respectively.

The school's willingness to grant me a year's leave from teaching while I myself was its Director of Research has been instrumental in completing *Secret History*.

The Brotherton Library, University of Leeds, purchased an important digital document resource on my behalf, making writing *Secret History* a much more efficient process than it otherwise would have been. The School of History's Staff Research Fund and the research support fund of the Faculty of Arts, Humanities, and Cultures for the benefit of the Professor of International History and Politics enabled the purchase of digitized documents and high-resolution images. Such support ultimately derives from the Quality-Related (QR) Research Funding provided to the University of Leeds by Research England.

I am grateful to the trustees of the Liddell Hart Centre for Military Archives, King's College, London, for permission to quote from the diaries of Major-General F.H.N. Davidson.

I was enormously pleased when Richard Baggaley commissioned *Secret History* for McGill-Queen's University Press. I would like to thank the press's anonymous readers for taking such care and time with my work. Their reasoned and helpful reports have greatly improved this book.

The completion of *Secret History* coincides with the thirtieth anniversary of my first meeting with my wife, Helen. She has been trying to improve me as an historian and a stylist ever since we were students at Cambridge. *Secret History* is our ninth book project together. I don't know how she has put up with it, but *Secret History* is dedicated to her, with all my love.

Secret History

Introduction

Secret History shines an intense light on the secret histories of Britain's intelligence machine. The mid-twentieth-century British state commissioned numerous, interlocking, not-for-public-consumption, internal histories of intelligence, with a variety of goals in mind. Some histories were created to show that intelligence was a vital tool in the defence of national security, and should be well funded. Some were written to remind policymakers of the dangers that can result when intelligence is ignored. Others were designed to ensure that the institutional memory about intelligence was recorded, and would not be lost when people retired or moved to other corners of Whitehall. In short, there was a complex 'politics' behind the production of internal histories that has not been properly understood or appreciated. In a phrase recently applied to intelligence history, 'the very power structure worked as a great recording machine shaping the past in its own image.'[1]

Secret History argues that a critical scrutiny of the various internal 'after action' assessments of intelligence prepared by British officials provide an invaluable and original perspective on the emergence of British 'intelligence culture' in a period stretching from the First World War to the early Cold War. These internal studies also provide a new angle from which to understand the history of the British government machine. They therefore deliver rich insights into the evolution of official administrative culture relating to both internal and external security.

The histories under consideration created a powerful, persistent, self-serving, 'triumphant' story about the role of intelligence in informing military and political decision-making. They consistently emphasized the dangers of neglecting either the state machinery that produced intelligence or the intelligence that it provided. This narrative was both a record of the past and an agenda for the future.

However, the secret history changed in crucial ways over time. By the end of the Second World War, the internal studies had evolved from histories of the role of intelligence in its wider military or political contexts to become histories of Britain's intelligence machinery, written by members of the machine under investigation. The prime audiences for the internal histories written in the wake of the First World War were military and political *consumers* of intelligence. By the middle of the Second World War, that audience had widened to encompass intelligence practitioners. The aim of the studies produced after 1943 became not only to underline the importance of intelligence to policy and to military operations, but also to map the field of intelligence itself.

It is important to avoid teleology. The history constructed reality just as much as it reflected reality. *Secret History* takes care to shed light on the role and perspective of armed-forces intelligence in this historical process, a role that tends to be neglected by those who focus on the now-more-glamorous civilian agencies. It thus strives to avoid the pitfall of writing winners' history for the winners. This is an all too easy pit into which to tumble.

Historians of military intelligence suffer from what they themselves describe as a 'neglect complex'. However, this complex is often exacerbated by attempts to 'filter out' security intelligence, counter-intelligence, deception, and special operations. The historical study of intelligence sometimes hobbles itself with ahistorical definitions used by contemporary practitioners.[2]

Yet these definitions were consciously constructed, as *Secret History* will show, to engineer high and low status for certain intelligence agencies and types of intelligence. There is a relative dearth of good military intelligence history for a reason. During the Second World War, bodies such as the Joint Intelligence Committee in Whitehall or Bletchley Park in Buckinghamshire serviced the armed services. This fact was skilfully obscured by post-1943 histories that looked forward to a time when strategic and political intelligence would be a priority for Britain's intelligence machinery.

Intelligence historians worry that they have neglected their own subject, too often giving in to an insatiable 'desire for discovery' and framing their approach to existing literature, 'by the discussion of absence'.[3] In one sense, however, the history of the history of intelligence has not been a neglected topic. In the opening paragraphs of *The Honourable Schoolboy*, published in 1977, John le Carré's fictional intelligence 'hard men' acknowledge that it was the 'case histories', rather than their personal knowledge of operations, that had real influence on the intelligence machine.

John le Carré had served as an intelligence officer, first in MI5 and then in MI6, during the late 1950s and early 1960s. By all accounts, he was already fascinated by the distinction between the officers who had run intelligence operations in the Second World War and those who had merely read about those operations.[4]

Le Carré's fiction was shaped by his personal observations of the world of British intelligence; but such fiction also influenced the historical scholarship that followed in its wake. The novelist's insight was echoed in the formative years of academic intelligence studies. In 1983, Michael Handel observed that 'most new knowledge will inevitably be based on historical case studies.' The case history has remained central to modern intelligence studies.[5]

The usual application of the 'case history model', however, has been an attempt to do intelligence 'better'.[6] History has had to be 'value added'.[7] In the exhortatory phrase of David Omand – an intelligence mandarin turned academic – 'learning lessons from history is the most important task of security professionals in the early part of the twenty-first century.'[8]

In intelligence studies, the study of the history of intelligence has become entangled with the analysis of the 'failure' to learn the 'lessons of history'.[9] Michael Goodman and Robert Dover's reflection on the issue, *Learning from the Secret Past*, concluded that 'various attempts to extract the wider lessons have been utilized at various points in the past, but their common problem is that they are forgotten as fast as they appear.' Goodman and Dover believed this was 'partly because of the time pressures on intelligence officers – they simply do not have the time to sit back and reflect on these lessons, and partly a problem of selection – how to select someone to conduct the research necessary to construct these historical case studies.'[10] In this view, the history of intelligence history has been the failure either to draw, or remember, valid practical lessons. The failure of historical case studies to help practitioners has become some kind of normative test of their relative importance.[11]

Yet this 'intelligence studies' approach, seeing history as some kind of ancillary activity for the benefit of the currently existing British intelligence services, is not how professional historians should, or do, work. The Anglo-Canadian historian Peter Jackson has recently observed, correctly, that a stress on the 'value added' study of historical investigations risks suggesting that intelligence communities emerged and evolved outside politics, rather than investigating how an historical intelligence culture emerged within a given political system.[12]

Secret History starts with the assumption that the proper task of the historian is to analyse how and why the British intelligence machine was created from the British cultural matrix, and to explain why that matters rather more than the effectiveness, or otherwise, of contemporary spies.[13]

The main purpose of a history of how intelligence history was created is thus part of the broader historical project of understanding the mental furniture of the mid-century British élite, those who oversaw the rise of secret intelligence to the heart of the British state, reflected on that rise, and then used those reflections to buttress further the position of intelligence as a core function of the state.

Intelligence constituted itself as a distinct field, in part, through writing its own history. This history was not the 'official history' of the 1970s and 1980s. The key conclusions had already been written and disseminated by the early 1950s. In writing history, authors delimited the field of intelligence by describing the borders between intelligence and abutting fields, most notably politics and war. The historical record embedded value judgements about what or who could rightfully be called an intelligence agency or an intelligence officer, qualified to decide between effective and ineffective techniques and organization. History was thus a powerful form of 'cultural capital'.[14]

In approaching intelligence history as a form of cultural capital, *Secret History* self-consciously builds on some major works in the broader field of British and international history.

In *In Command of History*, his Wolfson Prize–winning study of Churchill, who was both statesman and historian, David Reynolds laid out an agenda for anyone presuming to write the history of a history.[15] Reynolds argued that a book about histories should take those histories seriously. He also pointed out that historians talking about histories could be a somewhat sterile endeavour. A book about the histories of the twentieth century has to tell one something about the two world wars that shaped the century, as well as addressing the subject of the Cold War, the formative context for nearly all important historical writing in the second half of the twentieth century.[16]

To be worthwhile, a history of histories has to give a 'glimpse' into the mind-set of the writers, explaining not only what they said, but how they constructed their own past, explained their present, and projected their future. James Bond made his debut in 1953, but so too did the phrase 'the past is a foreign country: they do things differently there.'[17] Such an approach excavates the neglected by-ways of how we know what we think we know. What people thought and said was often not what it was later assumed that they had thought or said. A close attention to such realities yields a more sophisticated account of a past culture.

There is inevitably a borderline between detailed investigation, represented by historical writing and discussion, and what became common assumptions. The key elements of culture, in the sense of distinct items of production and consumption, emerged on that borderline. On that border also are the more intangible elements of culture, 'the shadows rather than the substance of the thing'.[18]

The positioning of the borderline is particularly crucial for understanding the history of intelligence. Traditionally, the border has been placed at the point where secret knowledge crossed over into public discourse, as transmitted by the mass media and other forms of popular culture.[19] In Britain, particular attention has been lavished on commercially produced historical 'faction': novels that derived their claim on the public's attention from a knowledge that the author has 'worked in intelligence', or non-fiction from the same breed of author, spiced by fictional incidents.[20]

However, the borderland for intelligence history in twentieth-century Britain was particularly wide. The divide between secret and public knowledge existed, but it was permeable. Practitioners of intelligence needed to keep secrets, in order to pursue their calling, while sharing information, in order to define, refine, and enhance their profession. It then became a case of choosing what to share, with whom, and when.

The public release of old secret histories formed a swell in the second wave of modern British intelligence studies.[21] In the 1990s, the Conservative government of John Major made a commitment to 'open government', including official acknowledgement of the role that the intelligence services had played in British statecraft in the twentieth century. Among the histories that were parlayed into book form, either by the national archives or by commercial publishing houses, were those of William Stephenson's British Security Coordination (BSC), the wartime clearing house for British intelligence activities in the Americas, Jack Curry's history of MI5, William Mackenzie's of SOE, Robin Stephen's account of Camp 020, of which he was commandant, David Garnett's Bloomsbury Group–inflected study of the Political Warfare Executive, and Frank Birch's massive unfinished work on Bletchley Park.[22]

However, these publications rapidly fell victim to Richard Aldrich's influential jibe that 'historians are what they eat'. If intelligence historians gratefully consumed the processed pap of the state, they would have 'no external guarantee that what is presented there is necessarily an analogue of reality.'[23]

A couple of decades later, it is perhaps time to eat the dish with a little more discrimination. In the research for *Secret History*, the official archives were scoured for historical writing, either freestanding or, often, embedded, that gained any degree of traction (or failed to gain traction for interesting reasons). The core of this method has been to read the corpus thus created on its own account. This involves laying to one side some of the heuristics that intelligence historians have traditionally deployed. Such heuristics include the assumption that 'this is known'; the question 'is there anything new'; and the hope of finding new raw materials to support an account of the 'real' history of intelligence operations.

This close reading has nevertheless deployed the outstanding achievements of a generation of intelligence historians, fired by the 'desire for discovery', as some kind of reality check. The secret histories teach us something about intelligence operations, but they are primarily important artefacts of the culture that produced and used them.

The secret histories were a cultural product of mid-twentieth-century Britain. From their inception, there was a continuum of knowledge propagated about such secret histories, ranging from distribution, to the distribution of extracts, to the distribution of the knowledge that a history existed. In the middle of the Second World War, the army officer James Hanbury-Williams and the civil servant Edward Playfair coined the phrase 'appealing to the limited outside public' to capture this phenomenon.[24]

Secret history took on many forms. It was understood to comprise any work that imposed a narrative or analytical structure on the past. Some such histories were free-standing reports, or even books. Just as frequently, however, histories were embedded in other documents, as preamble, context, or illustration. *Secret History* includes multiple examples of all such formats. In this sense, history provided a particular type of framing device, enabling those involved to ask, 'what went on; what should have gone on?'[25]

Secret History also takes seriously the injunction of another Wolfson Prize–winning historian, the late Donald Cameron Watt, to engage with the 'cycle of contemporary history'.

Watt's ideas are particularly germane to the concerns of *Secret History*. In between Rugby and Oriel, Watt did his National Service in the Intelligence Corps, and retained a close interest in intelligence history throughout his academic career. Before he was raised to the Stevenson Chair of International History at the London School of Economics, Watt also worked for a time as an official historian. Seemingly, he was unimpressed by his experience within the Whitehall machine: despite an otherwise legendary productivity, he never produced the official history for which his services had been retained.[26]

Watt characterized the first stage of contemporary history as beginning with 'what British official military historians once called "first narratives." To these are rapidly added overt statements of government policy, analyses produced by government agencies (including research papers), some of which may be frankly apologetic, narratives and research analyses … these writings interact with each other.'

Watt went on to comment on the borderline between historical study and common assumption. In his cynical-but-plausible view, many of the initial studies were subsequently 'plagiarized, overtly or covertly', thus amplifying their influence.

The final stage of contemporary history arrives when a later generation of historians realizes that 'the myths and misrepresentations that were generated by the controversies surrounding the events they study' were 'themselves part of the historical process.' In this final stage of contemporary history, therefore, Watt concluded, 'the contemporary myths, misperceptions, and misunderstandings about events are reincorporated into the study of the political historical process.'[27]

Secret History is a book written in the final stage of the contemporary history of mid-twentieth-century Britain about the opening stage of that history. It shows that the secret historians were as important to the development of British culture as they were 'accurate observers and recorders of fact'.[28]

Secret History takes a particular interest in five 'myths, misperceptions, and misunderstandings' of the mid-twentieth century, some still resonant in the shadowy borderland between official history, authorized history, and popular history.

First, that Britain's intelligence efforts were focused on victory in war. The British occasionally became focused on that challenge, but abandoned it as rapidly as possible.

Second, that military intelligence agencies were, necessarily, less effective than civilian intelligence agencies. They were often worse at writing history – for specific reasons that we shall explore – and they were certainly less acceptable to the political and administrative elites. It is important, however, not to elide effectiveness and influence.

Third, that intelligence services were starved of money. The historical investigations of mid-century were often about money. The conclusions that they drew about finance did not necessarily align with the evidence they collected.

Fourth, that the British intelligence machine of mid-century was particularly paranoid about either Bolshevism or the Soviet Union. There were certainly individual intelligence officers obsessed by communism, as there were politicians, civil servants, military officers, and journalists, and they were often very quotable. However, the official machine as a whole was cold about the threat, often to the point of complacence.

Fifth, and linked to the fourth point, that British intelligence did not understand the penetration of the intelligence services – 'moles' in post–le Carré parlance – or did not investigate them until the late 1940s and early 1950s, when a lot of time and effort was expended on the history of penetration of service.

1

Oh! What a Lovely War

History from the Great War

The history of the history of modern British intelligence began in 1917. However, the post–Great War history of the intelligence services was notably shallow and lacking in detail. Few in power asked any serious questions about military, air, or naval intelligence after the conflict was done. When the post–Second World War secret historians tried to find out about intelligence in the First World War, they struggled to discover anything other than 'bare bones'.[1]

First World War–era politicians and senior civil servants were fascinated by the internal conflicts among the civilian intelligence agencies: MI1C; MI5; Scotland Yard; Indian Political Intelligence; and the Government Code and Cypher School (GC&CS). In 1919, when the First Lord of the Admiralty, Walter Long, pushed for a re-organization of the intelligence state, and the creation of an overall Director of Intelligence, he specifically ruled out detailed discussion of military and naval intelligence on the grounds that 'it is on the civilian side that there is an entire absence of authority to act.'[2]

The Prime Minister's Secret Service Committee, created in response to the agitation of Conservative ministers, such as Long, who held the whip hand over Lloyd George after the December 1918 general election, commissioned 'mini-histories' of eight intelligence services: 'the Secret Service', 'Contre-espionage' [sic], naval intelligence, military intelligence, air intelligence, war trade intelligence, Indian intelligence, and intelligence in Ireland. They had these histories before them when they first met in February 1919. They learnt relatively little from them.[3]

Mansfield Cumming of MI1C offered up the nugget that he had reorganized the Secret Service in November 1917, in order that each section mirrored a consumer department. He argued the case for a single Secret Service, drawing not on the basis of his own history but on the presumed history of the German secret services: German naval, military, and political intelligence had worked independently and lost the war. This argument was greeted with approbation.

Vernon Kell of MI5 limited himself to observations about the growth of MI5 – forty officers in the first year of the war, 140 in the last.

'Blinker' Hall, the Director of Naval Intelligence, revealed that the Royal Navy had not regarded the Secret Service as 'the Secret Service' and had set up its own overseas intelligence operations. The chief of these had been in Spain; he did not elaborate on what his other operations had been.

The India Office vouchsafed that it ran a secret service, with an office in London and operations in the United States and Persia. By way of contrast, the Indian overseas apparatus cost three-quarters of the total expense of MI5.

The Irish Office admitted that its police intelligence network was doing very badly against violent nationalist revolutionaries.

Basil Thomson of Scotland Yard offered by far the most detailed work history. Thomson was the entrepreneur of counter-subversion, whom Long and his Tory allies wished to set up as a domestic intelligence head. Thomson had little interest in talking about the war at all: his area was counter-revolution. He cost one-and-half times MI5.[4] As intended, Thomson wrung the title of Home Office Director of Intelligence out of the committee.[5]

The lack of sustained reflection on intelligence *within* the state helped to create the conditions for a misleading intelligence 'war-books' boom in the 1920s and 1930s. The intelligence war books were written as tales of personal exploits, without an underpinning analysis of either truth or relative significance.[6] Basil Thomson – for all his bombast, a keen observer of the scene – predicted what would happen as early as April 1918. The 'confessions of spies' were inevitable, and would be, inevitably, unsatisfactory. As he wrote in a review of one such title, 'Personal vanity,' a subject of which Thomson knew much, 'and the supposed demand that he compete with the writers of spy fiction seem to make it impossible for him to tell the truth.' Such books were, 'the most unsatisfactory of all documents fiction masquerading as truth.'[7]

In the aftermath of the First World War, classified histories of intelligence were written, but they were dusty and dry, while being confused and unrevealing. There was no appreciable rise in the status of intelligence officers. The official historian of the Great War, Sir James Edmonds, had in fact been an exceptionally influential pre-war, military intelligence officer.[8] However, the Committee of Imperial Defence's monumental history of the First World War, which he oversaw, stressed the importance of military *operations* rather than military intelligence.[9]

In his more personal role as an anonymous reviewer for the *Times Literary Supplement*, Edmonds wrote over four hundred reviews of war books. Only four of those reviews concerned military intelligence, three being hatchet jobs on the work of Colonel Walter Nicolai, the head of the German army's intelligence agency, OHL III.B.[10] Edmonds's output was representative: intelligence was a minor key in the history of the war.[11]

The history of British military intelligence produced by the War Office in 1921 was almost wholly an organizational narrative.[12] In November 1917, the controlling section of the Directorate of Military Intelligence (DMI), MI1, had formed a small unit to write histories for the directorate. Within three months, the unit was transferred out of MI1, because its work was not about the history of intelligence, but rather a compilation of what military intelligence had learned about other countries. In September 1918, Sir William Thwaites became the final wartime Director of Military Intelligence. He assigned one officer on his staff, Major Potts, the task of writing a history of British wartime intelligence. Potts merely solicited reports from each section head and compiled them into a narrative.[13]

His account of secret intelligence was drawn from the report submitted by the head of such intelligence at GHQ France, Colonel Reginald Drake. The British Expeditionary Force in France and Belgium had set up its own secret service in 1914–15 in response to the perceived incapacity of what was sometimes referred to as 'the Secret Service', the civilian organization run by 'C', the 'Chief', Mansfield Cumming.[14]

The history of GHQIb, the secret intelligence service of the British Expeditionary Force in France and Flanders, made it nearly impossible for a reader to understand what had happened, unless that reader had been personally involved.[15] Apart from an interminable account of pigeon usage, the main 'case history' concerned the setting up of a GHQ secret service in

1.1. Sir William Thwaites: the final Director of Military Intelligence appointed during the Great War, Thwaites was also the titular post-war historian of the Directorate of Military Intelligence.

Switzerland and Luxembourg toward the conclusion of the war. In the end, with much study, the reader could have worked out that GHQ secret intelligence boiled down to one main activity: train watching. It believed it had had about six thousand agents.[16]

The reader could gain no insight from the history about why what had happened in military intelligence happened. The only explanation ever offered about causation – and it was offered repeatedly, as if a mantra – was that the volume of work had increased. Only careful reading would reveal the overall goal of these historical efforts: incorporation into a planned post-war *Manual of Military Intelligence*. The history of military intelligence in the First World War was an exercise in very limited and narrow ambition.

In April 1922, Military Intelligence was merged once again with Military Operations. The Military Intelligence sub-directorate would publish two things in the entire inter-war period: *The Manual of Military Intelligence* in 1923 and its revision in 1939. All the interesting findings were placed in a 'secret supplement'. The secret supplement to *The Manual of Military Intelligence* began with a firm statement of what the army learned during the war of '1914–1919'. The most valuable military intelligence had been 'acquired by the studying of the signals communications of armies in the field'. Some 43 per cent of intelligence successes in the First World War were attributable to so-called 'Y' Intelligence.[17]

'Secret Service' in the sense of human intelligence-gathering through agents was, however, important, if it was properly integrated into the military machine. In the words of the *Manual*, Secret Service was 'not a thing apart'. It was 'merely the complement of other intelligence organizations and is never likely to achieve success unless employed in closest conjunction with the latter.' The *Manual* paraphrased the history of GHQIb in mocking the idea that a line on the map could be drawn between military intelligence – operating near the battlefield – and 'C,' operating further back. Indeed, much of the secret supplement was derived directly from the GHQIb history of 1919.[18]

William Thwaites was most definitely interested in the lessons underlying the history he had commissioned. Immediately after the war, Thwaites had intended to merge the Sub-Directorate of Special Intelligence in the DMI with C to create a proper military secret service, a 'Special Intelligence Service'.[19] He had also suggested, as a smaller subsidiary initiative, the merger of the cryptographic intelligence services of the army and the navy.[20]

The timing and direction of Thwaites's thinking was important. His vision of integrated intelligence explains why he had been so supportive of C in the spring of 1919. Thwaites's historians – with actual experience of intelligence during the war – were much less sanguine about C. The history that Thwaites eventually put his name to – essentially completed by the end of 1920, and promulgated in spring 1921 – was much more cautious about the integration of intelligence.

Of course C had powerful patrons on the civil side.[21] Thanks to the repeated interventions of Lord Hardinge, the permanent under-secretary of the Foreign Office, who, in his own mind, was the creator of the civilian 'Secret Service', Thwaites's plan for military intelligence had been stymied.[22] Hardinge argued that 'all things considered [the civilian Secret Service] has survived the war with fair measure of success.' Hardinge offered no sustained evidence for his contention.[23]

In 1919, William Thwaites's smaller initiative to create a single cryptographic agency had gone ahead, to the eventual disadvantage of the army, who lost control of cryptography.[24]

Malcolm Hay, the head of War Office cryptography, felt that Thwaites had sold the pass, and left military intelligence in a rage in the summer of 1919. As a result, the history of military cryptography was almost entirely lost. Hay had commissioned a five-page history of his unit, but there is no evidence that it was ever passed on to a higher authority or informed either the history of Military Intelligence or the *Manual of Military Intelligence*. MI1b, MI1e, and MI1d – the cryptographic bureaux – were thus destined to become 'the worst documented of British intelligence agencies between 1900 and 1945'.

These bureaux had been manned by army subalterns classified unfit for active military service. Their recruits had had low status in the army hierarchy, but that did not mean they had been ineffective. The secret history claimed that, by the end of 1917, they had been deciphering 'all long range wireless messages emanating from Germany'. The bureaux had developed a sophisticated network for sharing their intelligence with GHQ and, subsequently, with the Americans. There is every reason to believe that they were appreciated in their own time: the bureaux merely left little trace.[25]

In 1926, when a new military interception and cryptography station was started, it felt like a new creation, not a re-formation. Military Intelligence Y in the Second World War traced its lineal descent to the 1920s, when the War Office set up a centre in Chatham, not to the First World War bureaux with offices in Cork Street, London.[26]

In one sense Military Intelligence took a full part in the post-war war-books boom, thanks mainly to the celebrity of T.E. Lawrence. *Seven Pillars of Wisdom* was published in different versions in 1922, 1926, and 1927. Lawrence had been an intelligence officer reporting to the Director of Military Intelligence, Cairo. David Hogarth, Lawrence's mentor in the Arab Bureau, took pains to stress Lawrence's role as an intelligence officer: 'when he joined up in 1914 he had no thought of helping Arabs to freedom,' Hogarth wrote when *Revolt in the Desert* was published in 1927. 'That thought only came when … he had been sent out to Cairo to do Intelligence service, and there learned of … our anti-*jihad* overture to the Emir of Mecca. The little sub-lieutenant of Intelligence began to dream of a revolt.'[27]

Yet there was very little written about Military Intelligence *per se*.[28] The brand of political intelligence and special operations practised by Lawrence and his comrades in the Arab Bureau overshadowed General Allenby's skilful use of an integrated military intelligence system to help him win his battles in Palestine.[29]

Closer to home, GHQ Intelligence in France was on the defensive after the war, not least because of the public dissatisfaction with its former head, John Charteris, which was expressed by many politicians and journalists. John Charteris had been sacked as head of GHQ Intelligence in December 1917.[30] The political excoriation of Military Intelligence was, however, as much a proxy attack on the handling of *operations* on the Western Front by Sir Douglas Haig. It was assumed that Haig's opinions shaped the intelligence assessments rather than intelligence shaping Haig's decisions.[31]

The 'frocks vs. brass hats' *topos* hardly allowed for a detailed analysis of intelligence work. Such an analysis would have revealed that Charteris had relied on a system of prisoner-of-war intelligence. However, his conclusions were at odds with both those of the Director of Military Intelligence and the Committee of Imperial Defence. All sides had been involved in sophisticated intelligence analysis, but none could prove their point beyond reasonable doubt.[32]

When Winston Churchill inquired into the matter in 1926, the rights and wrongs of Charteris's analysis were still unclear. James Edmonds assured Churchill that there was 'nothing of any use' in the files of the official war historians. One day the Germans might provide some accurate figures, but their own official historians had just admitted that, 'the intention to present statistically important (influence-free) casualty figures has not been realized as very time-robbing verifications are necessary.'[33] A great deal more attention was therefore paid to the operations of the part of military intelligence that oversaw the detention of about 180 suspected German spies than analysed the role of intelligence in the deaths of nearly two million German servicemen.

There had been a 'service within a service' in the Directorate of Military Intelligence: the Sub-Directorate of Special Intelligence. 'Special Intelligence' was inaugurated as a term in 1915 in place of counter-espionage, 'owing to the latter term having led to misunderstandings' as being solely equated with 'agents' and 'plots'. It was a deliberate attempt to get away from the notion of 'spy-catching'.[34]

The 'secret' civilian MI5 had been nested within Special Intelligence, alongside MI6, MI7, MI8, and MI9. The sole claim made by the Thwaites history about the effectiveness, and wider influence, of military intelligence, appeared in the chapter on MI8, the part of the Sub-Directorate of Special Intelligence concerned with the interception of cable traffic.

According to the history, MI8 swung into action in August 1914 to intercept all the cable traffic from neutral countries bordering the Central Powers. The bulk and accuracy of the intelligence thus obtained had underpinned not only the naval blockade of Germany but also the creation of an entirely new apparatus in the British state to oversee and enforce that blockade. The interception of cable traffic by MI8 had operated unhindered throughout the war, controversies to do with press censorship being diverted to other agencies. It was only finally undone by unilateral American action against 'censorship' in the summer of 1919. 'Censorship', the history made clear, was a misnomer. The main business of the 'censors' was the interception of communications.[35]

Special Intelligence was not particularly secret. When it was wound up after the war, its former director, Brigadier George Cockerill, by then a Conservative MP, published his farewell address to staff in *The Times*. In wartime, Cockerill claimed, it had been right to be reticent, but as 1919 dawned, celebration was in order. Cockerill told his audience that Britain had had a 'special bureau' operating for five years before the war to 'trace and expose' many of the activities of the German secret service. He thus blithely confirmed the existence of the Secret Service Bureau, which had indeed been created at the instigation of military intelligence in 1909.[36]

Cockerill understood the importance of case histories. He had made effective use of history to demonstrate the importance of 'MO5 duties' – spying and spy-catching – as part of the military intelligence team pushing for the creation of the Secret Service Bureau in 1909.[37]

Cockerill boasted that the greatly enlarged Sub-Directorate of Special Intelligence 'had obtained information of incalculable value to the Naval Intelligence, the Military Intelligence, and the War Trade Intelligence Departments'.[38] He chose his words carefully and accurately. Special Intelligence had not, in the narrow sense, been collecting military intelligence. It had, however, become the predominant partner in military intelligence. By the end of the war, the Directorate of Military Intelligence had a staff of six thousand. Nearly five thousand of those persons were 'censors'. Cockerill, a career military intelligence officer, had demonstrated that the British Army was quite good at harnessing the work of the 'nation in arms', including civilians, volunteers, and conscripts.

In subsequent years, the army would be portrayed as the consumer, rather than the collector, of intelligence. It was not therefore an 'intelligence agency' in any significant sense. Yet MI8 and MI9, the postal censor, had been most definitely part of a major – and very successful – 'intelligence agency', in the sense of being collectors of intelligence sent elsewhere for analysis and use. That elsewhere had been, as Cockerill observed, the War Trade Intelligence Department (WTID), a civilian intelligence analysis centre, created in March 1916 and run for the benefit of the Foreign Office through its wholly owned subsidiary, the Ministry of Blockade.

The Ministry of Blockade produced its own official history in 1920. It confirmed that, by the autumn of 1916, the intelligence provided by MI8 and MI9 and WTID had allowed it to cut the 'enemy's financial lines of communication, and to dis-arrange and hamper … the financial system adopted by the enemy in the circumstances of the war.' A recent study of the blockade has concluded that 'blockade intelligence saw the most sophisticated and wide-ranging intelligence assessment activities ever done to that date, with remarkable performance in technical, collection, analysis and data processing.'[39]

Despite Cockerill's determination to elevate Special Intelligence into a logical new step for 'MO5 work' – a determination that shaped the official history of Military Intelligence and convinced his superior, William Thwaites, to support a 'Special Intelligence Service' – he ultimately failed to displace 'spy-catching' as the perceived main activity for a security organization.

At the same time as Cockerill made his pitch for Special Intelligence, Vernon Kell, the head of MI5, the small 'civilian' security organization for whom Cockerill was the 'paymaster', decided to take politicians – of all ideological stripes – 'into our confidence' and give them a detailed account of what had happened in the war, which was 'not really very secret'.[40]

In saying this, Kell was stating the patently obvious. On 5 August 1914, the then-Home Secretary Reginald McKenna had told the House of Commons that 'within the last twenty-four hours … no fewer than twenty-one spies, or suspected spies, have been arrested … some of them long known to the authorities to be spies.' McKenna had ascribed the arrests to police action, but the second part of his statement left MPs in little doubt that the government had some kind of dedicated counter-intelligence organization – a revelation of which McKenna's audience had heartily approved.

Kell's rival, Basil Thomson, conceded in the press that 'the special section of the War Office charged with counter-espionage had a fairly complete knowledge of what the Germans were doing before the war, and on the outbreak of hostilities nine or ten of the known spies were clapped in prison.'[41]

Kell himself had long been in the habit of increasing the cultural capital of his organization and its activities by inviting senior politicians, including the prime minister, to take guided tours. Such tours had been running since at least the beginning of 1915. He was also keen on publishing a history stressing the pivotal role of MI5. The history was to have been written by Sir William Maxwell, a military intelligence officer seconded to MI5 as a branch head, and disseminated in magazine and newspaper articles over

Maxwell's name. The project was, however, vetoed by the Foreign Office on behalf of C.[42]

This setback did not thwart Kell for long. He commissioned a massive internal history of MI5. He also collaborated with journalists to 'get the story out'. In February 1920, with Kell's co-operation, the journalist Sidney Felstead wrote a series of articles for the right-wing *Morning Post* about MI5's success in rounding up German spies during the war. The next month, the articles were published as a book, *The German Spies at Bay*. Throughout the 1920s, Felstead kept to his beat, which culminated in 1930 in a second volume, *Steinhauer*, named for the German police officer who had run one of the pre-war spying networks.[43]

Kell's self-promotional activities in 1919–20 remain controversial to this day, although there is in truth a fair measure of agreement among historians of MI5 about the general outline of MI5 operations. The needle in the modern dispute is the implication that, in the twenty-first century, MI5 has been paying academic historians to shore up their 'foundation myth'. A suspicion persists that Kell deliberately polluted MI5's own files, before his historians were allowed to see them, to ensure they matched what McKenna had claimed in 1914. In the hard version of this critique, 'the great spy round up of 1914 was complete fabrication by Vernon Kell.' In the softer version, MI5 – then the Special Intelligence Bureau – identified roughly the number of German agents it later claimed, even if the numbers and names did not exactly tally in the record. In neither version was 'spy-taking' a high-intensity business. The twenty-odd suspects, even if guilty, did not have access to any particularly interesting military or naval secrets. They were low-grade ore.[44]

There is a general agreement that Kell's main influence lay in advising politicians about the legal structures of the wartime state. In an inversion, what was then called the Preventive side of MI5's business, later accorded low status, was much more significant than the Detective side, subsequently the glamour boys.[45] An MI5 briefing in June 1918 noted that 'the Preventive Branch deals with *potential* suspects *in the mass*, and the Detective Branch deals with *actual* suspects *as individual cases*.' The writer of the brief went on to comment that the 'connected history of the important cases of actual Detective work during the period from February 1916 has yet to be collected.' On the other hand, the activities of the Preventive branch were already 'fully recorded'.[46]

Security-minded Great War politicians, acculturated to years of 'enemy within' spy scares in the press, did not need MI5's guidance, except on technical matters of legislative drafting and the mechanics of port control. According to the MI5 history, the organization's biggest success had been in helping to erect an administrative security state that allowed them to control tens of thousands of aliens, of whom less than two hundred, half of 1 per cent, were suspected of espionage.[47] MI5's own tally of spy catching in Britain – not for the controversial August 1914 round-up, but for the whole war – added up to twenty-three spies convicted and 157 suspects detained.[48]

The state of the case histories shaped the final form of the secret history. MI5 had started its history as early as 1917, 'the end of the War being in sight.' An historical section had been 'charged with the duty of writing up the history of the Security Intelligence work both before and during the War.'

In May 1919, in the aftermath of the abortive Maxwell history proposal, Kell had put Swynfen Jervis in charge of the history. It juddered to a halt in April 1921. Jervis noted that he ran out of time for the project, and the Detective case histories never recovered from their partial recording. Most effort had been expended on the pre-war and 1914 cases. There was very little from the period after Lloyd George became prime minister at the end of 1916. The Protective and administrative side had been fully covered;[49] the Detective history was never properly completed.[50] When the post–Second World War secret historian of MI5, Jack Curry, read the post–First World War history, he pronounced it 'diffuse'.[51]

The same problem bedevilled MI5's secret history as that which afflicted the other Great War secret histories: it lacked any analysis of the actual war just fought. There was no evidence that MI5 had known much about 'the German Secret Intelligence organisation with which it had to deal.'[52] This was unfortunate, since the stated purpose of compiling the detailed history had been to assimilate that history into training material, 'so that those who study it may learn the methods of the German Secret Service attack, and the methods of the British Counter-Espionage Service defence.'[53]

In truth there had been no such thing as the 'German Secret Service'. The Nachrichtenabteilung of the Admiralstab der Marine had been in charge of intelligence against Britain since 1901. Gustav Steinhauer was a policeman tapped by N in 1911 to add some agent reports to the successful naval-attaché and open-source work they had been carrying out for a decade.[54]

The occupation of Belgium brought the German army back into the picture. It established Kriegsnachrichtenstelle Antwerp in November 1914. It also created Kriegsnachrichtenstelle Wesel, but transferred it to Admiralstab der Marine in early 1915. Much of the early war activity that the British had picked up had been associated with KNS Wesel, in the person of its civilian employee, Hilmar Gustav Johannes Dierks, who operated as Richard Sanderson. The Dutch arrested Dierks in June 1915. At that time, MI5 believed he was head of the Antwerp operation against Britain, and did not contradict that impression in the history.[55]

Like the British, the Germans had relied on interception and cryptography just as much as they had on 'secret agents'. Army field units made the first breaks into British systems in 1915. In February 1916, the army and navy collaborated in the formation of the Beobachtungs-und-Entzifferungs-Hauptstelle, interception and cryptography centre, in Neumünster.[56]

Both Nachrichtenabteilungen had toyed with 'special operations'. MI5 could hardly fail to notice their New York operation. In June 1916 Manhattan was literally shaken by the explosion of the Black Tom Island arsenal complex. American investigators could never definitively work out if the explosion had been sabotage or an accident, although they presumed the former. What was undeniable was that, in December 1915, the American authorities had expelled both the German military attaché, Franz von Papen, and the naval attaché, Karl Boy-Ed, for suborning both espionage and sabotage. The accident-prone von Papen then lost his correspondence with Boy-Ed in Palestine in 1917, and GHQI recovered the documents and passed them on to MI5. They were published in the *English Review*.[57] This *cause célèbre* had played a part in generating the idea that German military and naval intelligence had been incapable of collaborating. Papen and Boy-Ed had run separate and rival networks in New York.[58] In truth, their robust rivalry was atypical. German intelligence organizations had preferred espionage to sabotage.

The issue of sabotage was a sensitive one for the MI5 historians, since the main point of the Preventive Branch was to prevent sabotage. But there had been very little to report. There had been no German conspiracy: merely radical left-wing trade unionists.

There had been a sabotage scare in British munitions factories in 1915, which in turn led to the accusation that MI5 was not up to the job. As a result, the Ministry of Munitions had set up its own counter-sabotage intelligence unit in February 1916, naming it PMS2 in June 1916. When Lloyd George moved from the Ministry of Munitions to Downing Street in December 1916, PMS2 was handed over to Basil Thomson. Its legacy was the discovery of a left-wing plot to assassinate Lloyd George: the plotters had been convicted of conspiracy to murder in spring 1917. The records of PMS2 were transferred to MI5, which destroyed them.[59]

MI5's main source for the 'other side of the hill' was Col. Walter Nicolai, the head of German military intelligence. Colonel Nicolai's book on German counter-subversion, *The German Secret Service*, was published in Germany in the summer of 1920.[60] In parallel to the history, a handbook of the German 'police system', based on Nicolai, was hastily compiled in 1921. In the absence of 'definitive information', the 'writers … were compelled to a conjectural description of the German organisation in certain respects.' In any case, research on the history was over by the time the Nicolai study was written: there is little evidence that it had much influence on MI5's historical understanding of itself. Nicolai's detailed account of German operations against Britain was not published until 1924, long after the history had been assimilated.[61]

Nicolai himself had long since been frozen out of the German army intelligence community. He was pointedly excluded from any role in compiling the history of German army intelligence completed in 1927. Nicolai was more of a far-right political activist, himself relying on published popular accounts of the war. As James Edmonds noted, Nicolai was little more than a clanging brass, making noise in the conspiratorial echo chamber of the early 1920s.[62]

In very general terms, MI5 understood that it had been dealing with only part of the German intelligence apparatus. The arrest of a small number of German naval intelligence officers, had revealed 'a good deal … as to German methods.'

However, other organizations had done more counter-espionage than MI5. In 1915 the postal censors of the Sub-Directorate of Special Intelligence had taken on much of the caseload of what was then MO5. Interception of disguised mail to neutral countries had revealed that German intelligence was running its agent networks from Holland and Scandinavia. In 1916, the Germans realized that these networks had been compromised. They had also realized that the British were zeroing in on the Antwerp naval intelligence centre. Thereafter they had increasingly run anti-British operations from Switzerland: as a result, MI1C had done most of its counter-espionage work from 1916 onwards. It was MI1C and Naval Intelligence that had worked out that there was a 'big and dangerous' German naval intelligence network in New York, reporting to Antwerp.[63]

The history of MI5 was thus diffuse: the only hard facts offered were the number of detentions in the United Kingdom.

Despite its vicissitudes, however, the MI5 secret history did establish some very clear lessons for the future, not least because the fingerprints of Eric Holt-Wilson, Vernon Kell's faithful deputy, were left all over it. The various branch histories in their varying degrees of completion captured two important lessons for MI5 to live by.

First, there must be but 'ONE contre-espionage [sic] organisation'. It had to be MI5, and it needed to wangle a proper title, such as 'Defence Security Intelligence' for itself. This was because the most fearsome enemy of MI5 was the Directorate of Military Intelligence. In spring 1917, when Kell had been off sick with asthma, military intelligence pointed out that the job of the Preventive branch could be done just as well by the army from its own resources; and the Detective branch did not have much to do. Military Intelligence did not need the civilian cuckoo in its nest and could dispense with it, 'a course of action which would have been an irrevocable mistake as it would have brought the counter-espionage service entirely within the orbit of the War Office and would have severed its connection permanently with the Admiralty and other Government departments.' 'It is almost certain,' the history concluded, 'that if another war occurs similar attempts by other branches will be made and it is useful to be forearmed to this effect.'[64]

Second, and somewhat uncomfortably, C had done the real Detective work. From 1916 until the end of the war, nearly all espionage had been 'detected on information received from the Intelligence Service abroad, and the work of this Department grew to be of the greatest importance to the G [Detective] Branch of MI5.'[65]

This much was apparent to others. When Basil Thomson pitched to become Director of Intelligence in early 1919, he boasted that he ran agent networks overseas. There was no other sensible way of doing counter-intelligence work.

Seemingly secure in his new title of Director of Intelligence, Thomson had immediately moved to expand his intelligence work overseas. This manoeuvre, however, precipitated his own downfall. From the spring of 1921 onwards, senior civil servants were plotting to rein Thomson in. He was accused of acting *ultra vires* and forced to resign from government service in October 1921. Kell took the more prudent course of not challenging C. He did have an overseas intelligence arm, but chose not to push its claims too hard.[66] His caution proved to be a good survival tactic, but it did rest on an explicit understanding that survival equalled ineffectiveness. That dilemma was to haunt MI5 until it was officially empowered to spy overseas after the Second World War.[67]

In the 1920s, chatter about counter-intelligence overseas was hard to avoid. In March 1916, Special Intelligence had gone global, notably from the base in Egypt, where the Eastern Mediterranean Special Intelligence Bureau (EMSIB) had been formed. The EMSIB had attracted a particularly loquacious bunch of officers. They published books; they reviewed each other's books.[68] Notoriously, a modicum of control over the EMSIB community was achieved only in 1933 through a joint MI5 and C initiative to prosecute Compton Mackenzie, the wartime head of EMSIB in Athens.

Mackenzie's unique vulnerability was that he had been using EMSIB as a cover for C. 'His most damaging indiscretion' was to reveal that the official designation of the Secret Intelligence Service was MI1C.[69] He had, in the eyes of SIS, invited 'the searchlight of foreign attention on a system of intelligence, of which our present system is after all the lineal descendant and inheritor of many family traits.'[70] Mackenzie started publishing his story in 1929, but the EMSIB 'Club Med' had been at it since 1920.[71] They made little secret of how many intelligence agencies had been active in the Mediterranean, including 'the local representatives of that mysterious organization which was known by a group of letters allotted by the War Office and was commanded by a naval officer.'[72]

'Club Med' was highly politically motivated, usually denouncing the iniquities of British diplomacy and its local associates. The British taste for petty dictators was the 'chapter of the history of the War the least creditable to the Allies and richest in uncomfortable and possibly awkward precedents in International Law.'[73]

1.2. Our Man in Athens: Compton Mackenzie. Mackenzie is pictured in 1916 when he was C's man in Athens and head of EMSIB in the Greek capital. In 1933 he was convicted under the Official Secrets Act for publishing a book about what he had done in 1916.

Many members of EMSIB had served as naval officers: Compton Mackenzie himself had been commissioned into the Royal Marines. The Royal Navy was much feistier about intelligence than any other service. Their feistiness was, however, ambivalent. What the Royal Navy wanted to talk about in terms of the Naval Intelligence Division (NID) was not what ended up being talked about.

The Director of Naval Intelligence wanted to boast about world empire. Beginning in 1893 he had progressively divided up the world into sectors, with the system maturing in 1908. Naval intelligence officers had fanned out into each sector. They created Naval Intelligence Centres wherever they went. The naval intelligence officers also created a network of so-called 'Reporting Officers', 'untrained and unpaid as such' – in the parlance of Secret Service 'agents'. As Blinker Hall told the Secret Service Committee in February 1919, some of these initiatives had evolved into a true naval 'secret service'. The mission of the NID had been to 'collect, collate, disseminate'.[74]

In the main, however, 'reporting officers' had been friendly consular officials and employees of British-aligned private and public organizations. Wartime development of wireless communications and faster ships made this system even more pertinent in 1922 than it had been in 1914. The 'whole world' had truly been divided into 'areas for intelligence'.[75]

Sadly for naval intelligence, an expensive global-intelligence system was not what the political moment called for. Instead right-wing press magnates and coalition politicians campaigned against 'waste'. Lloyd George appointed the Geddes Committee of cost-cutting zealots in August 1921.[76] Imperial intelligence got caught in a lesser backdraft of the Geddes Committee, the Mond Committee, led by the industrialist Sir Alfred Mond with a view to rationalizing and streamlining 'backroom' services in the armed forces.[77]

Faced by Mond's challenge, the NID produced two short histories of itself.[78] On mature reflection, they decided not to share the internal history of NID – which described the running of the intelligence war from within the Admiralty – but promulgated the second history of global intelligence operations 'outside the Admiralty'. The history was designed to demonstrate 'the indisputable axiom that the smaller the naval forces of the Empire the greater must be the efficiency of the Intelligence organisation.' The result might be described as a score draw: Mond concluded that there was little point in trying to merge intelligence services, but was unconvinced by the grandiose ambitions of global naval intelligence.[79]

In any case, the Director of Naval Intelligence had already been overtaken by the efforts of others. In contrast to James Edmonds, the Committee of Imperial Defence's military historian, the CID's naval historian, Sir Julian Corbett, was a very fast worker.[80] Unlike the secret historians, Corbett was a professional writer, employed throughout the war as an historian and a propagandist. The first volume of the official history of naval *operations* was published in April 1920. It covered the outbreak of the war and the battles of 1914. Corbett had written two more volumes by the time of his death in 1923.[81]

Corbett thought of himself as an historian of naval strategy, but his naval readership was primed to argue about tactics. Corbett's work could not have been anything other than controversial. The naval historical debate of the 1920s was set up to be a series of controversies about the handling of the fleet in key battles. Since intelligence was a potent card in each of these controversies, it was rapidly thrust into the limelight. Personal reputations were at stake – most notably those of Winston Churchill, Lord Fisher, Lord Jellicoe, and Lord Beatty. The navalists were determined to thrash out their battles in public, and intelligence was particularly important to the stories of the German attack on British coastal towns in 1914, the battle of the Dogger Bank in January 1915, and the battle of Jutland in May 1916.

The would-be heroes of the naval war were unwilling to allow petty considerations of either secrecy or historical judgement get in their way. Indeed, when Corbett died with the work still in proof, Churchill and Beatty, by then First Sea Lord, agreed to insert a foreword that disowned both his factual accuracy and his opinions.[82] The naval war was fought with 'rumours which have passed from lip to lip'.[83]

The trick was in navigating both revelation and concealment. In the years before the First World War, the Naval Intelligence Division had suspected that the interception of wireless traffic might play some role in modern naval operations. They struggled, however, to define what that role might be. As a result, although the techniques of interception were well known to naval signallers, decoding and decryption tended to be the preserve of a vanishingly small number of intelligence officers.

In 1919, Admiral Henry Oliver provided a terse formulation of the situation. 'I was Director of the Intelligence Division at the outbreak of the war,' Oliver wrote, 'and I realised that there was no sufficient means of dealing with the work subsequently carried out successfully by the organisation known as Room 40. Before the war the War Office had a small section for the purpose, but not the Admiralty.'[84]

Many of the protagonists in the naval historical war were well informed about Oliver's initiative, both from personal experience and from subsequent accumulation of evidence. In 1919, Lord Jellicoe, the former commander-in-chief of the Grand Fleet, rushed into print with a memoir. He stated that improvements in British communications intelligence had 'led to our being able to obtain more reliable knowledge of the movements of enemy vessels. The result was that it had become unnecessary towards the end of 1914 to keep the Fleet so constantly at sea in anticipation of enemy movements.'[85]

In August 1914, Oliver had asked the head of naval education and amateur cryptographer, Alfred Ewing, to 'have a go' at ciphered German wireless traffic. Ewing initially paired up with Military Intelligence's small band of cryptographers, who were in turn being taught how to work by the French. In October 1914, however, the Imperial Russian Navy sent over two codebooks that they had recovered from a German warship in the Baltic. At the beginning of November 1914, Ewing became head of his own bureau in the Admiralty, known as 40 Old Building, 40 OB, or Room 40.

It was a tricky business. Ewing was most aware of his own status, and had good relations with the First Sea Lord, Jackie Fisher. He refused to join the Intelligence Division, of which Blinker Hall was in charge, having succeeded Henry Oliver in October 1914. Instead he insisted on having a separate cryptographic bureau answering directly to Oliver as chief of the Admiralty War Staff.

The First Lord of the Admiralty, Winston Churchill, signed off on these arrangements.[86] Churchill kept much of the intelligence he received from Oliver, recovered more of it after the war – 134 items in all – and used it in his own autobiographical history of the war, *The World Crisis*, published in 1923.[87]

Churchill had a powerful-but-tenuous political position to defend. In 1923 he was transitioning from Liberal to Conservative, a manoeuvre that

1.3. Sir Alfred Ewing. Ewing is pictured in 1915 when he was head of Room 40, the Admiralty's cryptography bureau. He gave a public account of his work in Edinburgh in 1927.

would elevate him from his secondary, but well-informed, positions in the Lloyd George Coalition – Munitions, Colonies, War, Air – back to the political heights as Chancellor of the Exchequer. Churchill's particular historical burden was Gallipoli. But intelligence also played a significant role in Churchill's larger defence of his handling of the Admiralty.

In *The World Crisis*, Churchill was the man of insight, constantly being let down by dunderheaded operational commanders. In his first volume, he wrote extensively about the what-might-have-been of the German attack on British coastal towns in November 1914 and the first engagement between the battle fleets, the battle of the Dogger Bank, in January 1915.

On 14 December 1914, Room 40, operational for a fortnight, had decrypted the signals of Admiral Hipper's German battlecruisers as they had set out from The Jade – the bay of their base at Wilhelmshaven – to shell Scarborough and Hartlepool. Three British squadrons had been deployed in good time to trap and destroy Hipper, but had nonetheless failed in their mission.

On 23 January 1915, Room 40 had again decrypted similar signals. The British battlecruisers under Admiral Beatty once more deployed, but once again failed to engage properly. The anger in the Admiralty was white hot. Corbett wrote in 1920, that 'in all the war there is perhaps no action which gives deeper cause for reflection on the conduct of operations at sea.'

Churchill wished to make clear that the Admiralty had been brilliant under his control, the Fleet less so. He wrote that the Admiralty had been able to predict German naval movements because of the 'special study we had made of German wireless'. The 'one comfort' flowing from operational failures was that 'the indications upon which we had acted were confirmed by events. The sources of information upon which we relied were evidently trustworthy.'[88]

The operational commanders were justifiably irked by claims of Admiralty omniscience. They had had to fight for access to intelligence. They had operated under clear instructions that the source of their intelligence was to be protected by all costs. Their overall strategic directive had been to avoid loss of the Grand Fleet. This was more important than sinking the German High Sea Fleet. The overwhelming sense of wounded *amour propre* created a post-war environment in which intelligence was freely discussed, not only in public, but even more so in mess rooms and naval colleges.

Winston Churchill could hardly be blamed for the most combustible battle of naval egos – over apportioning blame for failures at the battle of Jutland in May 1916 – since he had been sacked long before it occurred. Churchill merely poured fuel on the fire. Once again, the Grand Fleet had been teed-up by Room 40, but had proved underwhelming as an operational force.

Partisans deployed disclosures about intelligence at two points in the battle for the battle of Jutland: first, regarding the intelligence about when the High Sea Fleet had left The Jade; and, second, the communication of intelligence that should have allowed Admiral Jellicoe to intercept Admiral Scheer on Horn Reef as he fled back to port after the battle.

Room 40 had detected that the High Sea Fleet was preparing to put to sea. It had warned Oliver, who had warned Jellicoe, who had sailed in full force in excellent time. However, Room 40 had been unable to gauge Admiral Scheer's timetable with pinpoint accuracy. They had guessed he was still in The Jade, whereas the Fleet had left some hours earlier. As a result, Jellicoe had not pushed on to intercept at the highest speed.

Instead, Admiral Beatty's battlecruiser squadron suffered tactical surprise when it encountered the German fleet. In the engagement that followed, Scheer realized that he faced the full British fleet. His only hope was to get back under the lee of the German coast. There had been excellent intelligence in the Admiralty as to his intentions, but it had not passed to Jellicoe in sufficiently precise form to enable him to intercept Scheer, who made his escape.

So intense and closely wrought were the battles over the battle in the 1920s that the layman could be forgiven for despairing.[89] In reviewing Corbett's official, but disclaimed, history of Jutland, the *Daily Telegraph* gave up halfway through with the cry that 'the story of later events is so complicated that it is hopeless to attempt to summarize the situation.'[90]

The historical situation in the Admiralty in these years was poisonous, with the First Sea Lord, Lord Beatty, ever ready to suppress or criticize anything he saw as a personal slight. Beatty blamed Jellicoe, Jellicoe blamed Beatty, Beatty and Jellicoe blamed Oliver, Oliver blamed Jellicoe and Beatty.

There was an effort to sort out the history of Jutland from the intelligence point of view from within Room 40, then still part of the Admiralty. Frank Birch and William Clarke, two Room 40 civilians, wrote a 'contribution to the history of German naval warfare' in 1920. They too had their axe to grind: they thought Ewing was a buffoon, and Oliver a supercilious dictator. They thought they had been misled by their superiors during the war – 'we … did not know the truth' – and were determined to put the record straight.

Moreover, neither Birch nor Clarke would ever let the record alone. Birch became the official historian of Bletchley Park after the Second World War. Clarke was still worrying away at the history of Jutland in the late 1950s. In part, they were frustrated by the outcome of their early effort. In 1920 the newly formed Government Code & Cypher School (GC&CS), of which Room 40 formed the core, had little interest in wading into the crossfire between the great naval men, not least because all sides were willing to concede that the cryptographers had done a sterling job.[91]

One of the main internal agreements on history in the Admiralty was also, in its own way, sensitive. Both the naval officers in the Intelligence Division and the civilian cryptographers in Room 40 could concur that Alfred Ewing had not been much good at intelligence. Blinker Hall had never accepted that Room 40 should not be part of Naval Intelligence, and continued to answer personally to his predecessor, Henry Oliver. Hall's solution had been to second an able naval intelligence officer, Commander Herbert Hope, to Room 40, to oversee, insofar as he might, its activities. Hope became the *de facto* boss of Room 40.

Hall and Hope had been able finally to winkle out Alfred Ewing in May 1917. Thereafter, Room 40 was controlled by ID25, a regular section of the Intelligence Division. It had reached its highest intensity of decryption at the end of 1917, but 1918 provided slenderer pickings, because the Germans became chary of transmitting important messages by wireless. Indeed, the Germans knew that the British had been decrypting their communications, because they had been decrypting British communications, which the British had known because of their own decryption.[92]

In July 1918, the head of ID25, Captain 'Bubbles' James, had decided he had trained enough 'intelligence officers' that he could discontinue the practice of handing raw decrypts to the War Room. Instead, 'a branch of Room 40's Intelligence Section was set apart to survey and examine all wireless messages as they arrived and to report from time to time as necessary on the development of the situation.'[93]

The Admiralty had thus ended the Great War highly satisfied with a Naval Intelligence Division that had barely existed during that war. The 'old system' had only come to an end in the summer of 1918, in time for the Armistice. No real history of either the old diarchy or the unified Naval Intelligence Division was ever written.[94] Hope wrote up some notes on Jutland. However, it was only in the 1930s, when he was deputy chief of the Naval Staff, that James wrote down some reflections on the Great War. By that time Alfred Ewing had come roaring back into the picture, backed by Arthur Balfour, who had held office as First Lord of the Admiralty between May 1915 and December 1916.[95]

In the 1920s, both Ewing and Balfour had a vested interest in recentring attention on naval cryptography as it had operated during their term in office. They also had a joint interest in stressing the importance of the 'Zimmermann Telegram', an intercepted German foreign office message urging Mexico to wage war on the United States. The greatest achievement of Balfour's foreign-secretaryship, to which he had proceeded from the Admiralty, had been the entry of the United States into the war as Britain's ally in April 1917.[96]

Balfour and Ewing had a pulpit in Edinburgh University – Ewing as principal, Balfour as chancellor – from which they could propound their views. Balfour revealed in Edinburgh in 1925 that the Zimmermann Telegram 'had been discovered through the Intelligence Division of the British Admiralty.'

On 13 December 1927, Ewing rose before an audience of fifteen hundred at the Edinburgh Philosophical Institution to insist that it was not the Intelligence Division but he who had handed Britain victory in the war. He was careful to dismiss any imagined complaints about the discussion of intelligence agencies. Winston Churchill had already highlighted the operational naval intelligence work of Room 40 in 1923: Lord Balfour revealed its strategic diplomatic work in 1925. Ewing was there merely to ensure that credit flowed to those to whom credit was due.

A substantial part of the lecture was devoted to the organization of British intelligence. Room 40 had been a 'big affair'. It had been a 'separate branch of the Admiralty under my direction'. It had been an 'independent branch of the Admiralty, placed definitely in my charge by the order of the Board.'

According to Ewing, Room 40 had done its greatest service before 31 May 1917, when 'I ... handed over the command to Admiral Hall.' The staff had been overwhelmingly civilian: 'peers, professors, and college dons; civil servants from other Government offices; one or two publishers; a parson, lawyers, schoolmasters, officers disabled from war service of a different sort; men of other trades or of none'.

Ewing identified Mr Nigel de Grey as the 'specially able' man who had decrypted the Zimmermann Telegram: he did not mention that Lieutenant-Commander de Grey had been in uniform at the time of his success. Ewing's men had been 'have-a-go' amateurs drawn into 'secret service' by the war, and who had dispersed back into all fields of educated British society at its conclusion.[97]

Ewing prepared a brochure of the lecture, but it was not published because of an objection from the Admiralty.[98] Nevertheless, Ewing did his job well. *The Times* described Ewing's address as the 'first authentic particulars' of the 'most important' British intelligence agency of the war.[99]

No one was shy in boasting about 'naval intelligence' in its broadest sense. These boasts were woven into published accounts – much more gripping than internal reports – by journalistic former naval intelligence personnel – including Hector Bywater, subsequently famous in the United States as 'the man who predicted Pearl Harbor'. Bywater's reminiscences of spying in Germany were published in 1931 and 1932.[100] They were hailed as 'the best serious study of the work of our Secret Service during the war'.[101]

Hugh Hoy's *40 O.B. How the War Was Won: The Story of the Secret Service Department of the Admiralty* was published in 1932. At publication, some reviewers noted its combination of dry factual information about the NID, with outlandish claims to omniscience.[102] Notably, Captain von Rintelen, 'the Dark Invader', a former German naval intelligence officer sent to assist Captain Boy-Ed in 1915, who had been expelled by the Americans and captured by the British, objected to his portrayal and produced his own account from 'the other side of the hill'. In the subsequent libel case, Hoy and his publisher admitted that everything they had said about Rintelen, apart from the fact that he was a German naval intelligence officer, 'was untrue from beginning to end.'[103]

The war-books boom created more heat than light, even for Naval Intelligence. When the Naval Intelligence Division of 1943 tried to understand the Naval Intelligence Division of 1917, they concluded that no one had written it up to any great effect. Most of their information came verbally through the naval intelligence old-boys network.[104] John Godfrey, the wartime Director of Naval Intelligence (DNI), wrote that

> up to 1947, notwithstanding the importance of good intelligence to the country and the Navy, notwithstanding the references made to it by the Press, in government publications, and in books, there was practically nothing published that could tell you anything beyond the merest ABC of nomenclature and practice. There was nothing to tell you what part the DNI should play, what are his problems, and how these problems might be solved in the future.[105]

In a later era, the First World War would be reharnessed to the story of the rise of British intelligence. In the 1930s, however, the history of intelligence appeared to be petering out. This was not because the British government prosecuted Compton Mackenzie, blocked the release of Alfred Ewing's lecture text, or persuaded some intelligence officers to keep their mouths shut.[106] Rather there was a sense of ennui surrounding intelligence. Cyril Falls, the critic who did so much to define the canon of Great War literature, complained in 1930 that 'books on secret service are seldom wholly satisfactory … a diligent student of the matter in the Press will already know most of what they have to relate. Where they have something new to tell they have an unfortunate habit of treading in each other's footsteps and giving us stories such as the arrest of the German spies at the outbreak of the War over and over again.'[107] The former military intelligence officer Orlo Williams called *Ashenden*, Somerset Maugham's fictionalized account of working for GHQI, then C, 'dull'.[108]

Intelligence's notoriety, and its scattering of alumni to both the state and the literati yielded some cultural capital. The source of this capital caused its own problems. The regular British army, navy, and civil service had mobilized intelligence effectively. Yet the impression left on both commentators and participants was that intelligence was a rather amateurish and part-time affair. In 1931, Hector Bywater claimed that all the overseas personnel of the NID were civilians, 'this, no doubt, accounting for its intelligence.'[109] Just as Alfred Ewing had portrayed Room 40 as a tangentially naval operation, his fellow Scot, Harry Pirie-Gordon, the spokesman for EMSIB's 'Club

1.4. Our Man in St Petersburg: Somerset Maugham. Maugham is pictured in 1929, the year after he published *Ashenden*, a fictionalized account of his activities as representative of GHQ Intelligence and then C in 1916 and 1917.

Med', opined that, 'in fine, one may take comfort and hazard the opinion that an upbringing on the Humanities fits a man to deal with the rough and tumble of war ... [better] than some of those who have been hampered by an intensive but up-to-date training on specialized lines.'[110] 'Intelligence Officer' had become a carefully curated designation. In the aftermath of the Great War, it was still unclear whether 'Intelligence' or 'Officer' would be the better part of the equation.

2

Talking about a Revolution
History from the 1920s

The 1920s did not have much of a secret history. This might, at first glance, seem a surprising statement. More was said about intelligence operations in the 1920s than would become normal thereafter. Intelligence was a subject on which politicians would comment, a subject upon which journalists were well informed. In the period between 1918 and 1932, a series of books on intelligence – written by acknowledged intelligence officers – appeared. Although many were evanescent, some caught the imagination of a younger generation. Part of their charm was a barely understated eroticism. Agents fished in a pool of exotic lovers, enriched by the turbulence of revolution: one of their main activities appeared to be the rescue of mistresses.[1]

Yet the 1920s lacked the punctuation of war. War had made a rattling good yarn. However, the lack of underlying formal reflection by the state meant that the intelligence stories became repetitive. The same stories were told so many times, often by the same people, that they lost hold of the imagination. By the end of the decade, there was a significant amount of historical information with which to work, but there was simply no requirement to engage critically with it. The case histories settled into a pattern, without much analytical reflection.[2]

An enduring feature of the decade was a lack of desire for reflection from those given the oversight of the intelligence services. They met frequently and, on occasion, argued bitterly. They remained content that most of the information necessary for decision-making was already in their own heads. An aristocratic Foreign Office official, called upon to brief Lord Curzon, observed that any written brief he might offer was beside the point, since all the knowledge resided in the brain of Lord Hardinge, the permanent under-secretary.[3]

Hardinge had marshalled the working groups of the committee under Lord Haldane that had recommended the creation of a Secret Service Bureau in 1909. The same ministers and officials dealt with intelligence again and again. It was not that they were uninterested in the past, far from it: they merely believed that they already knew all about that past. Therefore, they tended to focus on contemporary history, the details and meaning of recent cases.

The historical investigation of intelligence in the 1920s can be understood in terms of two interweaving processes: first, the production of the contemporary history of the Russian Revolution; and second, the series of internal inquiries into the place of intelligence in the British state.

In the first process, intelligence agents reported to their intelligence agency, their reports were passed on to the Foreign Office or even the War Cabinet, and versions thereof were then published in newspapers, journals, or in the form of books.

This public history of intelligence had several definite characteristics. The focus of the inquiry was revolutionary Russia. The authors' duties might have included military intelligence, but they all ended up working on political intelligence. The agents concerned were mostly associated with MI1C, the civilian secret service. The authors were intelligence representatives of a particular type. Such 'superstar agents' were both representative and unrepresentative.[4]

In January 1918, the 'permanent agent' of MI1C in the United States, Sir William Wiseman, wrote a short account of the work of his 'chief agent' in Russia, the novelist and playwright W. Somerset Maugham (S).[5] Both Wiseman and the Foreign Office realized this account must be regarded as 'of only historical interest now', because it summed up Maugham's work before the Bolshevik Revolution.[6] Maugham himself believed that the time for secret operations had already passed. Only a military uprising could stop Bolshevism. Maugham would turn his experiences into *Ashenden* in 1928.[7]

On 7 November 1918, Jock Bruce Lockhart sent an account of his work in Russia to the War Cabinet. Bruce Lockhart was a discredited former consular official, appointed to serve as the War Cabinet's interlocutor with the Bolsheviks in January 1918. In September 1918, the Bolsheviks had accused Bruce Lockhart of being a British intelligence agent and imprisoned him.

Lockhart was the odd man out in the secret history, since he was not a member of any intelligence agency, merely accused of being so, and of co-ordinating 'plots' in Russia, which, to an extent, he had. Bruce Lockhart later played with this ambiguity when he published the last significant contribution to the secret history of the Russian imbroglio, *Memoirs of a British Agent*, in the autumn of 1932.[8]

A few days after Lockhart reported to the cabinet, Captain George Hill, who had escaped Russia as part of a deal that freed Lockhart, provided a more detailed report on the underpinning intelligence operations that had landed Lockhart in the Lubianka. At the time of the report, Hill was serving three intelligence masters: the Russian section of the DMI, known as MIR; the GSO1 (Intelligence) of the North Russian Expeditionary Force; and MI1C. As much as anything, the report was a history of Hill's journey out of military intelligence and into MI1C, which he completed officially upon his return to London. Hill's report was circulated to the political departments of the Foreign Office.[9] Hill published his own account of his operations a few months before Lockhart in 1932.[10]

In February 1919, the journalist Arthur Ransome re-entered Russia as a MI1C agent to re-establish relations with the Bolsheviks. He had been sleeping with Trotsky's secretary, and thus knew the Bolshevik milieu, intimately. Ransome had previously provided the maps for Bruce Lockhart's November 1918 report to the War Cabinet and had shared lodgings with Hill in Moscow. Ransome continued to report as a journalist during his posting in Russia. He delivered his official intelligence report, the 'State of Russia', on 2 April 1919. In June 1919 he published his findings as an 'instant history': *Six Weeks in Russia*.[11]

In September 1919, Paul Dukes, a former Foreign Office employee, recruited by MI1C because of his language skills, escaped from Russia. Dukes had entered the country in 1918 as a MI1C undercover agent, after other intelligence officers such as Hill had been expelled. In the first part of his mission to Russia, Dukes had been able to report regularly, indeed had travelled out to Finland to do so. Latterly, he had been a hunted man. He was greeted in London with both relief and a degree of hero worship. Dukes briefed Lord Curzon, the Foreign Secretary, and Winston Churchill, the Secretary of State for War, in person.

In early October 1919, the Political Intelligence Department (PID) of the Foreign Office provided the War Cabinet with a synoptic 'report of reports' from Russia. The PID analysis boiled down to a comparison between Ransome's 'State of Russia'/*Six Weeks in Russia* and Dukes's debriefing. It was not a disinterested comparison. The PID set out to destroy the reputation of Ransome and to elevate that of Dukes. It argued that, by virtue of being a MI1C 'secret agent' rather than merely an 'agent', Dukes was the sole source of worthwhile human intelligence from within the Soviet Union.[12]

Two days *before* the PID analysis was sent to the Cabinet Office, Dukes began a twelve-part series in *The Times*, describing the Russia he had seen and offering his analysis of the political situation. *The Times* trailed the most important element of Dukes's reportage as its 'astonishing details of the Extraordinary Commission'. This was important, because it suggested that the most important conflict was not between nations but between intelligence agencies – the 'Extraordinary Commission' being the *Cheka*, the secret police, the official name of which was the All-Russian Extraordinary Commission for Combating Counter-Revolution, Profiteering, and Corruption.

In his articles, Dukes claimed that he had gone to Russia 'simply because I wanted to see what it was like,' with 'very little encouragement [from]… British authorities.'[13] In April 1920, however, he corrected himself with a public statement that 'until September [1919] I was in sole charge of British intelligence in Russia.'[14] In November 1920, he was knighted for his services to His Majesty's Government. In May 1922, having resigned from MI1C, Dukes published a personal history of his mission, *Red Dusk and the Morrow*.

The various circulated and public accounts of the years 1919 to 1922 reflected on the genuine development of intelligence. When the Secret Service Bureau had been established in 1909, it had been as a very small part of British intelligence, its purposes and agents defined in clear categories. The leaders

2.1. Our Man in Bolshevik Russia: Paul Dukes. Dukes is pictured in 1920 when he was both a serving and publicly acknowledged officer of C. Dukes was knighted both for his work in Russia and for writing about that work in the press.

of the bureau were to be retired officers – or officers placed in the Reserve for the purpose. In Britain, 'detectives', retired policemen, would assist the former officers. Overseas, the retired officers would retain the 'permanent agent', the *chef*, the *Mittelsmann*, the 'big man'. The 'big men' would control the spies and informants. The 'big men' did not necessarily have to be British. The defining characteristic of both agents and spies was that they would commit illegal acts.

The exigencies of war had thrown this neat scheme up in the air. There were still multiple intelligence agencies. Their senior inhabitants either were, or wished to be, called 'officers'. The indigenous, now often *émigré*, 'big men' and spies still existed, but had been knocked down the pecking order.

Two new layers had been added to the system: 'permanent agents' were now British, often officers, and were classified as such. Their 'chief' or 'leading' agents were – usually – British civilians, considered qualified in some way, usually by mastery of languages, to act as interpreters of native custom. The latter, representative of a genuine change in intelligence practice, became the self-elected spokesmen of intelligence. As one such, George Hill, remarked, one had to properly understand the typology of spies, traitors, agents, and patriots.[15]

The voices of the 'permanent agents', the 'station chiefs', such as Lieutenant Ernest Boyce of MI1C or Commander Francis Cromie of NID were rarely heard.[16] These characters certainly appeared in the reports circulated around the British government; it was merely that they were portrayed as peripheral to the main action.[17]

Readers of Hill's 1918 account would be aware that multiple British intelligence agencies had been – and were – operating in Russia. They would also be aware that Britain had recruited some flamboyant agents, and that these agents were not freelancers but accredited representatives of the British state. They would have some insight into the fact that the celebrity British leading agent was part of a broader networks of agencies, controlling officers, permanent agents, big men, agents, and spies.[18]

In the second process, a small group, comprised at first mainly of ministers, but later including senior civil servants, met to analyse what the intelligence agencies had done and decide what, if anything, that state was going to do about it. The meetings of this group were, and are, usually characterized under the heading of the Secret Service Committee, but the same groups also met in parallel, under different auspices, to discuss the same issues.[19] The groups were well aware of the accounts of how intelligence operations had evolved, disseminated in the first process of celebrity agent reports.

There were five periods of reflection over the decade. The first Secret Service Committee convened in the early spring of 1919 and continued to meet until May 1919.[20] It was paralleled by a cypher conference to discuss the creation of a signals intelligence agency, the Government Code and Cypher School (GC&CS).[21] Ministers also met to thrash out the intelligence budget.[22]

In March 1921, Lloyd George established a second committee of investigation, led by the permanent secretary to the Treasury, Warren Fisher, in order to sort out the funding of the secret services.[23] At the same time, Lord Curzon demanded that the GC&CS should be handed over to Foreign Office control.[24] Over the summer of 1922, Fisher reported on how the intelligence services worked, having significantly expanded his brief beyond the budget.[25] The GC&CS was transferred from Admiralty to Foreign Office oversight.[26] Ministers, led by Curzon, reconvened themselves as a new Secret Service Committee. In turn the Fisher group re-assembled.[27]

The third period of reflection was prompted by the attempt of the new head of MI1C, Hugh Sinclair, to unify the 'secret services' under his control. This time the Secret Service Committee *was* the Fisher group.[28]

In 1927, the prime minister, Stanley Baldwin, ordered Fisher to have another go at investigating the intelligence services, because he was worried about their impact on British domestic politics.[29]

The Secret Service Committee launched its final inquiry into British intelligence in April 1931. For the first time, they turned over the stones on behalf of a Labour government. They finished their work before that government fell in August 1931, but the implementation of the committee's recommendations took place under the National Government, formed later that month.

To the frustration of some at the time, and many since, the final iteration of the Secret Service Committee seemingly kept very bad records. Since its members, the civil service heads of the Treasury, the Home Office, the Foreign Office, and the secretary to the Cabinet, were quite capable of keeping records if they so chose, it is presumed that they did not wish others to read their final reflections.[30]

If one interweaves the two threads of the secret history together, an overall pattern emerges.

In the first period of reflection, the Lockhart and Hill personal histories were submitted before the Secret Service Committee convened. Arthur Ransome reported for MI1C during the sittings of the 1919 Secret Service Committee. While the committee was in session, George Hill, now working for MI1C, also returned to London from Southern Russia with reports from himself and Sidney Reilly, another MI1C agent who had featured significantly in the Lockhart and Hill histories.[31] William Wiseman's anti-Bolshevik operations in the United States restarted while the committee was writing its report. Soon after the committee concluded its work, Wiseman and his chief subordinates were publicly exposed as secret-service agents by Irish republicans.[32]

By the time the 1921 committee gathered for its second round of reflection, Arthur Ransome had turned his Russian reports into a book. Paul Dukes had written a slew of articles for the press and had publicly identified himself as a senior British intelligence official, while continuing to serve operationally as a MI1C officer. In the summer of 1920, Reilly and Dukes toured east-central Europe recruiting agents for use against Russia.[33]

In August 1920, someone – possibly Sir Basil Thomson, the Home Office director of intelligence – leaked decrypts of Soviet messages to *The Times* to prove that George Lansbury, the editor of the trades-union newspaper the *Daily Herald* was taking a subsidy from the Bolsheviks.[34]

While the Secret Service Committee was in session, Lord Curzon confronted the Soviets with thirty-five documents detailing their hostile actions against Britain. Unfortunately, the documents turned out to be forgeries palmed off on SIS by anti-Bolshevik Russian *émigrés* in Reval and Berlin.[35] Rather unfairly, it was Basil Thomson – who had been doing rather well in the courts and the press – who was blamed for trading in forgeries.[36]

In the third phase of reflection, the Home Secretary gave a public speech to assure the world that 'so far as this country was concerned its secret service was never more efficient than it was to-day, but it was never more necessary than it was today.'[37]

A few days after the Home Secretary's speech, Dukes published *Red Dusk*. Basil Thomson supported Dukes's view of the world in his own memoirs, *Queer People*, published later in 1922. Thomson had been the main butt of the 1921 Secret Service Committee, but still had more credibility in public than in Whitehall. He argued that 'the real government [of Russia] ... is the Tcheka, the Extraordinary Commission, which has changed its name [to OGPU] but not its nature ... when its new name becomes as much hated as its old name, it will change it again.'[38] *Queer People* was well received as 'level' and 'authoritative'.[39]

Little was added to the sum of easily available knowledge in the fourth or fifth periods of reflection. Instead there was a blizzard of public speculation and comment flowing from the publication of the Zinoviev letter of October 1924, yet another forgery palmed off on C from the Baltic, Riga in this case.[40]

Sidney Reilly's posthumous 'memoir' of his work in Russia, the Hill memoirs, and, finally, the Lockhart memoirs were all published after the final Secret Service Committee had completed its work.[41] They were thus a codicil, no longer anchored to the genuine workings of the state. For both practical and perhaps symbolic reasons, the file on Sidney Reilly was closed during the sitting of the 1931 Secret Service Committee.[42]

The 1920s secret history was disjointed. Rarely was a reflection begun before someone took the discussion off on a different track. Threads were lost, and sometimes never picked up. The immediate was usually more compelling than the important. However, it was possible to see discussants, whether in the bowels of the state or in the pages of the press, coming back to the same set of questions.

First, what was intelligence for? Few in the political mainstream doubted that 'intelligence' was a good thing: one should have it. What one might want to do with intelligence was less clear in detail. In broad brushstrokes, there was a negative answer. Intelligence was not about war; it must therefore be about politics.

Second, what kind of people should do intelligence? And most pressingly, how much money should one spend upon these people? This second question of type, status, and character took up the bulk of the time for discussion. Personalities, their backgrounds, and their flaws were a topic of enduring fascination. There was a clear, if even more negative, answer to this second question: intelligence officers should not be policemen.

Third, what do we really know about the enemy, especially the Bolshevik enemy? In many ways this was the defining political debate of the 1920s and, because of that debate, intelligence services were highly visible. Whether they were any better informed than journalists, or the politicians themselves, was less clear. The overall conclusion was that, in the broad, the enemy was understood, but in detail his actions were occluded.

Finally, were the intelligence services effective or ineffective? Reflection on the final point was episodic and inconclusive, not least because the discussion was so often diverted into the question of personalities and loyalties. Politicians, civil servants, and soldiers spent so much time criticizing the police that they rarely moved beyond constabulary deficiencies to consider how the whole system was supposed to work.

By 1918, most intelligence stakeholders had agreed that they needed to discuss the role of intelligence in revolutionary peacetime. Intelligence was a spaghetti of multiple wartime agencies, but there was no consensus about what to do with the spaghetti or how quickly it should be disentangled, given the looming peace conference in Paris.[43]

Military personnel, politicians, and civil servants quickly and easily agreed that they wanted to add another strand: a permanently established cryptology agency.[44]

At the beginning of 1919, discussions between ministers revealed a lack of appetite for dissecting the armed-forces intelligence agencies of the navy and the army, and, in nascent form, of the air force.[45] They did return to the study of these agencies in 1921, but more with a view to cutting costs than effecting change. Neither did the intelligence departments of specific ministries and boards come under sustained review. Some faded away with their hostilities-only parents, others were wound up by their continuing department.[46] The Political Intelligence Department of the Foreign Office, for instance, had but a brief efflorescence between March 1918 and October 1920.[47]

The scope of discussion tended to be narrowed to equate intelligence with secret intelligence. However, as Hugh Sinclair, the DNI who became head of the Secret Intelligence Service (SIS), complained, this still left Britain with five 'Secret Services': SIS, MI5, GC&CS, Indian Political Intelligence (IPI), and Special Branch.[48]

The political purpose of intelligence was clearly established in the early 1920s, the most revealing discussions centring on the new GC&CS. In April 1921, Lord Curzon moved to establish complete control over GC&CS and its activities. The service was, he stated baldly, 'now purely political'. In other words, the service existed to break the cyphers of opposing powers in order that Britain might gain political advantage over them. The GC&CS was thus an old-fashioned 'Black Chamber'. It did not exist to accumulate data on military threats.

The Foreign Office took over GC&CS from the Admiralty in August 1921, on the same day that Hugh Sinclair retired as Director of Naval Intelligence. In a revealing exchange a few days later, the secretary of state for India, Edwin Montagu, commented to Curzon that the cryptographers were whining about how their work would be used, and they should be put firmly in their place. 'Well, well, this is quite characteristic,' Montagu wrote patronizingly: 'rather than jeopardise for a single instant their methods … they are quite prepared … there should be no useful results from their laborious work … They would rather work at their jig-saw puzzle in obscurity than … their labours should be any use at all to their employers.'[49]

Cryptographers were technicians – well-paid technicians – and their views were of little account. They were not intelligence officers. It was the immediate purposes of 'their employers' – Curzon and Montagu – that mattered.

At least some members of armed-forces intelligence were willing to acquiesce – if they had any choice – in this judgement. The 1921 Secret Service Committee had been quite open in rejecting any claims for a secret service with military purposes. 'Great importance is attached by the fighting services to this system of intelligence and the fact that it is still maintained on its present scale is due mainly, if not entirely, to their opposition to the reductions,' it noted. It did not consider such a system desirable or feasible.[50]

In June 1923, Hugh Sinclair was brought back as head of SIS. The next month he was given personal control of GC&CS. Sinclair's impeccable naval background – he was a much more accomplished naval officer than had been his predecessor Mansfield Cumming – did not change the primacy of politics for the two services he now controlled, however. The service origins of GC&CS were quickly erased. When the permanent secretary of the Admiralty decided to review the naval history of GC&CS during the discussions held in the summer of 1923, he found that very little was left in the files.[51]

In 1925, it was left to John Anderson, the permanent under-secretary to the Home Office, to conduct the historical review.[52] Anderson, an increasingly influential member of the Secret Service Committee, had little interest in military intelligence. His Home Office was still smarting from the loss of 'their' own intelligence department, first to Basil Thomson, and subsequently to the Metropolitan Police.[53] The Home Office wrote their own history of intelligence to demonstrate that they had had an intelligence service, older than the military police and johnny-come-lately secret intelligence services, operating in both Britain and abroad.[54]

Anderson certainly believed that the purpose of intelligence was political. He did, however, argue that the committee should not be misled into thinking that what the intelligence services were doing was all that they might be called upon to do. 'There were two separate and distinct aspects of secret service,' Anderson argued, 'that which was concerned with our relations with foreign powers and that which dealt with security at home. The relative importance of these must vary from time to time, but if and when an internal crisis arose, the importance of the latter would be paramount.'[55]

Anderson's conceptualization of intelligence was important. The exiguous records of the 1931 Secret Service Committee reveal that it was Anderson who explicitly argued that Britain needed only two intelligence agencies: MI5 for Britain and the Empire, SIS for foreign countries.[56]

In contrast to the bare-bones reflection on the purposes of intelligence, the argument about money – and, in particular, people – was persistent and almost overwhelming in its detail.

Hugh Sinclair said that everything came down to money.[57] The formal purpose of many of the reviews in the 1920s was to set a value on, and thus a budget for, intelligence. That budget comprised two parts, the first of which was monies allocated to intelligence by government departments, such as the War Office. The second part came under the heading of the so-called 'Secret Vote'. This was a sum of money voted on by parliament, but which did not have to be accounted for, on the understanding that the activities it covered were 'secret'. The 'Secret Vote' had a long tradition, stretching back into the eighteenth century, and its mechanisms were left deliberately vague. The overall amount of the Secret Vote was, however, presented to parliament and reported in the press. This allowed public commentary to run alongside internal debate.[58] Nearly all discussion used the Secret Vote in 1913–14 as a benchmark. A Secret Vote of £50,000 per annum had been 'normal peacetime expenditure'.

However, commentators on intelligence could agree that 'normal peacetime' after the war was not the same a 'normal peacetime' before the war. Vernon Kell of MI5 pointed out that 'there were more nations known to him to be carrying out it [espionage] today than before the war, when, he thought he was right in saying, Germany alone was in the field. The active powers were working more scientifically and knew what better to work for than the old.'[59] The journalist and former intelligence officer Ferdinand Tuohy argued that 'it is next to impossible to survey the map of post-war Europe without discovering fresh causes to account for the general increase of espionage ... *Fascismo*, the Reds, Restoration Movements, Territory that has changed hands, the League of Nations.'[60]

Even those who disliked Kell and deprecated his organization, admitted the likely truth of this analysis. In March 1925, 'Sir Maurice Hankey suggested,' to Hugh Sinclair, 'that it was the growth of communism which had so materially changed our requirements in regard to Secret Service since the war and C agreed.'[61] 'Normal peacetime expenditure' was thus assumed to be an order of magnitude double of that of 1914.[62]

In 1919, the Secret Vote was £200,000. Members of the Secret Service Committee lobbied hard for that figure to be more than doubled.[63] In December 1919 it was doubled to £400,000, albeit on the understanding that this was not 'normal peacetime expenditure'.[64]

Some of the same political figures lobbying for more Secret Vote expenditure – up to £475,000 – were also vociferous champions of a reduction in overall government expenditure. It was in order to reconcile the demands for more spending with the demands for economy that Lloyd George reconvened the Secret Service Committee as a 'Committee to Examine the Secret Service Expenditure'.

Led by Warren Fisher of the Treasury, the new committee wanted to return to 'normal peacetime expenditure': the 1914 level adjusted for inflation. They recognized however, that this would be no easy task.

A great deal of exceptional expenditure was being generated by the revolutionary crisis in Ireland: British intelligence had recently been partially decapitated by IRA assassinations, and there were urgent attempts to rebuild.[65] The army's history, written in 1922, concluded that

> the murders of the 21st November, 1920, temporarily paralysed the special branch [of Dublin District]. Several of its most efficient members were murdered and the majority of others resident in the city were brought into the Castle and Central Hotel for safety. This centralization in the most inconvenient places possible greatly decreased the opportunities for obtaining information and for re-establishing anything in the nature of secret service.[66]

Not cutting expenditure on Ireland was little more than crisis-driven common sense. However, the Fisher Committee did draw a more important conceptual conclusion with regard to military intelligence: the intelligence services were there for politicians to use, not for military purposes. On the other hand, it was plainly undesirable to deprive, 'General Officers commanding British troops in foreign territory of the means of maintaining an adequate intelligence organisation.' The committee thus fixed on a specific category of intelligence that they called Field Intelligence. Field Intelligence included the running of both human secret services and military signal intelligence.

If the real goal were to be a return to 'normal peacetime conditions' as defined by an understanding of 1913–14, the Secret Vote would pay for such activities. In order to get the Secret Vote back to 'normal peacetime expenditure', however, Field Intelligence had to be excluded. It was thus no longer 'secret' or 'special' but a regular activity of the armed forces that they would pay and account for themselves.[67]

In one sense, the senior civil servants were not completely out of tune with military thinking. The writing of the *Manual of Military Intelligence* was already under way. It gave pride of place to Field Intelligence. However, the military saw Field Intelligence as an expansive activity that would subordinate any civilian service in time of conflict. The civil servants regarded Field Intelligence as a useful-but-secondary activity that they hoped would wither away as Britain's end-of-war commitments, in places such as Turkey, came to an end.

This view was by no means the inevitable conclusion to be drawn from the figures they had before them, however. Field Intelligence cost about £90,000, equivalent to the entire planned budget for SIS.[68] To designate one a core intelligence activity and the other a peripheral activity was a definite preference rather than the consequence of actual intelligence work.[69]

The final outcome of these deliberations was that the 'normal peacetime budget' for a now tightly defined set of five civilian intelligence services was set at £180,000 per year, a figure proposed by the Treasury and the Committee on National Expenditure. When he became C, Hugh Sinclair had asked for budget stability, and that was exactly what he was given.[70] Sinclair remained in charge of the Passport Control Office, which he described as a 'possible sixth' secret service. Passport Control was a front organization, and it also yielded handsome fees to be retained by C.[71] The budgetary settlement endured for the rest of the decade.[72]

Handily, not only did the Treasury base the Secret Vote on multiples of the 1914 figure, but it also published the first British price index. It was thus relatively easy to calculate the cost of the intelligence services in historical terms. Cash expenditure on secret service had peaked at a time of high inflation, so the high cash figure of £400,000 was a little misleading. At peak expenditure, the Secret Vote was roughly three-and-a-half times higher than it had been in 1914. In 1929, expenditure was double what it had been in 1914.

The British state delivered exactly what it had set out to achieve in 1919: a tolerable, but much higher, level of expenditure on secret service. Subsequent histories, however, would claim the impoverishment of the intelligence services, and, in comparative terms, their budget was vanishingly small. The entire Secret Vote was worth less than one-tenth of the cost of a Royal Navy cruiser. Army Field Intelligence amounted to 0.1 per cent of the Army Estimates.[73]

However, this was not how matters seemed to those reviewing the intelligence services in the 1920s. When they wrote their assessments, it appeared that more tightly defined secret services were much better funded than their predecessors had been on the very brink of a catastrophic war. Then they had cost one-twentieth of a cruiser. The performance of those predecessors had been rated, rightly or wrongly, as reasonably good. The intelligence services were not preparing for an imminent war; their agreed purpose was solely political. They would only seem lacking in terms of a changed narrative on intelligence created two decades in the future.

In recent years, it has become a cliché to describe British intelligence as 'in the grip of paranoia'.[74] It only appeared this way to the Left in the 1920s. Those reviewing the history of intelligence expenditure were not paranoid: complacent, possibly, but hardly paranoid. They made a 'material change' to the funding of British intelligence that seemed appropriate to changed political circumstances.

British cryptographers tried to track the scale of a comparative opposition. They discovered that in 1920, in the first year of its existence, the Communist Party of Great Britain (CPGB) received approximately £60,000 via the Soviet trade delegation, largely a front organization for intelligence agencies. What they could not know – but merely intuit – was that Soviet intelligence had a huge budget. One modern calculation has put the budget of one of the major Soviet agencies, the Razvedupr of the Red Army, at one million pounds in 1925, dwarfing the Secret Vote by a factor of five.[75]

As to the kind of people doing intelligence and the kind of intelligence they were doing, the disengagement of the armed forces was plain to the 1925 committee.[76] Summoned to give evidence, Alan Hotham, the DNI, responded witheringly that 'it's wasting the Committee's time asking me to come over … to be interrogated.' 'NID,' he further remarked, 'makes use of C and MI5 as one makes use of a watch, i.e. knowing nothing in detail of the works. The latter are no concern of mine, and so long as the two departments give or get what they can for NID I am not mixed up with [them], except in the case of the Government Code and Cypher School, which I presume is not under discussion.'[77]

Although the committee was hardly likely to react kindly to such an attitude, Hotham accurately reflected how secret intelligence seemed to him after its politicization. He was forced to attend the committee, but sat through the session saying nary a word.

Hotham's opposite numbers from the army and the RAF were a little more forthcoming. They thought intelligence was now a curate's egg. On the disengaged level that Hotham had outlined, the Director of Military Operations (DMO) expressed himself reasonably content. The problem came when he needed actual intelligence on a problem that seemed to him pressing; then he 'got little information'. The other problem, added the Director of Air Intelligence, Air Vice-Marshal Steel, was that, although the intelligence services were fine for the political tasks they had been assigned, they were incapable of recruiting anyone with the ability to carry out the tasks that were actually necessary. Air intelligence, Steel argued, was 'so highly technical in nature that only persons of high technical ability and experience had the necessary qualifications for obtaining it. These qualifications had not hitherto been found in anyone with the necessary aptitude for Secret Service work.'[78]

When the committee reassembled in 1927, it was because Steel's contention had proved not necessarily true when applied to secret services in general. Stanley Baldwin reconvened the Secret Service Committee to consider the Stranders Case.

The Stranders Case threw very considerable light on the personnel of intelligence. One press commentator remarked that a pool of intelligence officers were still left over from the war: 'consider the vast pool of highly-trained ex-Intelligence Officers – some 3,000 there were, on both sides, at Armistice time – upon which the Secret Service chieftains may draw. Vivian Stranders, sentenced a few days ago in Paris, was such a former specialist officer turned back on civilian times with an expert "intelligence" mind still functioning within him.'[79]

Vivian Stranders was a well-qualified Territorial Army officer who had gone on to join the Intelligence Corps. He joined the RAF when it was formed in 1918 and specialized in air intelligence. His most notable intelligence work was as a member of the post-war Military Allied Commission of Control and the Reparation Commission. He had worked in Germany, primarily in Hamburg and Kiel, and was discharged in 1921.[80]

Unfortunately, Stranders had become rather too enamoured of the objects of his investigation; he remained in Germany after the end of his service. He had then set up private air intelligence bureaux in London – Brixton – Paris, and Brussels. It was never established for whom Stranders was working, but he was definitely carrying out technical air espionage for a German intelligence organ. Here was an experienced air intelligence officer with graduate qualifications – from University College, London – gathering technical data.[81]

Stranders had worked against both Britain and France. His main victims had been the French, who arrested him in Paris in December 1926. He was convicted of espionage by a French court in March 1927. Baldwin was concerned how the public revelation of Anglo-French collaboration in the pursuit of Stranders would play out politically. This was this 'grave concern' that prompted him to call the Secret Service Committee back into existence.[82]

Although subsequently overlooked, and unusual in being a case discussed by the Secret Service Committee that did not involve the Soviets, the Stranders case was exemplary in placing the focus of inquiry on police intelligence officers. The police had only five intelligence staff paid for from the Secret Vote, as opposed to thirty MI5 officers and thirty-three SIS officers. However, Special Branch had a further 136 officers.[83]

If the first Secret Service Committee had been set up to vault Sir Basil Thomson, assistant commissioner of the Metropolitan Police, into place as the pre-eminent figure in the intelligence firmament, the subsequent committees were devoted to damning his memory.[84] There was something about Basil Thomson that turned people against him.[85] He had managed to fritter away the enormous political capital he had amassed in the spring of 1919 in little under two years.[86] However, the Secret Service Committees were not inevitably anti-police. Thomson's nemesis, Warren Fisher, had gunned for Thomson in person, not the police.[87] His view in 1921 had been that the Metropolitan Police were quite capable of controlling all of Thomson's intelligence empire. He did not see much point in an independent MI5, and suggested that it should be placed under the control of the assistant commissioner of the Met.[88]

Denunciation of the police gained momentum only after Hugh Sinclair became C. In the 1920s, Sinclair was hailed as a 'remarkably efficient chief of the Secret Intelligence Service'.[89] There was thus something suspicious about those who disagreed with him. Sinclair and Thomson's successor as assistant commissioner of the Met, Fido Childs, clashed with Sinclair over who should control secret intelligence work in southern Ireland. Sinclair fuelled the feud with real personal animus.[90] The key factor in destroying the reputation of policemen as intelligence officers, however, was that the Secret Service Committee concluded that they were buffoons.

The problem started at the top. In full view of the Secret Service Committee, the commissioner of the Metropolitan Police, Sir William Horwood, muddled up the three intelligence agencies he had under his control, SS1, SS2, and Special Branch.[91] Horwood plaintively remarked that 'it is not always possible to keep fresh in one's mind the details of things which may have happened some months or even two or three years ago.'[92]

The Secret Service Committee hoped for better luck in talking real cases with Fido Childs. They focused on three: the Zinoviev letter, the O'Leary case, and the Avenno case. It was clear from the committee's line of questioning that their primary concern was how the various secret services articulated across the three domains of 'abroad', the Empire, and Britain.[93] Given that Britain's enemies travelled among the three, this seemed to them a reasonable line of inquiry.

Childs, however, was dismissive of their concerns. The Zinoviev letter had exercised everyone in the political nation, but Childs described it as 'childish'. He did not see why the committee was interested in the O'Leary case: it showed MI5 and Special Branch collaborating on Irish terrorism. The role of MI1C was 'minute'. As for the Avenno case, he had never heard of it.[94]

There was an element of fair comment in Childs's remarks. The Zinoviev letter was indeed a forgery that C had foisted on the government, the Conservative Party, and the press; and MI1C was, arguably, 'childish', in a malevolent way, in its handling of the case. The O'Leary case was obscure. It referred to a Sinn Fein organizer who had used youth clubs in Liverpool as cover organizations for IRA recruiting in Britain.[95] The Avenno case has entirely escaped the attentions of modern historians: we are no wiser than Childs. The important point, however, was that the senior civil servants were singularly unimpressed by Childs's mastery of his brief.[96]

They insisted that both he and C should get their case histories into a proper state and brief them properly. Beyond the Zinoviev letter, the O'Leary case, and the Avenno case, the committee threw two more cases into the mix. The Hais case concerned the leaders of the Czech Red trade unions, MVS, and their role in laundering Bolshevik money for British trade unions.[97] The

Counsell case dealt with a similar subject. John Counsell was a Canadian lawyer, described as 'the chief Canadian communist' involved in setting up front organizations to fund pro-Bolshevik trade unionists.[98]

The case-history meeting lasted for over three hours and ran out of time because of the difficulty of getting clear answers. Notably, the committee finally ended up inviting Captain Miller of SS1 into the room, since Childs appeared incapable of talking to the brief that Miller had prepared for him. It was Miller who took the committee through the case histories.[99]

The committee's third attempt to get to the bottom of the case histories was an interview with Colonel Frank Carter, the deputy assistant commissioner of the Metropolitan Police. Carter too failed to impress. He admitted that SS1 and SS2 were rogue units, of which he had lost control. The latter – supposedly the service devoted to the analysis of the Communist threat – he dismissed as 'two ladies'. Carter tried to jolly the committee with a ritual denunciation of Basil Thomson – a subject on which all could agree. He further attempted to cheer them up with the thought that he had created another 'secret service' within Special Branch.[100] It was at this point that the committee agreed that there was no point in asking the police any more questions: they were idiots.[101]

Instead the committee sent in Russell Scott, the controller of establishments at the Treasury, a long-time hatchet man for both Fisher and Anderson, to conduct a hostile investigation of Scotland Yard.[102] Scott confirmed the suspicions of the committee that Scotland Yard was running three, barely connected, secret services.[103]

The whole political point of the Stranders case was that the articulation between the secret services had visibly and embarrassingly failed. The involvement of Britain in the case had supposedly reached the press because a reporter for the *Evening Standard* heard two policemen talking about Stranders on a public telephone at Trafalgar Square tube station. That, at any rate, was the conclusion of an investigation by the director of public prosecutions, Archibald Bodkin.[104] Naturally, the Secret Service Committee – or indeed anyone else – did not believe a word of that cock-and-bull story. They believed that Special Branch leaked stories to their friends in the press as a matter of course.[105]

Fido Childs had further discredited himself by the time the Secret Service Committee met for the final time. In April 1928, the Labour politician Sir

Leo Money had been arrested in Hyde Park with a prostitute. Money was acquitted in the subsequent court case, and the minority report of a tribunal of inquiry – written by the Labour MP Bertie Lees-Smith – found that the police had shown excessive zeal in pursuing the incident. Childs was blamed and was forced to resign.[106] Again, he might be considered simply unfortunate, since Money was a serial – and subsequently convicted – sex offender.[107] Childs successfully sued the *New Statesman* for libel.[108]

Sir William Horwood retired on the same day as Childs resigned.[109] The only surviving member of the police triumvirate of the 1920s was deputy assistant commissioner Carter. The 1931 committee concluded that Carter remained as ineffective and inefficient an intelligence officer as his former colleagues,[110] and SS1 and SS2 – the agencies paid for by the Secret Vote – were finally removed from the control of the police. It was at this point that Vernon Kell, who had spent the 1920s in search of special titles, latterly billing himself as 'chief of special intelligence', the old wartime term, was able to declare that MI5 was the '*the* Security Service'.[111] Although the papers of the 1931 committee were nugatory, it was clear that the British state finished the 1920s with the firm view that real intelligence could not be police-led intelligence.

The final judgement that the Secret Service Committees were called upon to make was how much intelligence work British intelligence had actually done. In 1918, Jock Bruce Lockhart had framed his report as an apology for the failure of his mission, redeemed by the collection of good political intelligence. The apology was self-serving. He apologized for his failure to keep the Bolsheviks in the war on the Allied side, his failure to overthrow the regime, and for having been embarrassingly caught. He believed himself responsible for none of these failures.

Lockhart had been, nevertheless, serious about good political intelligence. By going to Moscow in person, by being a prisoner of the Cheka, he, his staff, and those purporting to be members of his staff, had amassed 'valuable material and information … concerning a movement that constitutes a menace to the whole civilised world.' Lockhart warned that, despite reports from the ill-informed and politically motivated, Bolshevism was not going to fail any time soon.[112]

Paul Dukes had also made a fetish of reporting from within Russia as a source of authority in political intelligence. He went one step further than Lockhart in claiming that only secret political intelligence was worthwhile. There had been no point in meeting Soviet leaders to gauge their political intentions: only reports on objective conditions, gathered surreptitiously, counted. He explicitly denounced the work of his fellow MI1C operative Arthur Ransome, because he had gone openly to Moscow under journalistic cover. Dukes had further warned against relying on Russian *émigrés*.[113] The Political Intelligence Department's October 1919 analysis of intelligence from Russia for the cabinet had been outspokenly supportive of the Dukes model. All other intelligence was useful merely as confirmatory evidence for on-the-spot reports.[114]

The era of the superstar 'man on the spot' had been brief. In November 1919, GC&CS had made its first significant break into Bolshevik communications. In early 1920, GC&CS broke into the high-grade Bolshevik diplomatic cypher. From that point onwards, the British government had some direct insight into Bolshevik thinking, rather than having to rely on their own expectations or the interpretations offered by their agents and analysts.

In 1922, Sir Eyre Crowe, the permanent under-secretary of the Foreign Office and a member of the 1921 and 1925 Secret Service Committees, had said that 'intercepted telegrams' were 'a much more valuable source of information' than 'Secret Service reports'.[115]

However, agent reports and the decryption of Soviet telegrams could offer only a general warning of the shape and direction of the Bolshevik threat. This, ministers, and certainly the press, could have worked out for themselves. What the political situation required was not good intelligence but forensic proof of Bolshevik guilt.[116]

Sir William Tyrrell, the permanent under-secretary of the Foreign Office, and a member of the Secret Service Committee, said that the task was to catch the Soviets 'in flagrante delicto, which will enable us to clear them out of this country with almost universal consent.'[117]

This was why British governments proved willing repeatedly to reveal the gleanings of their decryption efforts. For this tactic to work, the government of the Soviet Union had to be unmasked as the aggressor, not a particular intelligence agency. There thus seemed little curiosity in the Secret Service Committee about who was actually threatening Britain. The

Secret Vote was set on the basis of general presumptions about how the world had changed since 1914, not as a result of a detailed threat assessment.

The Cheka had been made famous by the initial reports of the superstar agents.[118] The Cheka, however, formed in December 1917 and commanded until 1926 by Felix Dzerzhinsky, evolved. In February 1919, while Dukes and Ransome were in Russia, it spawned military counter-intelligence, known as OO, to run alongside its political counter-revolutionary function. The OO eliminated the non-Bolshevik actors of whom Dukes had had such high hopes. In December 1920, OO, while continuing as military counter-intelligence, formed the basis of the INO, the foreign-intelligence wing of the Cheka.

When the INO was formed, Lenin told Dzerzhinsky that the primary mission of the Cheka was to destroy *émigré* forces outside the Soviet Union. The Cheka's vehicle for this plan was Trest, or the Trust. The Trust was a wholly owned shell organization aimed at convincing *émigrés* and their Western supporters that the oppositional forces in the Soviet Union that had been eliminated at the beginning of 1920 had, in fact, survived.[119]

Finally, and most obviously to the British, the Communist International, the Comintern, had its own clandestine service, the OMS. The Comintern had been formed in March 1919: Paul Dukes was at hand in Petrograd to observe its first meeting. He wrote in 1922 that it stood for 'world revolution forever'.[120]

Vernon Kell told the 1925 Secret Service Committee that, as soon as the Communist Party of Great Britain had been formed in August 1920, Special Branch, MI1c, and MI5 had all recruited informants, either within the CPGB or in Soviet House, the base of operations for the OMS. In fact, the agents were in danger of tripping each other up.[121] However, the insight that decrypts and informants provided on the hostile activities of the Communist Party in Britain could be as much hindrance as help in understanding the threat in detail.[122]

We now know that the INO and the OO, each part of the Cheka, the OMS of the Comintern, and the Fourth Directorate of the Red Army all had a hostile interest in Britain. In the formative years of the Soviet state, all these agencies were mixed up in overseas *rezidentury*. This was illustrated to the world in April 1927, when a Chinese warlord sacked the Soviet embassy in Peking, turning over the *rezidentura* and distributing a massive haul of documents to the winds. Many Fourth Directorate and OMS transcripts made their way into the pages of the *Straits Times* in Singapore. The Fourth Directorate was the agency that paid most attention to Britain. It was interested as much in political infiltration as in espionage, and often used the OMS as a front.[123]

The British state seemed to have little detailed knowledge of Soviet organization. Or, if some of the hard men of British intelligence possessed it, this knowledge did not make its way into reflections on British intelligence. The Secret Service Committee picked up that the Cheka became the GPU in 1922 and the OGPU in 1923: an informant inside Soviet House provided a list identifying specific inhabitants as 'GPU' in 1927.[124]

Certainly, MI1C attempted to understand the Soviet foe, but as Dukes had warned, British agencies found themselves in 'the darkness' outside Russia, attempting to peer within. Some members of the British trade mission sent to Moscow in 1921 were MI1C agents. When the delegation was withdrawn in 1927, the Foreign Office noted that, 'before the break our [secret service] in Russia were extremely reliable, but now they have to send in much less stuff.'[125] Thereafter, SIS was based in a chain of residencies, under the cover of Passport Control Offices, around the Baltic. The PCOs were the 'permanent agents,' but they were now more than ever reliant on their *émigré* 'big men'.[126]

The moment for profitable reflection in Britain on Soviet intelligence came between the end of 1927 and the beginning of 1930. In the autumn of 1927, Josef Stalin carried out his long-prepared coup within the Soviet Union, purging the Bolshevik leaders most associated with noisy Comintern operations: Lev Kamenev, expelled from Britain in 1920, and Georgi Zinoviev of the eponymous 1924 letter.

The backwash from the coup was a dislocation in the Soviet intelligence agencies. The Trust was closed down, throwing some of its agents onto the international jobs market. In June 1927, the *émigré* victims of the Trust launched a series of bomb attacks against OGPU within the Soviet Union, and the *émigrés* received some support from SIS in Finland. Stalin, as ever combining genuine paranoia with savvy tactics, used the attacks as proof of the failure of his rivals. 'The course towards terror taken by London's agents,' he warned Molotov in June 1927, 'changes the situation fundamentally.'[127]

However, the timing was off from a British perspective. The main visible action occurred after the 1927 Secret Service Committee had completed its work. In September 1927, the Bolsheviks named Ernest Boyce, their long-standing enemy, now Passport Control Officer in Helsinki, as the chief agent-runner in Russia. Boyce was finally forced to resign from SIS.[128] A sample of his correspondence with Sidney Reilly was published in Pepita Bombadilla and George Hill's 'Reilly memoirs' in 1931.[129]

In November 1927, Special Branch arrested Wilfrid Macartney and his Fourth Directorate handler in London. Macartney was a member of 'Club Med', having served in EMSIB. This was the case of a former British intelligence officer and a 'gentleman', like Stranders, gone to the bad.[130]

Macartney was a straw in the wind. However, the intelligence history of the 1920s was written through the lens not of the Macartney case but the Ewer case. The Ewer case broke when two senior members of Special Branch were arrested as Soviet agents in April 1929. Their 'big man' was William Ewer, a Cambridge-educated journalist, a founder member of the CPGB, and the foreign editor of the *Daily Herald*. He had also, it became clear, run a very sophisticated intelligence – and notably counter-intelligence – agency under the cover of two private-press bureaux. The Soviets had funded the operation. The recovered diary of one of his employees revealed that, not only had Ewer found informants in Special Branch, the Foreign, India, Colonial, and Post offices, and the Admiralty, gleaning intelligence along the way on all five of the British 'secret services', he had actively targeted those agencies.

His private detectives had kept a watch on 'secret service' offices, followed officers, and logged who they were and with whom they were in touch. They had also run counter-counter-intelligence operations to make sure that Ewer himself was not observed.[131] The 'history of a section of the Russian Intelligence Service operating in this country under the management of William Norman Ewer, 1919–1929' was written up by MI5 to try and understand what had gone on over the decade. They did not get very far. Although it was clear that Ewer had been an important Soviet agent, it remained unclear for whom he had actually been working. In fact, it was the INO.[132]

The 1931 Secret Service Committee was assembled after the trail had gone cold and, in any case, was particularly unreflective. The exact role the Ewer case played in the deliberations of that Secret Service Committee is unclear, because of the terseness of the record: it most certainly did not enhance the reputation of Special Branch. There was no change in the Secret Vote in response to a greater threat. All seemed business as normal.[133]

The highly fragmented history of the 1920s presented the intelligence state as useful but not overly important. The conspiracy theories of the Left – or indeed the Right – had little influence on that history, except inasmuch that the political 'police state' became a very touchy subject. Having said that, the role of intelligence was defined as almost entirely political. It had little role in acquiring military intelligence. Accordingly, the military-intelligence agencies, and military intelligence, faded almost entirely from the discussion.

On the other hand, there was a general assumption that the ideal intelligence officer would be ex-military. There were hesitations: Sidney Reilly, Vivian Stranders, and Wilfrid Macartney had all held commissions, but their unreliability was subsequently held to be a personal, rather an institutional, problem.[134] 'Later, I was to know much more of Reilly than I did at the time,' Lockhart wrote in 1932. 'He was a Jew with … no British blood in his veins.'[135]

Basil Thomson had warned in 1922 that one result of the establishment of a Communist Party in Britain had been 'to augment the little band of intellectual revolutionaries who have always bloomed amongst us modest and unseen.' 'Not a few' of the new Communists were 'ex-officers in the navy and the army'. There were even recruits from 'among the undergraduates at Oxford and Cambridge and in one or two of the public schools'. However, most of the 'intellectuals' had been purged from the party in 1924, including J.T. Walton Newbold, whose plan for infiltrating the universities was acquired by Special Branch in 1922. The post-1924 party could plausibly be seen as one of miners, engineers, and the unemployed. Because the various intelligence services took time to penetrate and investigate that party, they were able to portray the officer-gentleman-traitor as an occasional oddity.[136]

The British state did not have an overheated view of what its intelligence services might achieve. As soon as the post-war period had been declared at an end, with the signature of the last treaty of the Versailles process in

1923, the budget for the secret service was fixed, and then maintained at that fixed level, whatever the visible storms. The Secret Service Committee and the government decided that they were satisfied with the *status quo*.[137]

British intelligence might not be very good. But not too much was expected on the basis of the secret history. In 1932, Bruce Lockhart, by then a journalist working for Lord Beaverbrook, said his experiences had left him 'with a very poor opinion of secret service work. Doubtless, it has its uses and its functions, but political work is not its strong point. The buying of information puts a premium on manufactured news. But even manufactured news is less dangerous than the honest reports of men, who, however brave and however gifted as linguists, are frequently incapable of forming a reliable political judgment.'[138]

3

The Locust Has Eaten
History from the Phoney War

'Secret Services,' wrote Maurice Hankey, concluding his eight-month investigation into the intelligence services in May 1940, 'can only be judged by their results and it is only when the supreme emergency arises that it is possible to say they have proved themselves successful.'[1] Contrary to Hankey's own expectation, the 'supreme emergency' triggered by the German invasion of France and the Low Countries had occurred on the day before he finished his final report.[2]

The history of intelligence written in the early 1940s had its own particular flavour. Defeat lay at the heart of this history. Its overriding historical question was not 'Why was Britain good at intelligence?' but 'How had it become so bad at intelligence?'

The history of the early 1940s was a layer in a palimpsest, overwriting much that had come before, but rapidly being overlaid itself by the histories of 1945. It has thus been easy to lose sight of the fact that the history of these years was different in goal and procedure than the history that came a few years later, even though that later history cannibalized many of the earlier cases. Indeed, because so much effort had gone into the earlier history, the later history concentrated disproportionately on the early years of the war. Victory, although welcome, seemed paradoxically less interesting than the morality of defeat.[3] The historical effort of the early 1940s was, arguably, an ineffective means of making policy. The German foe was universally portrayed as formidable, but the German intelligence services were barely understood. It was, however, a compelling way of telling the morality tale.[4]

Later history bundled the intelligence history into an 'appeasement paradigm'. By 1945 the British intelligence services had laid the German

3.1. Man of Secrets: Maurice Hankey. The former cabinet secretary was author of two reports on the British intelligence services in 1940.

intelligence services entirely bare: in victory, they were seen as feeble. If the will and resources had been available, they and their masters might have been deterred. The history of 1945 also ransacked the history of 1940 to find the origins of later success, in particular, to identify those who had laid in good stores.

However, the use to which the early 1940s history was later put concealed to a degree what that history was primarily for. Cases later dismissed as unimportant loomed much larger at the time. Organizations later held to be 'reforming' were then seen as satisfactory in their own right; organizations that had once flourished were seen, by the end of the war, as minor stepping stones in the evolution of other agencies, of which no one could have been aware in 1940.

Nevertheless, it was undoubtedly the case that some of the early historians were already writing the history of 1945 as early as 1940. As ever, Winston Churchill was fighting and writing. When the Director of Military Intelligence decided to keep a diary of the 'bedlam' of his first five months in office, everyone in adjoining offices was also scribbling away: the Director of Military Operations was keeping a diary; the vice-chief of the Imperial General Staff, himself a former Director of Military Operations and Intelligence, was keeping a diary; the DMI's boss from the end of 1941, the CIGS, Alan Brooke, proved to be the greatest diarist of the Second World War. The permanent under-secretary of state for Foreign Affairs from 1938, Alec Cadogan, the overseer of both the Secret Intelligence Service (SIS) and GC&CS, was keeping a diary. The deputy head of the Security Service's investigations branch, Guy Liddell, was keeping a diary. Most notably of all, the Director of Naval Intelligence, John Godfrey, commissioned a history of Naval Intelligence as early as 1940, predicated on the assumption of victory.

The morality play of intelligence was a contemporary phenomenon. The left-wing 'Guilty Men' critique of appeasement might be dated to July 1940, when 'Cato's' pamphlet with that title was published. The Conservative critics of Chamberlain had, however, homed in on intelligence much earlier. According to this early public version of intelligence history, venal politicians had betrayed British intelligence. In a lacerating attack on how Britain had been caught by surprise by the Italian invasion of Albania in April 1939, Winston Churchill claimed that the Royal Navy had been caught 'lolling about in Italian harbours'.[5]

Churchill went on, however, to exempt the intelligence services from blame for this spectacular failure. 'After 25 years' experience in peace and war,' Churchill said, 'I believe it to be the finest service of its kind in the world.' It was the politician's handling of intelligence that was at fault. Churchill spoke of a 'hidden hand … which intervenes and filters down or withholds intelligence from Ministers.' 'It seems to me,' Churchill concluded,

> that Ministers run the most tremendous risk if they allow the information collection of the Intelligence Department, sent to them I am sure in good time, to be sifted and coloured and reduced in consequence and importance, and if they ever get themselves into a mood of attaching importance only to those pieces of information which accord with their earnest and honourable desire that the peace of the world shall remain unbroken.[6]

The most effective attack on the Chamberlain government at the time of the Munich Crisis in October 1938 made much the same point about counter-intelligence. In the words of the aristocratic politician and soldier Sir Sidney Herbert, the British government was a 'tiny Tammany Hall ring' that misused intelligence officers to discredit its domestic enemies rather than to maintain military security. He could hear the 'little jowls' of these 'locusts' creaking behind ministers. Thanks to Chamberlain and his gang, British counter-intelligence was worthless. Not only was Britain's military weakness plain as a pikestaff to 'Herr Hitler', it was equally visible 'to the children in my village.'[7]

Neither Herbert nor Churchill was an intelligence *ingénue* when they made their remarks. Churchill's history with intelligence was well known, because he had already written about it. In addition, he was receiving highly illegal secret intelligence briefings from the head of the Industrial Intelligence Centre, Desmond Morton.[8] Herbert was speaking on behalf of Anthony Eden, the minister who oversaw SIS and GC&CS until his resignation in February 1938: Herbert himself had been Stanley Baldwin's parliamentary private secretary.

Maurice Hankey was one of the 'locusts' to whom Herbert referred. He had moved seamlessly from the secretaryship of the cabinet into Neville

Chamberlain's cabinet as minister 'without portfolio'. From September 1939, one of his tasks was overseeing SIS operations that required additional Treasury funding. His more historical inquiries into secret intelligence began in the same month. History and operations thus ran side by side.[9]

Chamberlain told Hankey to carry out a full inquiry into the secret intelligence services in December 1939. Hankey's investigating officers were Gladwyn Jebb, Cadogan's principal private secretary, through whom all SIS affairs were funnelled in the Foreign Office, and Herbert Brittain, the official who dealt with SIS in the Treasury. They all worked in 'close collaboration' with Stewart Menzies, 'the recently appointed "Chief of the Secret Service"'.[10]

Neville Chamberlain's fixer, Sir Horace Wilson, warned that they all needed to take their task seriously, since so many individuals around Whitehall were smarting from the Foreign Office grandfathering in of Menzies as C in November 1939.[11] As a result of that exercise, there had been no proper stock-taking at the end of the long tenure of Sir Hugh Sinclair as C.[12] The dying Sinclair had merely passed on the final thought that each of his section heads would have to make their own case as to their efficiency and worthiness to be his successor.[13] Menzies was the continuity candidate: the long-term head of SIS's Section IV (Army).[14]

Hankey's report served as the long-overdue stock-take. He completed the first draft by mid-February 1940 and delivered the final report on 11 March 1940. He immediately began a second investigation into counter-intelligence.[15]

Hankey himself was careful to assert his personal history as a long-term 'man of secrets'. In his first report, he mentioned, seemingly casually, that he was a 'former member of the Naval Intelligence Department'. His terminology was exact: as a Royal Marine officer he had served in naval intelligence in the early years of the twentieth century, before the department was reclassified as a division of the naval staff.[16] In his second report, he told an anecdote about being ferried about in an MI5 car bought with the money extracted from German naval intelligence to pay for a fake agent network in the First World War.[17]

Hankey had been a fixture on the Secret Service Committees of the 1920s: his remit and procedure were determined by those first established in 1919. Most notably, the intelligence agencies of the armed services were called as witnesses: the subject of the inquiry was narrowly defined as 'the secret services'. However, Hankey was the first important investigator of intelligence to refer to something he called the 'intelligence machine'.

Hankey's first report began, explicitly, with a history of the secret services since 1909. The second report referred the reader back to the history offered in the first. Hankey set 1909 as the canonical foundation date for the 'secret services': 'the Secret Services were formed in the year 1909 as the result of an inquiry by a Sub-Committee of the CID.' He also offered an analytical historical narrative distilled from what had become the tradition of historical reviews established by the Secret Service Committees, and previously delivered by Sir John Anderson. That 'sleek superman' was now Hankey's cabinet colleague as Home Secretary.

Hankey wrote that the Haldane Report of 1909 had, in his own view, defined the proper role of the secret services: 'to deal with espionage and to act as a screen between foreign spies and Government officials.' On the other hand, the Haldane Report had also recommended the creation of a single Secret Service Bureau. The bureau had 'very soon' fallen into two compartments. In Hankey's retelling, this was both an inevitable and a desirable development.

He went on to derive some crucial distinctions from this early history. The two natural compartments of a secret service were 'Foreign Intelligence' and 'Home Security'. 'Foreign Intelligence' was the primary focus of Hankey's historical review. He claimed that Britain had developed a 'Secret Foreign Intelligence Service' with two branches, which he called 'Secret Service proper' and the Government Code and Cypher School.

Hankey went on to observe that, 'with experience and the march of science, round them have gradually grown up, as a result of war experience and technical development, a cluster of other secret or quasi-secret services.' This construction of history was focused on primacy and legitimacy. The core secret services were the 'Secret Foreign Intelligence Service', with its two branches, SIS and GC&CS, and 'Home Security (MI5)'. There *were* other secret services, but they were subsequent, secondary, and ancillary.

Hankey gave his core secret services names other than those they actually traded under. In 1940 there was no 'Secret Foreign Intelligence Service', and neither was there anything called 'Home Security (MI5)'. This was an ideal vision created by historical elision. Hankey's was very much an SIS, Foreign

Office, and Treasury version of history. It was becoming, and became, the dominant version of intelligence history, although many participants in the inquiries doubted its veracity and raised those doubts with Hankey.[18]

Although Hankey's primary focus was on historical continuity, he was certainly sensitive to change over time, especially the 'march of science'. He took care to inquire into the state of scientific intelligence, making a personal visit to Bletchley Park. He correctly reported that there were 'a cluster of other secret or quasi-secret services'. Their most important foci were cryptography, wireless interception, wireless direction finding, and the detection of illicit wireless telegraphy (W/T) stations.

Hankey chose to discuss GC&CS, a long-term formal element of his 'Secret Foreign Intelligence Service', at some length, despite his frequent statements that it was too secret to write about. He said he was unwilling to discuss his findings further, except 'verbally in an unrecorded meeting'.[19] He urged that all mention of GC&CS should be expunged from papers seen by the cabinet.[20]

The history that Hankey was unwilling to write down was that of the Pyry meeting of July 1939. At that meeting, Polish military intelligence handed over their reconstruction of the Enigma mechanical ciphering machines of the German armed forces. This history revealed certain interesting facts. First, GC&CS had been unsuccessful in both method and result in trying to break Enigma. Second, the successful Polish reconstruction had in turn been based on French intelligence operations in the 1930s. These intelligence operations had relied on 'secret service proper' of a kind SIS could have mounted – but did not. The French had found a corruptible human source in the Chiffrierstelle of the German armed forces: he sold them the information necessary to attack Enigma. Thirdly, the Pyry case was not wholly an SIS initiative. The head of Admiralty technical signals intelligence had accompanied the head of GC&CS to Poland as the nominee of the DNI.[21]

Fourth, and most significantly from a wider point of view, the bowdlerized history of GC&CS did not reveal much about its essential nature. In the 1930s, GC&CS had attacked machine encryption with skill and energy. Its failure against Germany had not been representative. Also in the 1930s, GC&CS had enjoyed its greatest successes against Japanese machine-enciphered diplomatic communications.[22]

The 'drug of addiction' at Hankey's time of writing was not Enigma – prospect rather than retrospect – but Blue Jackets, deciphered diplomatic correspondence presented in blue folders. The Japanese Gaimushô decrypts had been an outstanding source for European, as much as Far Eastern, intelligence, because Germany and Japan had signed the anti-Comintern Pact in November 1936, and Italy joined in 1937.[23]

With regard to diplomatic intelligence, there was much truth in Churchill's April 1939 assertion that Chamberlain and his allies chose to ignore the work of the 'intelligence department', rather than being starved of such intelligence. One of GC&CS's leading Japanese specialists noted that the codebreakers' analyses were reproduced with some accuracy by *The Times*. It was not as if any interested politician had had to be misinformed.[24] However, the Japanese diplomatic intelligence bonanza had ended in May 1939, when the Gaimushô adopted a new cipher. The GC&CS tried and failed to break it, and was forced to admit defeat.[25]

Hankey wrote of cryptology that, 'in the late war, as is well known, by good fortune combined with the patient effort of an exceptionally able staff, it became the most reliable of all our secret sources of information.' But that was armed-forces cryptology, organized by and for the services.

In August 1939, GC&CS had moved to its 'war station' at Bletchley Park. When war broke out the next month, Bletchley Park had a staff of two hundred. This was a good-sized 'black chamber', but it was a small agency for military intelligence.[26] At the same moment, the most effective of the German cipher agencies, the Kriegsmarine's B-Dienst, had five hundred personnel. Unsurprisingly, German naval signals intelligence was, by an order of magnitude, superior to that of their British rivals in 1939–40.[27]

Hankey wrote at a time when the extreme fragility of decryption as the main driver of intelligence appeared all too evident – not only to the British but to their allies.[28] There was general agreement around his table that cryptography would become a very useful tool. However, few believed that Britain's military enemies would be so stupid as to repeat the mistakes of the First World War that had allowed British naval and military intelligence to decrypt their communications.

'I doubt,' John Godfrey wrote to Hankey in February 1940, 'if we are ever likely to be able to regain the priceless source of information which was available to us in the late war. The Germans are thoroughly on their guard, and have developed a technique which is difficult if not impossible to break.'[29] Godfrey was expressing not just the long-held NID view, but the formal position adopted by the final pre-war meeting of the co-ordination of interception committee chaired by the C of the time, Sir Hugh Sinclair.[30] In the First World War, Room 40 had often operated as a black chamber. That seemed the most likely future usefulness of GC&CS. It was what it had been designed to do.[31]

Although Hankey learnt a lot about technical-intelligence organizations outside the 'Secret Foreign Intelligence Service', and what they were doing, he chose not to highlight them. He was mainly exercised by the fact that GC&CS had been so focused as a 'black chamber' that its presumed co-ordinating role for all Y had been neglected. His solution was an inter-agency Y committee with a powerful independent chairman.[32]

The technical-intelligence organization he specifically named, other than GC&CS, was Section VIII of SIS itself. Section VIII had been the last initiative of Hugh Sinclair,[33] who had brought in talented communications specialists from the private sector. They had developed relatively portable radios that allowed SIS heads of station to keep in touch with London. These advanced radios continued to work even during crises, and thus were much sought after by non-SIS officials who desperately needed to radio home. There was genuine agreement about the excellence of Section VIII. John Godfrey remarked to Hankey that it was the 'one really bright spot, in fact', and added, 'all praise to Colonel Gambier-Parry'. Richard Gambier-Parry was the head of Section VIII.[34]

Most notably absent from Hankey's account of technical intelligence was the Radio Security Service (RSS), a military intelligence agency created in September 1939. It was run by MI8 of the Directorate of Military Intelligence, and its recruiters were officers who had done army wireless-intelligence work in the First World War. Most of its recruits were Post Office civilians and amateur radio enthusiasts. Its most important members, however, were executives from private British radio companies, inducted on the same model as SIS's Gambier-Parry, and Oxford academics. Hugh Trevor-Roper was MI8's star Oxford catch. He came to RSS from the Oxford University OTC, and so was not a civilian spook but a commissioned army officer.[35]

In March 1940, while Hankey was working on his second report, MI8 set up a meeting between RSS, MI5, and GC&CS to report that, although there were no German agents in Britain using wireless transmitters, it was beginning to understand the set-up of German armed-forces intelligence, Abwehr, by intercepting and decrypting its radio messages to and from other countries.[36]

As Hankey started work in November 1939, the Royal Navy and the RAF generated one of the great intelligence coups of the war. The naval attaché in Oslo received an inquiry from a write-in source as to whether he would like secret information on German technical-weapons development. Two memoranda duly arrived and were dispatched to NID in London. No one knew the source of the memoranda and there was no further contact.[37]

The documents were written by Hans Mayer, a research scientist working for the German firm Siemens, who was on a business trip to Oslo, but this fact was not known until the 1950s. Given the provenance of the memoranda, the Admiralty was sceptical of the reliability of its own intelligence.

However, as one of Hankey's witnesses, the Director of Air Intelligence, Air Commodore Buss, explained, the lack of any secret intelligence on German weapons developments since 1937 had prompted the RAF to appoint a scientific liaison officer with SIS. The head of SIS Section II (Air), had told Buss that scientific air intelligence 'seriously interfered' with his other SIS work.[38] The contents of the Oslo memoranda convinced the new RAF scientific liaison officer, Dr R.V. Jones, of their veracity and accuracy. They discussed the Luftwaffe's research facility at Rechlin, and the bombing navigation aids it was developing. The memoranda also gave technical details of the, hitherto unsuspected, German radar air-defence system. Jones started bleeding their revelations into air intelligence reports.[39]

There was some sense that the Oslo dossier did not 'count' as secret intelligence. It had come in via a naval attaché, as a windfall, and had been championed by the scientific liaison officer of a new service. However, naval attachés had been deployed since the 1890s to receive such windfalls. The RAF had appointed Jones for exactly the purpose he fulfilled.

As with RSS, the military were demonstrating the desire and ability to seek the secret intelligence that the 'Secret Foreign Intelligence Service' had failed to provide. In the 1930s, both naval and military intelligence had relied mainly on their own sources, attachés prominent among them, for gathering intelligence.[40]

Hankey pronounced himself 'uneasy' about whether SIS was collecting the information that the armed forces actually required. He sought to quell this uneasiness by balancing the services off against one another. Buss had briefed him on the failure of technical air intelligence.[41] The Director of Naval Intelligence was vocally dissatisfied. On the other hand, Paddy Beaumont-Nesbitt, the Director of Military Intelligence, was 'fairly satisfied', as was Desmond Morton, the head of the intelligence department of the new Ministry of Economic Warfare. Morton, most certainly not a head of armed-forces intelligence (indeed a former senior SIS officer, but undoubtedly a 'customer'), was used to balance off the revelations of Buss and Godfrey.[42]

At the time of the first Hankey report, John Godfrey, the DNI, was by far the most articulate critic of British secret intelligence. This point was muddied in later histories, because Godfrey changed his position a few months later and became a staunch defender of the SIS. He certainly worried about his own tergiversations in his historical writings: for much of the 1940s he defended his change of heart, only to conclude at the end of the decade that he had been right in 1939. Although Godfrey had not been sorry to see the Admiralty's particular candidate for the post of C fail, he was undoubtedly deeply unsettled by the transfer of the post from the late Hugh Sinclair – former Director of Naval Intelligence – to Stewart Menzies, a member of SIS since the First World War.

Godfrey took a close interest in the history of naval intelligence: having found little of value in the Admiralty papers, he relied on the personal memories of those who had run the division – in particular Blinker Hall, DNI throughout the First World War; Hall's personal assistant, the stockbroker Claude Serocold; and Bubbles James, head of ID25/Room 40.[43]

Godfrey's conclusions were bleak. Naval intelligence in 1939 was much worse than naval intelligence in 1914. It had lost both its system of running agents and its ability to do cryptography. In particular, no one was tracking German naval movements through The Sound, the narrow waterway between Denmark and Sweden that granted egress from the Baltic into the North Sea, although 'we had a very good system in 1914–18.'

In August 1939, Godfrey had made a personal tour of inspection of SIS offices in the Baltic. Although the 'head agents' were agreeable, they had been also, less than a month before the outbreak of war, completely concentrated on gathering political intelligence. There was no up-to-date information about the German U-boat programme. In the First World War, naval intelligence had tracked German U-boat construction through Switzerland, where Imperial Germany had insured its engines. Nazi Germany no longer insured submarine power plants.[44]

There was no secret intelligence.[45] The navy did not know the state of readiness of the Kriegsmarine. It had little idea where to find German ships. After three months of war, Godfrey wrote, he could definitely report to the Board of the Admiralty that naval intelligence was failing. 'I find myself with deep regret,' he admitted, 'unable to tell the Board anything of value.'[46]

Churchill shot down Godfrey's proposed solution, the recreation of a Royal Navy Secret Service, not least because Godfrey rather implied that the 'guilty men' should be sought in the immediate post–First World War period, when Churchill had been Secretary of State for War and the Colonies, and no friend to the Admiralty. The 'idea of starting a service of our own would not succeed,' Churchill commented tersely. He also dismissed Godfrey's next plan, to flood SIS with senior naval officers. He told him to try and introduce a few new naval faces to SIS at a relatively junior level.[47] One of these junior officers subsequently reported back that SIS was 'worthless, and frequently so entirely worthless as to provoke laughter.'[48]

When Godfrey met Hankey for the purposes of the inquiry, he was already on a short leash.[49] Churchill had reined in Godfrey and shifted the focus of blame from the post–First World period to the late 1930s. It was during 'the declining years of Sir Hugh Sinclair' that intelligence on naval affairs had failed. 'Information about the movements of German ships, about the number of U-boats building, and above all about the dates of completion of their new capital ships' was 'lamentably meagre'. Cryptography was 'a blank so far as we are concerned,' and had 'become mainly political'. Churchill professed 'shock' that the 'DNI had no original intelligence to give me, but only what was passed on to him [by C].' British intelligence was 'altogether inferior to what we had in the last war'.[50]

Hankey's description of Paddy Beaumont-Nesbitt as 'fairly satisfied' was based on deliberate misreading of the evidence. Beaumont-Nesbitt may have found personally agreeable the appointment of a former army officer, a fellow guardsman – and the army had seconded many more officers to SIS than any other service – but he was no more enamoured of the organization than Godfrey. Like his naval opposite number, he told Hankey that SIS was a political, not a military, intelligence service.[51] However, Beaumont-Nesbitt's reading of history, and thus his expectations, differed from those of Godfrey. Unlike the DNI, the Directorate of Military Intelligence had no continuous existence. It had re-emerged from the Directorate of Military Operations and Intelligence only in September 1939.[52]

Just before the separation, Beaumont-Nesbitt, as Deputy Director of Military Intelligence, oversaw the update of the *Manual of Military Intelligence*. The manual crystallized the army's historical experience. Its – and Beaumont-Nesbitt's – main assumption was that, although SIS would continue to exist in wartime, the army would be running its own intelligence operations, as it had during the First World War. Armies 'in the field' had their own intelligence apparatus, usually referred to by 1939 as GSI, General Staff Intelligence. Their predecessors, GHQ Intelligence, had created secret services, and the army saw no reason why it should not replicate that practice. The lessons of history were that this intelligence operation would be based around technical intelligence-gathering. As Beaumont-Nesbitt's deputy put it, 'there are so many difficulties in the way of agents these days that their usefulness is past.'[53]

Based on historical experience, the two most important means of gathering intelligence would be wireless interception – Y – and prisoner-of-war interrogation. The War Office already had its own Y service based in Chatham: more importantly each army would be dispatched overseas with Y intelligence units manned by signallers.

In March 1939, the War Office had convened a meeting with the Admiralty, the Air Ministry, the Home Office, and MI5 to discuss an investigation of prisoner-of-war interrogation during the First World War. In the Great War, each service had interrogated its own prisoners, but tentative discussions had begun by 1918 about pooling efforts.

The five departments had agreed that they should start where their predecessors had left off. The War Office undertook to organize a UK-based prisoner-of-war interrogation centre on an interdepartmental basis. The other services were happy to see the army take the lead, because the experience of the First World War had been that most prisoners were military. The Combined Services Detailed Interrogation Centre (CSDIC), run by MI9, opened at the Tower of London on the outbreak of war. A few days before Hankey interviewed Beaumont-Nesbitt, it moved out to a stately home on the northern outskirts of London.[54] Beaumont-Nesbitt's successor thought that 'Cockfosters' was his most impressive achievement.[55]

This is not to suggest that all was sweetness and light in the British army. There was a group of intelligence 'radicals' in the middle-high echelons of the army who believed that they would need to push decentralization even further than the *Manual of Military Intelligence* envisioned. Their problem was with the War Office, as much as with the seemingly irrelevant SIS or GC&CS. 'London,' as a whole, was a 'congealed mass of fat'.[56]

The best-known leader of the radicals was Archie Wavell, from August 1939 commander-in-chief, Middle East. In November 1939, Wavell argued that the armed forces needed to ignore the ineffective central organization of intelligence in London. Instead, they would set up their own field intelligence system based on their First World War experience, specifically, he suggested, that of armies which had conquered the Middle East under Lord Allenby in 1917–18. The army should take the lead in developing inter-service intelligence agencies that would gather intelligence and carry out deception and sabotage operations. Wavell acknowledged that 'Whitehall' would try to sabotage such initiatives, in order to preserve its own power, but in his view that was just too bad.[57]

Hankey's history demonstrated that British intelligence had been primarily political intelligence since the First World War. He believed that this was a perfectly defensible position, and put a positive slant on Britain's blinded state in time of war. This was the unfortunate 'technical position' that needed to be remedied.

Of course, that still left Hankey with the explosive task of explaining the conduct of political intelligence. 'There is general agreement that the service of information of a general and political character is very satisfactory,' he wrote: everybody was 'well content with supply of political intelligence.' That was a rather strained reading of the evidence that he received, and of the cases he cited in his report.

The hub of the system of political intelligence was plainly the so-called Passport Control Officers. In 1921, SIS had been awarded control of the Passport Office. Thereafter, the Passport Control Officer in capitals around the world had been a cover for the SIS head-of-station. The trouble with this system was that the cover was laughably thin.[58]

The system sometimes broadcast its embarrassments. The first SIS head of station in post-war Berlin, forced to resign for embezzlement, had emigrated to the United States, and had written extensively about running a MI1C network in Belgium during the First World War. E.A. Dalton, the PCO in Holland between 1924 and 1936, had committed suicide in July 1936. Dalton had been regarded as a man of 'conspicuous ability', who had served in MI1C since 1917. He had also been skimming off the fees paid by Jews desperate for visas to go to Palestine. After an inquiry, SIS repaid Dalton's 'grave defalcations' to the Colonial Office.[59]

It was plain that all foreign powers understood that the PCO represented the SIS. Frederick Winterbotham, head of SIS Section II, remarked in 1938 that 'everyone in China knows who and what "Steptoe" is!' Steptoe was head of SIS in Shanghai.[60] The same year also brought the publicly reported Kendrick case. The Gestapo of the newly unified Reich picked up Thomas Kendrick, the PCO in Vienna, questioned him for a couple of days, and then expelled him as a spy, which he was. Kendrick and his ilk were easy prey for enemy political police.[61]

Gladwyn Jebb, the secretary to the Hankey inquiry, wrote the report on the Kendrick case. In his subsequent investigation of the PCO in The Hague, he further confirmed that 'the Dutch government apparently knew all about the Passport Control Officer long ago.' He also found that PCOs' wives, who accompanied them abroad, talked about their husbands' secret work among their social circle.[62]

The case that Hankey could not avoid was the Venlo Incident of November 1939. On 9 November 1939, unknown Germans kidnapped the PCO in The Hague, along with another SIS officer, in the Dutch border town of Venlo. The Germans had also killed the Dutch military-intelligence officer who had been accompanying the SIS men.

On 22 November 1939, the 'German Secret Police' sent a message over a radio link that had been supplied by the SIS to what they believed was an anti-Nazi group of Wehrmacht officers: 'corresponding with conceited and foolish people becomes boring in the long run,' the Germans had written. 'You will understand us breaking off relations. Best wishes from your friends in the German Opposition.' At the same time, German press and propaganda outlets had identified the two kidnapped Britons as officers of the 'British Intelligence Service'.[63]

After an intense debate in the cabinet, the Foreign Office confirmed, in an 'off-the-record' press briefing, that the missing men were intelligence officers. Its main concern was to refute the second German accusation: that these particular British intelligence officers had organized an assassination attempt on Hitler in Munich.[64] The foreign editor of the *Daily Herald*, W.N. Ewer, previously the Soviet Union's 'chief agent' in the UK, orchestrated press management on behalf of the Foreign Office.[65] In December 1939, the Germans told the Dutch that they had taken the British officers alive.[66]

The Venlo Incident revealed some salient features about British political intelligence in the 1930s. First, and most importantly, it had demonstrated that the SIS had gathered very little good political intelligence from Germany, and thus British foreign policy had been based on whatever diplomats and politicians had garnered from their own experience, observation, and expectation. Political intelligence on Germany had been neither very good nor very important. Responding to a report on the state of political intelligence from Germany, put together by Jebb, Lord Halifax had commented that, 'we are moving in a mental atmosphere with which a child might be surrounded in which all things were both possible and impossible and where there were no rational guiding rules.'[67]

Second, policy-makers with an interest in political intelligence were reduced to seeking it for themselves. The Venlo Incident was linked to the Putlitz case. The British had an effective spy in The Hague, the first secretary of the German embassy, Wolfgang zu Putlitz. Recruited in 1934, Putlitz was a source of British political intelligence, but not an SIS agent.[68] Rather he had been run by MI5 as part of the 'private' intelligence organization created by Sir Robert Vansittart, permanent under-secretary to the Foreign Office between 1930 and 1938. Since the PUS was the overseer of SIS, it hardly said a lot for his trust in SIS that he had developed his own political intelligence network in Germany.[69]

Justifiably spooked by the dangerous turbulence in The Hague, von Putlitz flew to Britain in September 1939, and took refuge at Vansittart's country estate. The wrangles about von Putlitz's status were continuing at the time the Venlo case broke.[70]

Finally, the Venlo Incident showed how little British intelligence had discovered about their German opposite numbers. In his final testament of November 1939, Hugh Sinclair declared that SIS faced an, 'all powerful and ruthless contre-espionage service'.[71] The intelligence services presumed that the Gestapo were the enemy at Venlo. They assumed the Abwehr was the 'German Intelligence Service'. They did not suspect – and did not even know the name of – their actual foe, the Sicherheitdienst.

The combination of these factors was to make Venlo the centrepiece of historical investigations into British political intelligence for years to come.[72] Much more information about the Venlo Incident would come to light in subsequent histories, but even on the basis of the case history assembled by Jebb, Hankey had to admit that something was wrong. He concluded that PCOs 'were not sufficiently informed' to effectively carry out intelligence work. He was 'not satisfied that the present system of engaging personnel' had worked.[73]

In response to this emerging conclusion, C, Stewart Menzies, decided to provide Hankey with a 'brief historical sketch of what we now know as SIS.'[74] Hankey reproduced the history in full as an appendix to his report. This was SIS's view of its own history, finally committed to paper, rather than confined to verbal briefings. It revealed, among other things, that the SIS took its foundation date to be October 1909, when the Secret Service Bureau split into Home and Foreign sections after only two months of existence. It stressed the importance of the 'charter' the Secret Service had awarded itself in 1919, to 'supply all authorised Government Departments with any information that they may require which is not readily obtainable through official channels.' The SIS history clarified that SIS had adopted its current name in 1921, and thereafter preferred to be called by that name rather than its official cover designation of MI1C.

The purpose of the history, Menzies explained, was to demonstrate that 'over and over again we learn the same lesson, i.e. that one must plan for the future and that success in SS work must always be the result of years of patient work and not of improvisation.' Since that work had not been done, the 'improvisation' of which people like Godfrey spoke was unachievable. Menzies effectively admitted that SIS would be of very little use in the war, because the spadework had been left undone. The SIS had been a political intelligence agency, so it could not be expected to become an effective military intelligence agency.

The SIS history then tacked briskly in the opposite direction. It insisted that SIS *was* primarily a military intelligence agency. It had not been created for political intelligence, and in the First World War the Foreign Office had prevented it from doing such work, preferring its own Political Intelligence Department. The SIS history cited three historical authorities for its status as *the* leading military intelligence agency. The authorities were reproduced in appendices, all of which found their way into Hankey's final report.[75]

In chronological order, the first historical exhibit was a 'classic' minute written by Colonel Macdonogh of MO5 in October 1910, found in SIS's early records. Macdonogh had observed that, 'our Secret Service system compares unfavourably with that of other first class powers' and stated that 'the first essential is thorough organisation in time of peace.' George Macdonogh was an odd choice as an historical authority. He had undoubtedly been an early champion of the Secret Service Bureau, but he had also been the head of GHQI, and subsequently DMI, who had created his own secret service and had kept MI1C firmly in its place.

The second historical authority was the *Manual of Military Intelligence* that had 'incorporated the fundamental principle of a central control over all military SS wherever functioning at the various GHQs in war time.' The *Manual*, just revised under Beaumont-Nesbitt, was an even odder choice of historical authority. It certainly acknowledged SIS as an unavoidable fixture in wartime, while suggesting means by which it might be circumvented in order that the army could gather its own intelligence. 'It is sometimes supposed,' the 1939 revision observed, 'that secret service is something outside the rest of the intelligence system and that it works as an independent entity by many mysterious means.' This was false doctrine. 'The Secret Service' was 'only one of the numerous interdependent organisms whereby a commander seeks to obtain information about the enemy and to inflict injury upon him … not a thing apart.'[76]

The third authority was the oddest and most striking of all: none other than Colonel Nicolai, the disgraced former head of the Imperial German OHL IIIb. Seemingly, James Edmonds's exposure of Nicolai's mendacity, inaccuracy, and incompetence had long since been forgotten. Since he quoted Nicolai's 1924 work so frequently, it was somewhat unclear whether Menzies was citing him for advice as to how the British should act, or as the best source for how the Germans would already be acting. Probably both. At least one close reader of the document, John Godfrey, believed that the material drawn from Nicolai was the most compelling element of the Hankey Report.[77]

The SIS chose four main Nicolaian precepts. First, 'Espionage is of military origin. At all times and in all places, accurate information, supplemented by means of espionage among the enemy, has been an indispensable auxiliary help in military struggles.' Second, in order to be effective, secret services must be 'in full working order at the outbreak of war'. Third,

> The World War produced the proof that a struggle between nations had grown out of the narrow limits of decision by arms and had become a contest … in the very soul of the people. In the place of a military I[ntelligence] S[ervice] there arose a State Secret Service against surrounding countries. It concerned itself with all that might give the State an advantage over another, and equally with economics, politics and armaments. It did not limit itself any longer to the purely negative aspect of inquiry, but engaged in positive action in the economic struggle and in home and foreign political propaganda.'

Finally, 'the Intelligence Service is a service for gentlemen.'[78]

Alongside his historical philosophy of secret service, Menzies offered a more pragmatic historical defence of SIS's performance; it had been underfunded. Hugh Sinclair had first put this claim on the record in 1935. Sinclair had argued in 1935, and Menzies repeated in 1940, that in 1914 Britain had faced but one strategic threat: Germany. Now it faced four: Germany, Japan, Italy, and, possibly, the Soviet Union. This rather neglected the fact that, in 1914, the Habsburg Empire had been an enemy – a point that Hankey had to deal with for rather recondite legal reasons elsewhere in his inquiry – and Italy had been a likely enemy. But the reader could take his point.

Sinclair and Menzies argued that a small service, organized around the system of PCOs in politically important centres, was simply unequipped to deal with the magnitude of the threat. In 1935, Sinclair had wanted his piece of the re-armament pie, remarking, bitterly, that his budget 'only equals that spent every year on the *maintenance* (not the cost) of HM Destroyers in Home Waters.' He then put the cost of a decent SIS at £500,000 per annum.[79]

While Herbert Brittain did plenty of financial devilling for the Hankey Inquiry, providing breakdowns of the Secret Vote, he did not give much historical context. Brittain set the current financial year, 1939–40, as the baseline, and projected budgets forward rather than backward. When Sinclair had made his démarche in 1935, the Secret Vote had stood at £179,000, with SIS receiving two-thirds.[80] Brittain's figures revealed that the Secret Vote set in early 1939 was £700,000, although this had since been heavily supplemented. Of this overall figure, £93,298 was allocated to MI5. Other agencies, such as IPI, had received negligible amounts.[81] The GC&CS was not paid for out of the Secret Vote: it was funded by the Foreign Office from its own estimates, and cost a fraction of the SIS.[82] The SIS's final peacetime estimate had thus been set at around £600,000, a five-fold increase on the budget of which Sinclair had complained, and well in advance of the amount he had claimed would finance a first-rate Secret Service.

The argument for underfunding thus rested on the money being too late, rather than too little. Although SIS was re-armed at the same rate as the armed forces, it claimed it had been unable to use the money wisely, because agent networks required many years to build; they could not be turned on and off like a tap. In a testament to Sir Hugh Sinclair, C explained that the money had financed two worthwhile things: the 'peerless' Section VIII and 'the penetration of neutral Secret Services and the utilisation of *their* agents'.[83]

The Treasury figures showed that, in 1939, the Secret Vote was over seven-and-a-half times higher, in real terms, than it had been in 1914. Nevertheless, Hankey concluded that 'funds before the war were not sufficient'. 'I do not,' he wrote, 'think that Colonel Menzies' explanations can be contested.' In one sense, Hankey was right. Unlike many of his other judgements, the financial explanation for SIS's performance was not challenged – then, or subsequently.[84]

Neither the history nor the contemporary history of secret service ceased with the first stage of Hankey's inquiry. As he started work on the next stage of his work, the author, playwright, and leading member of 'Club Med', Compton Mackenzie, published another volume of his memoirs about MI1C in the First World War.

The Mackenzie Case had not ended in 1933. Mackenzie was still under surveillance, his meetings with Oswald Mosley, radical Scottish nationalists, and Communists, all regarded with deep suspicion. In the wake of the Munich Crisis, Vivian and Jasper Harker of MI5 finally persuaded the Attorney-General and the Director of Public Prosecutions that, as a matter of settled policy, 'we could not permit Intelligence Officers – particularly those entrusted with Secret Service work – to publish information obtained either from official documents or their own experience, which in any way might hamper the work of the Secret Service.'[85]

His conviction, and the general atmosphere of the late 1930s, made Mackenzie more cautious, but it did not stop him. *Aegean Memories* of March 1940 continued the story of the Eastern Mediterranean Special Intelligence Bureau into the later war years. No action was taken. Valentine Vivian of SIS commented that, 'I regret the publication of a work of this sort as in deplorable taste and as likely to be as deplorable in its effects. It merely does (but at a far more critical moment) what "Greek Memories" did, viz: invite the searchlight of foreign attention on a system of intelligence, of which our present system after all [is] the lineal descendant and inheritor of many family traits.'[86]

Just as Hankey was putting the finishing touches to his second report, the Rickman case broke.[87] The Rickman case had been bubbling up throughout the inquiry, not least because Hankey and Gladwyn Jebb were so closely involved with the operations that Rickman had been sent to carry out.[88]

Freddie Rickman, an 'illegal' officer of Section IX of SIS, was arrested in neutral Sweden. Hankey had spent an inordinate amount of time during his inquiry on the 'subterranean activities' of Section IX.

Rickman, whose purpose in Sweden was to blow up Swedish iron-ore facilities,[89] was caught with his stockpile of explosives. Sweden was a neutral country, and if Rickman had been successful, he would have killed many Swedes.[90] Apart from that awkward diplomatic complication, Rickman proved to be but one part of British secret service in Sweden. Through the documents he carried and his own statements, he managed to reveal, to the Swedes, to the Germans, to the British press, and to significant sections of Whitehall, not only the PCO operation but also those of other 'illegals'. Rickman made everyone look like amateurs.[91] He even managed to underline the louche reputation of British intelligence. Like so many of the First World War memoirists, Rickman acquired a secretary-mistress-partner-in-crime. No more than Mackenzie, was Rickman ever forgiven.[92]

The second part of the Hankey inquiry took place within a different context to the first. Events in Scandinavia were more profound than the bumbling of SIS in Stockholm. On 9 April 1940, Germany invaded both Denmark and Norway. As an addendum to the SIS history, Stewart Menzies produced, and Hankey endorsed, a history of intelligence concerning Norway.[93]

The main historical focus of the second Hankey report, however, was German penetration of Britain and the history of British counter-measures. There were German agents in Britain. The most recent prosecution of a German spy had been in May 1939.[94] On 2 September 1939, MI5's wiretaps on the Germany embassy detected calls into the press office of 10 Downing Street. The press officer who received the calls had previously been warned about his conduct of passing confidential information to German agents.[95]

The Germans most certainly had intelligence services. The press bureau of the Minister of Propaganda under Göbbels, DNB, collected intelligence and ran agents. The Auswärtiges Amt under Ribbentrop ran agents.[96] The British were most aware, and in many ways most fearful, of the Auslands-Organisation of the NSDAP. The AO was responsible for harnessing the potential of Germans and Nazis resident in foreign countries. In addition, Germany had formidable signal-intelligence agencies – B-Dienst, Pers. Z S, OKW/Chi, Funkorchdienst – targeting Britain.[97] Hansa-Luftbild-Abteilung B had started making covert photographic reconnaissance flights over Britain in 1938.[98]

In September 1939, Heinrich Himmler succeeded in pushing through the creation of a Nazi national security agency, the Reichssicherheitshauptamt (RSHA), under the command of his protégé, Reinhard Heydrich. The RSHA was a merger of state and party agencies and included both the Gestapo – the political police – and the security service, Sicherheitsdienst, the SD.[99] The RSHA VI was an aggressive foreign-intelligence agency, which had been responsible for the Venlo Incident.[100]

The Germans also followed the same practice as Hugh Sinclair had recommended: using other people's intelligence agencies. In August 1939 they had received intelligence from their 'sure source' within the British Foreign Office.[101] This was the Foreign Office cipher clerk, John King, who was being run by the Soviets.[102]

However, what the Hankey inquiry referred to as the 'German Intelligence Service', OKW Foreign Information and Counter-Intelligence Office, Amt Ausland/Abwehr, did not attempt to send agents into Britain by covert means until September 1940.[103] Gruppe I of the Abwehr conducted espionage, Gruppe II, sabotage. The agents sent to Britain were from Gruppe II.[104]

Hankey's reliance on Nicolai for the history of German intelligence in the First World War demonstrated how imperfect was the grasp of the British on the history of enemy intelligence, let alone its current reality. The British analysts of 1940 embraced the concept of 'totalitarianism': this sidestepped the requirement for seeking information that they did not possess.[105]

Hankey did not request a history of counter-espionage from MI5.[106] However, Vernon Kell began the first official session of the inquiry by offering an 'historical sketch'. As he had been doing since the First World War, Kell rehearsed the story of the capture of twenty-one out of twenty-two spies in Britain in 1914. He went on to explain that MI5 was planning on running deception operations against the Germans, as it had done in 1914–18, although he complained of 'indiscretions committed by ex-members of the Security Service after the last war, as a result of which we were now unable again to make use of certain invaluable ways of outwitting the enemy.' As regards more recent history, Kell stated that MI5 had taken over counter-subversion from the police in 1931.[107]

Hankey subsequently elaborated on these events from his own memory. As he had in the case of SIS, Hankey concluded that MI5 was important because of its 'purely military work', even though during the past decade it had been a small agency devoted to countering Soviet subversion.[108] Kell said that MI5 had started preparing for war in 1937, although his portrait of those he had recruited – 'barristers, solicitors and retired Indian and Colonial police officers' – still suggested counter-subversion among the civilian population rather than an agency devoted to supporting a war effort.[109]

When asked, the armed forces remarked that MI5 had very little presence in their sphere. They were rapidly creating security agencies other than MI5, such as the Inter-Services Security Board and MI11.[110] The War Office informed Hankey that they planned to subsume MI5 in a Deputy Directorate of Military Intelligence for Security.[111]

Kell himself, on the other hand, now argued that the conclusions drawn by his own historians at the end of the First World War should be ignored. The most important branch of MI5 was now the 'detective' or 'investigations' branch under Jasper Harker, rather than the security branches.

The main purpose of Kell's 'historical sketch', however, was to demonstrate that the past had been misunderstood by others. That misunderstanding of history was paralysing contemporary policy. In 1914, according to Kell, there had been forty thousand aliens in Britain, a relatively stable population, since few, if any, were refugees. Now Britain had seventy-five thousand aliens, three-quarters of whom were refugees. Kell called for immediate internment of these aliens.[112]

Kell's verbal history of the problem was followed by a written MI5 history of the alien question. The history outlined the uncertainty of policy in 1914, with the Home Office portrayed, as in 1940, as the villain. It confirmed that, in September 1914, the Asquith government had decided to intern enemy aliens who were registered as reservists in the armies of their own country, and explained how this internment was expanded to cover all enemy males of military age after the sinking of the *Lusitania* in May 1915. Over thirty-two thousand Germans and Austrians had been interned.[113]

Hankey probed this history, generating an 'answering' addendum about the differences between 1914 and 1939. In 1939, Britain had, in fact, arrested many more suspect Germans than it had in 1914. But because no one had any real knowledge of the German intelligence effort, 'the claims of security are very far from satisfied'.[114]

The question of aliens dominated the historical side of the second Hankey inquiry. Hankey announced that it was so critical that he could not confine himself to merely investigating MI5: he would transform his inquiry into an investigation of the alien issue.

This caused two immediate problems. First, it brought Hankey into conflict with his old colleague on the Secret Service Committee, John

Anderson.[115] The Home Secretary did not appreciate Hankey's trespass.[116] Second, as soon became clear, Hankey's enthusiasm for propagating MI5's policy prescription on aliens blinded him to the fact that MI5 was unprepared for the implementation of that policy. Its Registry in Wormwood Scrubs prison, which Hankey visited, was already showing signs of collapse, as the reality of mass internment caused it to implode. Some of Hankey's witnesses realized that there was a problem and warned him.[117] Instead of heeding those warnings, however, he went out of his way to praise the MI5 Registry and its head by name.[118]

This piece of wishful thinking, as much as anything else he wrote, made Hankey appear ludicrous. The cruellest contemporary judgement on his efforts was delivered by the private secretary whom Churchill inherited from Chamberlain: 'Lord Hankey was appointed to overhaul Secret Intelligence, but his reports were not very helpful, and in fact the only recommendations he made were trifling.'[119]

Not only did Winston Churchill sack Vernon Kell, he also sacked Maurice Hankey, and appointed Desmond Morton as his personal intelligence adviser.[120] The sustained attempt to create a 'settled history' of British intelligence ended with Hankey's ouster. The rhetorical emphasis shifted from defending the past to dismissing the past.

However, more particular exercises of historical reflection continued, as did suggestions for future inquiry. One of Hankey's parting shots was the observation that the real Pandora's Box of intelligence was armed-forces intelligence, not civilian intelligence agencies. This conclusion was hard to ignore, given not only the palpable failure of operational military intelligence during the Norwegian defeat, upon which Hankey based his observations, but also the even-more-glaring failure of military intelligence – indeed of everything military – during the disastrous campaign in France in May 1940.[121]

The changed status of the military proved a major dividing line between the intelligence histories written up to May 1940 and those produced thereafter.[122] The inter-war tradition of investigation had focused on civilian secret services, and had treated military-intelligence personnel as disinterested witnesses. After May 1940, the army, navy, and RAF were the subject of writing by critical civilian officials. This in turn created a defensive mode of historical writing within the armed services.[123] It also made a clear difference in how authoritative military and naval history was considered when treated as a source for intelligence history.[124]

The outgoing Director of Military Intelligence, Paddy Beaumont-Nesbitt, was palpably dismayed when the Director of Investigation and Statistics, a civilian official answering to the permanent under-secretary at the War Office, gave him low marks.[125] He complained that the DIS had overstepped a red line.[126]

The War Office review was based on questionnaires to, and interviews with, officers serving in the directorates of Military Intelligence and of Military Operations. It conceded that the DMI still had the problem Beaumont-Nesbitt had described to Hankey: the SIS was useless.[127] It doubted, however, whether the directorate itself was particularly well organized. There was no shortage of intelligence officers. The DMI was now 'considerably larger' than it had been in 1918. But Beaumont-Nesbitt had 'caused branches to multiply to a greater extent than was found necessary in the war of 1914–18.' There were branches collating intelligence on places where there would never be military operations. Many military-intelligence branches, according to the DIS, could be packed off to civilian agencies without any appreciable loss.

Even worse, the DIS openly doubted if military intelligence officers were really much good, or even if they needed to be in the army. Most of the officers in the Directorate of Military Intelligence held wartime commissions. The investigators were not convinced by the argument that intelligence 'duties … are best carried out by officers wearing the King's uniform and subject to discipline.' Army officers, whether holding permanent commissions on the active list, or temporary, had not really been trained for this task. The 'good intelligence officer' was 'something of a *rara avis*'. Owing to shortage of supply of these rare birds, they were kept exclusively on intelligence work for a large part of their careers. The unhappy result was that 'Intelligence is regarded as a backwater and is not readily undertaken by ambitious officers.'[128] Beaumont-Nesbitt was livid, 'I[ntelligence] *must* remain a military organisation in which military thought and method predominates. It must not,' he expostulated, 'degenerate into an emasculated civil branch.'[129]

In November 1940, the Chiefs of Staff reviewed their intelligence apparatus more broadly.[130] On the whole, they professed themselves as satisfied as they had been in May 1940. Clement Attlee, the senior Labour member of the cabinet, commented to Churchill, upon reading their report, that the armed forces were complacent. The Chiefs seemed determined to defend a status quo that had failed to deliver.[131]

These failures of military intelligence became the butt of criticism, not only internally, but in parliament and the press too. In April 1941, there were a slew of press articles asking why British military intelligence was so bad. The occasion was the 'unexpected' arrival of Rommel and German troops in Libya, hitherto an Anglo-Italian battleground. Both the DMI in London and the autonomous intelligence apparatus that Wavell had erected were caught in the crossfire.[132]

The minister charged with managing the public relations of Rommel's first offensive crisis wrote that 'the Libyan news is worse than I had supposed … we have a serious inquest upon the handling of the Libyan news … dreadful shock … we have very meagre information and Cairo has dressed those slight pudenda in the most foolish and unnecessary frills … The fact is we have been taken by surprise and badly beaten.' A few days later, having read the newspaper articles, he added, 'Norway was a nasty knock, but Libya was a nastier knock. "How", they ask, "was Germany able to land four divisions in Libya?" There are many explanations of this feat but none of them really disposes of the question.'[133] The DMI's own 'introspection meeting' concluded that their 'deductions' had been 'OK up to a point but we had not categorically uttered warnings in black and white to COS though often done verbally to VCIGS [vice-chief of the imperial general staff].'[134]

In the middle of this crisis, GC&CS made its first spectacular breakthrough into the German Enigma machine. The Director of Military Intelligence, F.H.N. Davidson, described his own disgust at seeing Stewart Menzies and Desmond Morton placing carefully selected 'words' – short Enigma decrypts – in front of Churchill during meetings, as the prime minister declared – inaccurately – that with such information Wavell was bound to beat Rommel. 'Can the PM see these men for the "charlatans" they are?' Davidson wondered. Davidson characterized himself as an actor now taking part in an historical drama of which others would write the history.[135]

Desmond Morton wrote that they were entering a new world. In contrast to the past, 'the fault of our Intelligence lies far less in a dearth of information than in failure to collate and appreciate information made available.'

This, in the view of the civilian intelligence official, Morton, was due to 'a mistaken view that Intelligence is mainly a function of the Service Departments. It is a function of State.' Britain had been guilty of 'over-stressing the responsibility of Directors of Intelligence Departments for organising and gathering information.' The Services were not competent at Intelligence, and they had only themselves to blame for the 'appointment to "Intelligence" ... of the less able staff officers.' The most pressing need was for a civilian 'nucleus' to run the intelligence machine.[136]

In this new world, fresh commentators could push themselves forward, and the first of this breed was R.V. Jones. Jones was only formally recognized as an 'intelligence officer' at all in May 1941. After much effort, he finally secured a transfer from scientific research to intelligence. He was given the title of Assistant Director of Scientific Intelligence – ADI (Science) – reporting directly to the newly created Assistant Chief of the Air Staff for Intelligence – ACAS (I).[137]

Jones's section of ACAS (I) was tiny, but it did some things exceptionally well, allowing it to loom much larger in the consciousness of Whitehall. From the point of view of secret history, Jones's most notable ability was the construction of readable scientific intelligence case histories aimed at the layman. He perfected the art with his history of the Bruneval Raid in February 1942. Bruneval was the operating station for Würzburg, a new type of German radar used in the short-range detection of sorties penetrating German-controlled air space.[138]

As important as the achievement of understanding the radar system itself was the careful way that Jones showed how each part of the scientific intelligence machine interacted with the others. The Oslo Dossier, he explained, had warned about the development of the radar; Enigma decrypts had confirmed that the radar was being deployed; RAF PRU – the Photographic Reconnaissance Unit – had started searching for the radar; CIU – the interservice Central Interpretation Unit – had identified the installations. CCO – Combined Operations – had agreed to mount a raid to seize a working model. The head of CCO, Lord Louis Mountbatten, understood the propaganda value of such a raid within Whitehall. He wanted to push 'the PR side of I'.[139]

The raid took place on 27 February 1942. The commandos captured the radar and took a radar operator prisoner. The apparatus was sent to the TRE – Technical Research Establishment – at Farnborough, the prisoner to ADI (k) – RAF prisoner interrogation. The technical research and the interrogation reports were collated by ADI (Science). The examination pinpointed the radar's performance. It thus also established the proper counter-measures: a radar-evading flight profile and the use of 'window', foil strips that created 'noise' on the radar screen.

Within a few days of the raid, Jones had written up and circulated a full case history.[140] Churchill specifically asked for a copy, and pronounced the author worthy of 'high honours'.[141] At least forty-seven copies of the report were distributed around Whitehall, reaching every known intelligence department and many 'users'.[142]

Jones was a case-history innovator, in terms of topic, approach, and method. He was also the first person to write effectively about the impact of Bletchley Park on the wider structure of intelligence. However, Jones was an individualist in his approach to history: institutional innovation came from elsewhere in Whitehall.

Charles Morgan finished the first draft of his book *Naval Intelligence, 1939–1942* in February 1942.[143] This date of production was significant. Early 1942 marked the first crash of Bletchley Park's ability to decrypt German signals, of which the pessimists had warned.[144] Menzies sacked Alastair Denniston, head of GC&CS since 1919, in February 1942.[145] This manoeuvre allowed C to cling on to his control over Bletchley, but in the short term it was also an acknowledgement that Bletchley needed to be run as an armed-forces intelligence operation.[146]

The Bletchley crash had a disproportionate effect on naval intelligence. On 1 February 1942, the Atlantic U-boat fleet changed to a four-rotor Enigma machine, effectively blacking out British efforts to track the submarines. The U-boats would enjoy an increasing record of success, reaching a crescendo in December 1942. Also in February 1942, the Kriegsmarine and the Luftwaffe successfully orchestrated the so-called 'Channel Dash', the transfer of their warships *Scharnhorst* and *Gneisenau*, along with the *Prinz Eugen*, from Brest on the Atlantic coast of France back to their home port in the German Baltic. A large-scale radio screening and jamming operation blinded British intelligence.[147] The political fallout was so intense that ministers began openly discussing the failures of British intelligence, skirting dangerously close in public to the revelation of Enigma.[148] Morgan wrote a specially extended section on the Channel Dash in *Naval Intelligence*, explicitly because NID needed to assemble the case that it had not been caught 'unprepared'.[149]

Morgan was one of those civilians brought into NID by John Godfrey at the beginning of the war. There was a hint of vainglory about the secret history of naval intelligence, inasmuch as it focused on the words and deeds of John Godfrey himself. Kenneth Strong, the head of MI14, later dismissed Godfrey as 'the master of the "broad brush"'. 'There was a tendency for Naval Intelligence to feel itself superior, in efficiency and influence, to the Intelligence departments of the other two Services,' Strong wrote, but 'in fact, there was no justification at all for this attitude.'[150] However, most notably, Godfrey was convinced about the need to get the history 'right' from the very beginning of the war.[151]

Godfrey recruited Morgan from *The Times*, along with others such as Pirie-Gordon, of 'Club Med', and Donald McLachlan, the eventual public-facing historian of naval intelligence.[152] Morgan was a moderately well-known middle-high-brow novelist and playwright – his novel *The Voyage* won the James Tait Black Prize in 1940. He kept writing for the *Times Literary Supplement* throughout the war.[153]

Godfrey had originally envisioned the 'historical' role of the NID Information Section as maintaining the war diary for an eventual history of naval *operations*. He was acutely aware of how badly the conflict over the Corbett history, and particularly regarding who would have access to which Admiralty documents and when, had embittered personal relations in the Royal Navy throughout the 1920s.[154]

As a result of his experiences of the Hankey Inquiry, Godfrey changed his mind. By the time Morgan started work on the NID history, he was writing a pure history of intelligence, not an intelligence contribution to some future official history of the Royal Navy in the war. Indeed, he poured scorn on such a project as 'digging in the ruins of Nineveh and Tyre', noting that, when historical record-keeping was transferred out of NID, it was little more than the 'removal of a corpse'.[155]

Although he disclaimed his own novelistic talents in his role of intelligence historian, Morgan wrote the naval history *con brio*. Morgan kept working after Godfrey's term as DNI finished in November 1942, and he

3.2. Charles Morgan. Novelist and pioneering intelligence historian: the first version of his history of the Naval Intelligence Division was completed in 1942.

produced a second edition of the history for Godfrey's successor, 'Rush' Rushbrooke, in August 1944. Yet, despite some later reflections, the history remained focused on Godfrey and Godfrey's tenure of DNI.[156]

A great deal of the material Morgan collected mirrored that which had been used for the Admiralty contribution to the Hankey inquiries. Indeed, part of his purpose was to write Godfrey's *apologia* for his conduct during those inquiries, in which he had ended up siding with the civilian intelligence agencies against his service colleagues.

The second major theme in the Morgan history was NID's pioneering role in creating an Anglo-American intelligence alliance. It focused in particular upon the visit John Godfrey and Ian Fleming made to the United States in June 1941, and how they had tried to sell an ideal vision of an intelligence machine to the then-sceptical Americans.[157]

The Morgan history was a turning point. It was the last history that had to deal with the old question of why the British had become so ineffective at intelligence. By the time Morgan wrote the second edition of the history, it was from the perspective that the British were very good at intelligence: early war failures had merely been an unfortunate blip caused by a lack of resources and political will. The British intelligence organizations needed to remember their own failures in order to avoid them in the future.

Above all, Morgan pioneered a new approach to intelligence history. This history of intelligence would be a history of intelligence, not a history of intelligence's contribution to operations.

4

The Audit of War

History from the Year of Victory

The first draft of the history of intelligence in the Second World War was written before 1945 was out. Most of the 'secret histories', as usually understood, were not completed – or in many cases even begun – by that date. However, in some ways the early historical writing was more compelling than what came afterwards. The 'instant history' of 1945 created a mould. Much of the molten infill had already begun to harden by Christmas.

Timeliness was important. The career MI5 officer Jack Curry began ponderously writing a history of his own organization, only to discover that the senior civil servant, Sir Findlater Stewart, convinced that a solid historical underpinning was necessary for an inquiry he was running on security, had commissioned his assistant John Drew to write one too. Curry had to hustle round to Drew to share his notes. Thus the DNA of the unfinished MI5 history made its way into the Findlater Stewart Report. In that report, Stewart declared that the 'security history' of Britain, for the whole period 1919 to 1945, must now be regarded as 'settled'.[1]

The historians of 1944–45 were a group diverse in enthusiasm and aptitude. Some of them were very talented. J.C. Masterman, who wrote a history of deception, was a history don at Christ Church; his former undergraduates had recruited him into MI5. Others were on the brink of successful careers as academic historians: Harry Hinsley and Jack Plumb at Bletchley, Bill Williams at 21st Army Group, and Hugh Trevor-Roper of SIS.

Some of the historians were egotists determined to showcase their own wartime achievements, notably Masterman and Ewen Montagu of the Naval Intelligence Division. Some wished to write an *apologia pro vita sua*. Others were reluctant historians. Jack Curry believed, correctly, 'that if he took on the writing of the history of the office he would be overlooked for any other job.'[2]

Although the historical output of 1945 was vital in framing the past and future of intelligence, the work itself was drudgery, and the individual authors derived varying levels of satisfaction from doing it. Their historical writing was by no means independent: committees or other hierarchies oversaw most of the historians.[3]

Many wrote histories because they were ordered to do so. This often led to visible unevenness in the same history. For instance, the history of the Central Interpretation Unit, which generated image intelligence derived from aerial photography, was mainly a series of rapidly completed *pro forma* accounts – until one came to the account of railway intelligence written by Major Moody, a man who had plainly enjoyed both his job and his writing. In fact, he had written his history some months before the official instruction to do so reached CIU.[4]

Despite the personal specificities of each history, a number of identifiable strands coalesced. Thus there was an SIS version of history, a Bletchley Park version of history, a Naval Intelligence version of history, a JIC version of history, an SOE version of history, and, finally, an MI5 version of history. Although the strands were distinct, however, the process of creating them was intertwined.

The dominant versions also left out a great deal. In September 1945, Churchill's personal adviser on intelligence, Desmond Morton, once influential but by 1945 peripheral, quipped about the neglect of his former agency, the Industrial Intelligence Centre, '*Undank ist der Welten Lohn*' ('Nothing is so hard as man's ingratitude').[5]

Most notably, military intelligence, and to an extent RAF intelligence, found themselves once more left out in the cold, both as a result of their own decisions and decisions made on their behalf.[6] No one even considered the police.[7]

The 1945 history of British intelligence was a history of how certain voices had come to speak for intelligence. It limned out the boundaries of the field, striving to define who had been 'in' and who had been 'out'. In one of his own reflections on intelligence, R.V. Jones observed that 'the worldly wise are such rogues.'[8]

Sir Nevile Bland, for instance, was certainly, 'worldly wise'. Bland was the first of a trio of men commissioned to impose narrative and analytical order on the past, present, and future of British intelligence. In October 1943, Sir Alec Cadogan, the permanent under-secretary at the Foreign Office, commissioned Bland to write a report on SIS. Bland delivered the Bland Report in October 1944.[9] In the 1920s, Bland was the secretary of the Secret Service Committee. In 1939, he had found himself ambassador in the intelligence hotspot in The Hague. He had thus been swept up in the Venlo Incident.[10] In 1944, while still ambassador to the Dutch government-in-exile, he was closely involved with the revelation that British intelligence operations in occupied Holland were controlled by the Germans.[11]

Neither of the other two men charged with investigating the history of British intelligence were any less worldly than Nevile Bland. Findlater Stewart presided over the Home Defence Executive. A former permanent secretary of the India Office, trusted by his peers in the higher civil service, he had been brought fully into the intelligence fold 'by name' in 1941, 'partly on his official position as assistant to Sir John Anderson who was in charge of Home Security … partly on the sort of duties that he carried out for the Government and partly on his personality, record and knowledge of such work in India.'[12] In 1942 he had been touted as an official 'conciliator' when relations between SIS and SOE became unbearably poisonous.[13]

Denis Capel-Dunn was an army officer – a lawyer and clubman in civilian life – who served from 1941 as assistant secretary, then secretary, to the Joint Intelligence Committee. He handed over the day-to-day running of the JIC to another officer in November 1943, but remained in charge of the organization of both it and a series of other committees. Less well known to many, even in intelligence, Capel-Dunn was secretary to a Cabinet Office panel on security arrangements in government departments. The chairman of that panel was Sir Findlater Stewart.[14]

Capel-Dunn and Victor Cavendish-Bentinck, the chairman of the JIC, began discussing a report on the Joint Intelligence Committee in August 1943. Cavendish-Bentinck was a Foreign Office official who also reported to Cadogan. Capel-Dunn delivered their final report to the JIC in January 1945.[15]

By that time, Cadogan and Sir Edward Bridges, secretary of the cabinet, had tapped Findlater Stewart to carry out an inquiry into the Security

4.1. Sir Nevile Bland. Diplomat and author of the Bland Report on SIS.

4.2. Sir Findlater Stewart. Civil servant and author of the Findlater Stewart Report on MI5.

Service.[16] Stewart began work a few weeks after Capel-Dunn had reported and finished his inquiry in November 1945.[17] In Cadogan's quaint phrase, 'all the pigs are rounded up'.[18]

In the first report to be completed, Bland observed that there was not much point in pretending that he had been investigating a 'Secret Service'. The SIS had become, in the Blandian idiom, little more than a *secret de Polichinelle*. He confidently expected his readers to understand the allusion to Karl Wolff's 1903 play *The Secret of Pulcinella*, about the comic deceits of adultery. 'Pulcinella's Secret' was an 'open secret'. As had Lord Hankey before him, Bland poured scorn on the Passport Control Officer system. In his opinion, they might as well have put a brass plaque on their door, engraved with the title 'British Secret Service'.[19]

In less comic vein, Bland pointed out that the war had made the members of the 'secret services' well-known figures around Whitehall, as they dispensed intelligence, liaised with the foreign governments clustered in London, and worried away at the security of other departments. The identity of most intelligence officers did not 'need to be kept unduly secret, nor indeed can it be kept very secret.'

Bland thought that no purpose might be served in trying to bolt the stable door. The SIS would remain a semi-secret service, indeed a 'semi-public' organization. Bland turned his mind to how this status might be best exploited to wider advantage. He suggested that certain key figures in the British state should be prevailed upon to deliver public encomia on the key role that the 'secret services' had played in securing victory. His candidates for this role were the holy trinity of great leaders as it stood in 1944: Winston Churchill, Sir Bernard Montgomery, and Sir Arthur Harris.

Bland thus touched on three elements that would become central to the historical endeavour: the widespread knowledge of the intelligence services in Whitehall and Westminster; the need for some kind of broader public awareness; and, relating to both, and most important of all, the need to establish that intelligence had played an important role in military victory. The handling of all three, he realized, posed delicate challenges.

In 1943, Churchill, ever the cynic, declared that, 'every department that has waxed during the war is now considering how it can quarter its officials on the public indefinitely when peace returns. The less we encourage these illusions, the better.' He added that 'it will be quite easy to find the necessary

4.3. Heart of the Matter: Broadway Buildings. Here was the home of the Secret Intelligence Service, the Government Code and Cypher School, and (via an internal passage) the Passport Control Office.

personnel for such Security or Secret Services as we require.'[20] The history of the secret war was by no means a done deal. At an early stage, the need for 'positive information management', to use Richard Aldrich's perceptive phrase, in Whitehall, Westminster, and the press, had been laid down.[21]

History might be help or hindrance in addressing the third of Bland's challenges: how to establish that the secret service had made a contribution to military victory. The 1940 history had established that the British intelligence services were not really focused on assisting the nation's military effort in the inter-war period. Just as strikingly, by the time Bland reported, most intelligence agencies were busy shifting their focus away from assisting the nation's military effort. The turning point was in June 1944, when the U-boats had been defeated and a military expedition was safely lodged on the Continent.[22]

Part of Alec Cadogan's intention was to prevent broader inquiries, with a wider remit, and independent chairmanship. By 1944, Cadogan had drawn numerous threads of intelligence into his own hands, largely because his boss, Anthony Eden, kept accruing responsibility for intelligence agencies, while claiming to be overworked and uninterested. The Foreign Secretary had long been the minister responsible for SIS. In a personal capacity, Eden added responsibility for MI5 in December 1943. The Foreign Office took over the Enemy Branch – the intelligence division – of the Ministry of Economic Warfare in January 1944. Eden claimed ministerial responsibility for SOE in November 1944.[23]

Peter Loxley, Cadogan's private secretary, was the main drafter of the Bland Report, with significant input from Victor Cavendish-Bentinck. Cavendish-Bentinck was a loyal Foreign Office official, not some sort of honest broker. Cavendish-Bentinck advised that the Bland Report should be dressed up so that it did not look like the Foreign Office document it undoubtedly was. Otherwise it would invite the Service Departments to hold the fuller inquiry into the intelligence services that the Bland Report's whole purpose was to avoid. Cavendish-Bentinck undertook to lull his colleagues on the JIC into a false sense of security. He would briefly 'consult' them on the Bland Report and then pass off those discussions as 'full military consultation'.[24]

The authors of the Bland Report faced a tricky task They needed to demonstrate that SIS played a major role in the British war effort, while ridding it of the incubus of military influence. They needed to tell the story of SIS's ineffectiveness in order to demonstrate that Britain desperately needed a civilian political service. In Cavendish-Bentinck's view, SIS had 'failed badly'. This failure he ascribed to it being 'staffed with mediocrities' and 'starved of funds' before the outbreak of war. It was only through the 'good fortune which gave us Ultra and the miracle by which Ultra has continued during five years and the Germans have not tumbled to it, the senior members of SIS have saved their salaries.'

He argued that it was only since the invasion of Europe that SIS had started generating good agent intelligence, but that was solely because they were being supplied by European intelligence agencies such as the French BCRA.[25] 'In real enemy countries ... we have no agents and only obtain our information from neutrals who come out,' Cavendish-Bentinck lamented. The problem for SIS was that one did not have to be the chairman of the Joint Intelligence Committee to know any of this. The irrelevance of SIS and the dominance of signals intelligence was known around Whitehall and in the Services: 'the number of people who are in on this secret are legion.'[26]

The SIS version was most certainly a confection. The conclusions were reached before the investigation began. In retrospect, the motivation of the authors was fairly plain, although they sometimes cloaked them for tactical reasons. The Foreign Office wanted a secret service to gather political intelligence: the pre-war SIS, but actually effective. The SIS wanted to be that effective, well-funded, political secret service. It suited everyone's purpose to push the historical analysis of failure into the period before May 1940, largely to avoid discussion of the history of the war itself and to pick up the story when British intelligence was on top from the autumn of 1943. On the other hand, Loxley and Cavendish-Bentinck between them did know an enormous amount about the recent history of intelligence, and they applied that knowledge with effect. Their history of SIS integrated a much broader view of intelligence and the interrelationship between various agencies, rather than confining itself to the Secret Intelligence Service alone.[27]

Many of these issues were bound up with the history of the deputy directors of SIS, appointed in March 1942 at the insistence of the armed forces, who had found that SIS was incapable of supplying them with information useful to the conduct of the war. Cavendish-Bentinck claimed to have engineered the appointment of the deputy directors because he was so 'bored' by military complaints. The wrath of soldiers, sailors, and airmen would fall, ineffectually, on their own men.[28]

The SIS itself wrote the 'real history' of SIS. Major contributors included Menzies and Malcolm Woollcombe, the retiring head of Section I, the political section that collated intelligence for the Foreign Office and one of Loxley's Eton contemporaries, who wrote a 'valuable and amusing paper'.[29] Woollcombe pointed out that 'as in almost every government organisation, there are in SIS a number of excellent men who would probably be ready to stay on after the war subject to reasonable conditions of employment, provided an offer was made on them in time.' The SIS needed to pay well because the best officers could get better terms in industry: 'they cannot possibly be retired Indian Army or Service rejects.'[30]

The draft of the Bland Report opined that 'SIS officers became so impressed with necessity of anonymity and secrecy, that they became mere ciphers, living entirely on mediocre and meagre scale amongst non-entities. The whole environment tended to be a drab and second class world.'[31]

Menzies's own account fixated on the money. His goal was to secure a peacetime Secret Vote allocation for SIS double what it had been in 1939. And by a Secret Vote to SIS he meant purely SIS, excluding not only the other intelligence services he controlled – and wished to keep on controlling – GC&CS and RSS – but Section VIII of SIS itself. Section VIII alone now cost double the budget of the pre-war SIS. Menzies was thus imagining a peacetime SIS budget, in real terms, twelve times as much as it had been in 1914.[32] He was also assuming a much broader 'SIS empire' paid for by others.[33]

Apart from lack of money, Menzies laid the blame for SIS's poor historical performance squarely on the shoulders of the service intelligence departments: 'I would remind you,' Menzies wrote, 'that during the interval between the two wars, the War Office stated emphatically, on several occasions, that no information was required on Italy, whist the Admiralty decreed that Japan should be ruled out as an enemy.'[34]

Menzies argued that SIS had not had a performance problem; it had had, and still suffered from, a public-relations problem. It had been hoist on the petard of the Secret Vote. Politicians believed that most of the vote was spent on security, but nothing could be further from the truth: SIS had always consumed the vast bulk of the funds. It was Menzies who came up with the idea, subsequently expounded by Bland and Cavendish-Bentinck, that Churchill should provide a public tribute to 'Secret Intelligence' at the end of the war.'[35]

The one surprising aspect of SIS that Bland turned up, and Findlater Stewart confirmed, and which proved a bone of contention between Menzies and the otherwise supportive Foreign Office team, was just how few resources were being committed to espionage and how many were devoted to counter-espionage.[36] Cavendish-Bentinck attributed this evolution to the empire-building of Menzies's deputy, Valentine Vivian.[37] The figures were striking. In 1939, about 20 per cent of SIS officers in the London circulating branches had worked on counter-espionage. By 1945, 65 per cent of circulating branch officers were in counter-intelligence.[38] Meanwhile, as to the political intelligence reports, '90% of these were useless and a good many dished up out of works of reference.'[39]

The SIS had turned towards the sun of Bletchley Park. Whereas once Section I had been the main 'intelligence agency', collating and analysing political intelligence, mainly for the Foreign Office, now Section V was the main 'intelligence agency', collating and analysing counter-intelligence for SIS, excluding not only other analysts but other consumers.

As a result, probably the most hated man in intelligence was the head of Section V, counter-espionage, Felix Cowgill, referred to in private as SIS's 'sand-encrusted brain'. Doubtless, Cowgill was not an attractive person, 'a louse in the folds of a diseased dog's ear,' in the words of C's private secretary.[40] According to Cavendish-Bentinck, 'in the course of twenty-six years, I have never come across any institution or organisation in which the various members were so given to spitting venom about each other.'[41] Dislike of Cowgill built up to such an extent that Menzies removed him in January 1945, solving the human-relationship problem by replacing him with his much-better-liked deputy.[42] However, the real problem was not personality, it was the structural transformation of SIS. As the Bland Report was being written, Section V was, overwhelmingly, the dominant part of SIS.

At the end of the Bland process, Victor Cavendish-Bentinck reviewed the efforts and concluded that the core of intelligence was 'penetrating enemy service'.[43] Menzies homed in on Cavendish-Bentinck's phrase to reinforce his own contention that the history of SIS had been a history of insufficient long-term resources: 'penetration of foreign Intelligence organisations cannot be effected at short notice,' Menzies wrote. 'Continuity of effort is perhaps, more necessary in this branch of SIS work than in any others.'[44]

The historical cases that Bland picked out and cited – pre-eminently, of course, Venlo – concerned compromise or penetration. Loxley's predecessor as Cadogan's private secretary, Henry Hopkinson, had written a history of Venlo as far back as 1941.[45] The SIS responded with an alternative history of the incident.[46] Timing was important, however. Loxley had these early war histories in hand when he drafted the Bland Report, but the capture of the first German participant in the Venlo Incident occurred only in the week after Bland delivered the final document.[47]

Overall, Bland used the history in his report to make the case for a political intelligence service as intended. He recommended that Section V should be brought back to its proper status. Resources should instead be pumped into Section I – political intelligence.[48]

Bland laid the failings of SIS at the door of historical insufficient funding and unwise recruitment. 'We must never again,' Bland wrote, 'try to run the SIS on the starvation level of the lean years between 1920 and 1938.' He concluded that C had to stop recruiting men with private means or with an existing pension. Before the war, he contended, SIS had been overstaffed with ex-officers, and understaffed by those who knew about foreign countries. It now needed 'the best men', with 'first class pay and prospects' – indeed, men who would look remarkably like the denizens of the Foreign Office.[49]

Menzies, himself an ex-officer product of the very system that Bland criticized, thought this analysis was so much eyewash. In clubland he boasted that 'the only people he really relied on were those who had been with him for twenty years.' However, he was willing to accept the historical critique in order to get his hands on the money.[50]

Bland acknowledged that most intelligence had not come from SIS but from Bletchley Park. He reverted, however, to the pre-war argument that, 'we cannot count indefinitely on obtaining the bulk of our most valuable secret information through the GC&CS.'[51] It was thus by no means coincidental that GC&CS should begin to take an intense interest in its own history at the very moment Bland reported.[52] This was a new development in the autumn of 1944; hitherto, Bletchley had taken little explicit interest in history.[53] Frankly, its inmates were too busy machine-producing intelligence to have time to look over their shoulders. In September 1943, the head of Bletchley, Edward Travis, had written, 'we do not want to undertake any historical work now.'[54]

In late 1944, however, Travis's mind was acutely focused on history. He particularly wanted to retard the historical efforts of other organizations. The issue was pithily summed up in one of his briefs: 'WE MUST CONTROL THE DOCUMENTS.'[55] GC&CS's product had been scattered like chaff in the wind throughout Whitehall and British headquarters overseas. Anyone writing a history was bound to use it, and it was clear that many had already begun those histories.

Menzies and Travis agreed that all trace of decryption should either be destroyed or brought back to Bletchley. Menzies promulgated that edict at the end of 1944. Although the motive for this campaign was clearly the preservation of the 'Ultra secret', it did force Bletchley into some reasoning about the nature of history. Only Bletchley should be allowed to write 'true' intelligence history. For everyone else, intelligence history would merely be a means of writing the history of the enemy. Other intelligence organizations would 'compile their own Intelligence histories as was done after the last war'. However, since only Room 40 – the Bletchley analogue – and MI5 had done a thorough job, this was not too much of a problem. Bletchley would control the history of British intelligence.[56]

Like Travis himself, two of the three moving figures in the GC&CS history initiative, Frank Birch, head of Naval Section, and Alastair Denniston, now head of the Government Communications Bureau, had long personal experience of intelligence history reaching back to the First World War. The new boy was Gordon Welchman, the assistant director of Bletchley.[57]

Birch had the distinction of being the sole intelligence historian of the First World War who would go on to be an intelligence historian of the Second World War. He saw himself as repeating his Room 40 experience, combing through all the accumulated decrypts to produce a definitive blow-by-blow account. Such a process had taken – and would take once again – many years, not least because the scale of Bletchley was so much greater than that of Room 40.

Birch was an oft-ridiculed figure at Bletchley, labouring under the nickname Widow Twankey, after a farcical pantomime character: he had no role on the key policy committees that set the Bletchley agenda in late 1944.

However, Birch was thrust into a position of more immediate importance at the beginning of 1945, when the American representative in Hut 3 – Bletchley's 'intelligence centre' – Telford Taylor, proposed an 'Anglo-American research project on European ULTRA and ULTRA handling techniques … which would produce a historical record of the role of SIGINT in the European War.'[58] The project was approved in early March 1945, and American G-2 – military intelligence – and OP-20-G – naval intelligence – officers arrived in Bletchley to help with the project.[59] An 'historical committee' was to oversee the work.[60] The Bletchley Park Historical Committee was formally constituted under Birch's chairmanship in August 1945,[61] and Birch's Naval Section became the 'Historical Tasks Section' in October 1945.[62] Birch finally got the title 'Head of the Historical Section' in January 1946.[63]

Denniston took his cue from Bland's defence of the black chamber. According to Victor Cavendish-Bentinck's notes on the Bland Report, it had been Denniston's blue jackets – BJs – decrypts of diplomatic communications, that had delighted Churchill, more even than Ultra, and saved Stewart Menzies's bacon.[64] Menzies sacked Denniston as head of GC&CS in early 1942 and turfed him out of Bletchley. However, Menzies had set him up instead as head of the Government Communications Bureau – GCB – in London, universally known, from its primary address, as Berkeley Street. The GCB was exactly what GC&CS had been before the war – a black chamber. Denniston reported directly to Menzies, not to the head of Bletchley Park.[65]

Denniston was determined that early GC&CS should not be portrayed as the failure from whose ashes the triumphant phoenix of late-war Bletchley Park had risen. He was seriously perturbed by a remark by Eric Jones, the head of Bletchley Hut 3, that 'it would be a tragic and retrograde step for intelligence as a whole, and therefore – this is not putting it too high – for the future of the country, if GC&CS were to sink back into its pre-war position.' Denniston wanted a history that stressed GC&CS's long-term commitment to military intelligence, rather than portraying it as a mere black chamber. This history would take Jones's words '*not* as a general scathing criticism of the pre-war activities of GC&CS but as a warm tribute of the wartime development in GC&CS of its new function of "Intelligence" at the source, a tribute with which, I am sure, none of the Service Departments will quarrel.'

Denniston wrote the first history of GC&CS from his own memory, submitting it within weeks of the Bland Report. Its avowed purpose was to rehabilitate Hugh Sinclair in the eyes 'of those about to build the new GC&CS'. The GC&CS had gone over to the Foreign Office and diplomatic intelligence only because the Services had been unwilling to pay for it. In any case, 'there was no Service traffic ever worth circulating.'[66] The GC&CS had been held back by lack of funds, and because the armed forces had controlled interception. The army had had its own decryption effort both at home and in the field, while GC&HQ had only one interception station, acquired from the Metropolitan Police at Denmark Hill in 1924. The second station run by the GPO at Sandridge was not obtained until the eve of the Second World War. Between 1920 and 1939, the cable companies dutifully handed over all material routed through Britain: none of it had been read, because none of the Services wanted it read before 1938.

The GC&CS had been well aware of the German Enigma machine, but the Services had showed little interest in putting in the effort to gain intelligence from German military communications. In any case, being aware of Enigma and breaking into it were two very different things. The armed forces started sending some intercepts over only in 1937, and GC&CS had used the scanty material wisely. 'I think that it may be rightly held that this effort of 1938 and 1939 enabled the party at BP to read the current traffic of the GAF within five months of the outbreak of the war,' Denniston wrote.[67]

Of the trio, Gordon Welchman, a Cambridge mathematician, was the relative newcomer to GC&CS. As the head of machine decryption, however, Welchman was by far the most influential of the three architects of Bletchley history by 1944. He was not particularly interested in history *per se* – although it subsequently became something of an obsession – however, he had a keen understanding of the power of history to influence the future.[68] Welchman believed that everything Bletchley wrote or allowed to be written was important, because such histories would be the opening shots in a bid for effective control of British intelligence.

The history of Bletchley's triumph had to be hardwired into the belief systems of the British administrative, military, and political elites, for the very reason outlined in the Bland Report: it would not always be 1944. Bletchley had enormous cultural capital. It was easy to generate such capital 'when concrete results in the form of a large and valuable output can be produced as evidence.' However, Welchman warned, 'the development of a proper framework for another war will be largely a matter of abstract planning, and prestige in such matters is not easy to establish.'[69]

In September 1944, Welchman, along with Harry Hinsley, a Cambridge historian serving in the Naval Section, and Edward Crankshaw, a literary critic and military intelligence officer brought into Bletchley in September 1943, wrote a plan for the future that they sent to Travis and, subsequently, to Menzies.

Welchman, Hinsley, and Crankshaw forthrightly stated that, after five years of war, 'there was no conception of a proper intelligence organisation' in Britain. As they wrote, there was, in their view, 'a definite but fleeting chance of using wartime experience in one field of intelligence to obtain a proper development of all types of intelligence.' Bletchley Park should be the model and hub of that intelligence organization, 'the intelligence centre'.

The problem was that Bletchley Park, as the ideal intelligence organization, was at risk, because 'in high places the existence and value of this output are known to very few.' The Bletchley Park model had to be sold in the very near future: 'all the experience on which these ideas are based has been gained in several years of concentrated work and in secret. It will be no easy matter to explain all that has been learnt to a few people in high places who are allowed to know the secrets, and those who do not know the secrets will be highly sceptical.'[70]

The primary role of the intelligence centre would be the collection, analysis, and distribution of political intelligence, because 'Foreign Policy will be very difficult after the war: there will be a high demand for diplomatic intelligence.' The intelligence centre would be the core of the 'Foreign Intelligence Office' and answer to the Foreign Secretary. The secondary role of the centre would be the collection, analysis, and distribution of scientific and technical intelligence, since new weapons would make a surprise attack so much more devastating than it had been historically.

Welchman and his co-authors were particularly insistent that the armed forces should be excluded from, or play a very subordinate role in, the intelligence centre. They had no serious role in intelligence. They were merely 'users'. At most, the army might need some tactical signals units for the battlefield.[71] These arguments were explicitly deployed in Whitehall in the spring of 1945.[72]

Despite their very different motivations and approaches, Welchman, Denniston, and Birch agreed that Bletchley as it looked in 1944 was a problem. They feared that if decisions were taken on the basis of current performance, they would not reflect their own preferred 'reality' of a dedicated cadre of highly educated civilian intelligence officers. Bletchley in 1944 was a military camp, dedicated to armed-forces intelligence. The reforms of 1942–43 had completely transformed the organization. In order to become Bletchley, Bletchley had militarized itself. It was no longer about maverick civilian geniuses: Alan Turing had long since been removed as head of Hut 8.[73]

According to the figures that Birch collated, until the summer of 1942 Bletchley had been a predominantly civilian organization. By the summer of 1943 it had more than doubled in size and its personnel were fifty-fifty civilian-military. By D-Day it had grown by half again, with the military in the clear majority. By the autumn of 1944, the civilian establishment was actually decreasing, while the military establishment continued to grow apace: by VE Day, 63 per cent of Bletchley's establishment would be in uniform. Many of the officers and other ranks deployed to Bletchley were drawn from similar backgrounds to the civilians: there were very few 'professional soldiers' among them. However, their very presence demonstrated that Britain's armed forces were quite capable of mobilizing an effective intelligence effort in pursuit of operational intelligence.[74]

The historians of Bletchley wanted to reverse this process of militarization by claiming not only decryption, but interception, traffic analysis – W/T Intelligence in older jargon – and intelligence analysis for a civilian GC&CS.[75] The reverberations from the Bland process allowed the Bletchley historians to firm up their version of intelligence history. What made this exercise immediately relevant was Menzies's instruction to come up with a proper plan for the future of GC&CS, and Travis's decision to set up a series of working groups to flesh out that plan.[76] Clearly, the working groups' primary focus was on the future rather than the past. However, they had to clear a great deal of historical brushwood in order to function. Welchman and Hinsley sat on 'sub-committee B', chaired by John Tiltman, with Edward Crankshaw and Jack Plumb devilling on some of its reports.[77]

Their first challenge was to define what they had been doing. In one sense, Bletchley Park was, plainly, an intelligence organization, 'because its object is to produce "intelligence"'. But in Bletchley's own *lingua franca*, 'intelligence' had hitherto been used 'to describe the work of part of the organisation'; Hut 3 and Naval Section VI in Hut 4 were akin to the 'assembly department of a manufacturing firm' whose role was 'to hand over to a user'. The problem was that 'even after several years cryptographers of the old school were still regarding intelligence officers as an inferior breed of men with an easy job.'[78] John Tiltman still had a tendency to evince such prejudices at inauspicious moments.[79] An intelligence officer by this account was a failed cryptographer, someone who could not handle the mathematical, logical, and linguistic rigours of cryptography.[80]

Any useful historical narrative would have to be retrospectively converted to encompass a more capacious interpretation of intelligence and the intelligence officer. Not everyone working at Bletchley had been an intelligence officer, but intelligence officers, cryptographers, and traffic analysts could now all be recognized as such.[81] Being an intelligence officer was a prize rather than a booby prize.[82] By 1944, this was simple to agree to, but it had to be said in order to make clear that 'GC&CS should be finally and absolutely responsible for all Intelligence work and … for all Intelligence personnel.'[83]

The Churchill government agreed to Bletchley's role as 'The SIGINT Centre' in the spring of 1945.[84] In doing so, it adopted Welchman's argument that 'the value of Signal Intelligence is obvious to all who have had extended experience of the service during the war.' It stood high in estimation. 'But people would forget, governments would change, and it would be the inter-war years all over again.' They had to get the story straight now.[85]

This decision was followed immediately by the promulgation of the Bletchley 'history plan'. The plan was twofold. First, to chart the development of 'signals intelligence', particularly 'cryptanalysis', the term coined to replace 'cryptology', the word hitherto used for code and cipher breaking, into the beating heart of the 'intelligence machine'. Second, to control the flow of information to non-Bletchley historians. In 1945, the initial job of Birch's

Historical Committee was to control that flow.[86] No one – especially not other intelligence historians – was going to get any Bletchley documents: Birch would set up a 'filtering process' merely to prevent untrue statements.[87]

On a broader front, Travis issued his notorious 'law and honour' secrecy directive in April 1945. It first addressed the need to filter the historical record: 'no possible excuse,' Travis wrote, 'must be given to the Germans to explain away their complete defeat by force of arms. They will seize on any excuse to maintain that they were not well and fairly beaten, and the uncanny success of our Intelligence would offer them just such an excuse.' He only then went on to cite the various operational reasons why no one should blab about Bletchley. Thus, from April 1945, Bletchley's intention to warp history was made explicit.[88]

Frank Birch had his work cut out in his new role as intelligence historian-gatekeeper, not least because the intelligence histories of 1945 were being written in a kind of 'wild west' atmosphere.[89] However, Bletchley's new status as '*the* SIGINT Centre' certainly had an immediate effect on the histories of other signal intelligence agencies.[90] The Special Liaison Unit (SLU), the unit staffed by military personnel but controlled by SIS Sections II and VIII, which handled communications between Bletchley and military commanders in the field, passed under Travis's direct authority, while Anthony Gore-Browne was writing up its history.[91] The 'Wavell model', in which military commanders had maintained fully functioning interception and decryption units, was portrayed as a dead end.[92]

A proposed history of the Radio Security Service was stillborn. It would have concluded that the amalgamation of the service with Bletchley was probably a mistake: 'nobody denied that GC&CS had done a wonderful job but this had not been due to the organisation but rather in spite of it. Had the organisation been better the results would have been obtained with far less labour and been more intelligently used.'[93] It would also have argued that, although Trevor-Roper's section had been formally separated from RSS in 1941, 'being regarded as an Intelligence Section and not properly part of a technical organisation' and thus going to SIS Section V, while RSS came under the control of SIS Section VIII, this had made little practical difference. The Intelligence and Discrimination sections remained co-located in Barnet, 'fully integrated' and doing intelligence. The main targets of RSS had been the Abwehr, the SD, the intelligence service of the German foreign office, and the Italian Servizio Informazioni Segrete. From 1942, they had added allied governments in London – Polish, Czech, Yugoslav, French, and Russian – to the target list.[94]

On the other hand, the Royal Navy felt no such inhibitions. Ewen Montagu wrote a long and catty history of NID 12, the section of naval intelligence responsible for distributing Ultra, which he had headed from 1943 to 1945. Montagu most certainly did not return his documents to Bletchley: he broke them out and reread them. Commander G.E. Hughes wrote an equally catty history of NID 9, the naval signal intelligence agency. The SLU history remarked that the navy never 'played fair' and that the Admiralty acted as 'a Law unto itself, not subject to mere mortal control.'[95]

The naval signal intelligence history began with the sentiment that the GC&CS black chamber had not been of much use when it was really needed in 1940, and that it had become truly fecund only when its relevance was decreasing: 'at the beginning of the war we needed every scrap of intelligence we could get; at the end we could have reduced intelligence staffs by nine-tenths, and still have won.'[96] One had not needed special intelligence to understand the extent of Germany's difficulties from July 1943 onwards.[97]

Hughes concluded that 'the Services must control the national Signals Intelligence effort,' 'Communications Officers must learn … more and more about it,' and that 'only communications officers can produce communications intelligence intelligently.' In 1939, the Naval Y Service had had two hundred personnel, the same as GC&CS: in 1944 it had 5,500 personnel – not quite as big as Bletchley, but in the same order of magnitude.

Hughes, as he wryly admitted, very much a civilian in uniform, set out 'not to explain what went right but what went wrong.' In Hughes's view, the primary thing that had gone wrong was the breakdown of trust between signallers and intelligence officers. In part this had been due to professional naval officers looking askance at 'bloody amateurs'. However, hoity-toity intelligence officers had stoked distrust by going around with their noses in the air, too delighted with their Ultra.

Thus, many naval officers had known that they were getting high-grade decrypts, but were too often treated like idiots. Eventually a compromise was worked out by which all officers were told about the existence of 'special', though 'they had guessed long before'.

Montagu made much the same point. His butt was Captain Oliver Bevir, the director of Naval Ordnance who had distributed Ultra to his officers, and, when reprimanded, had written to the DNI 'for your information, and as an indication of the care taken in such matters, may I inform you that I have been wearing a false beard while dictating this letter.' 'It was obviously impossible,' Montagu concluded, 'to let officers with such an attitude of mind have such information.'

On the other hand, he cited the Director of Economic Warfare Division (DEWD) as someone who had been unfairly treated like an 'idiot'. Captain Oswald Hallifax 'knew' about Ultra because his collaborators in the Ministry of Economic Warfare had told him where their intelligence was coming from. In any case, 'DEWD like so many others had read the stories of Blinker Hall's work in the last war!' 'He was,' however, 'too much of a gentleman to display his knowledge when Lt Cmdr Montagu went through his camouflage stories with him.' It was only in November 1943 that NID had persuaded Menzies to be straight with DEWD.[98]

Hughes noted that, by 1944, the situation had stabilized, because both the Director of Naval Intelligence and the Director of Signal Division sat on the Signal Board, and all officers on the captains' course were taken to Bletchley to be told 'the facts of life'. There were a great many naval officers who knew a lot about intelligence. The 'unhealthy fog of ignorance and suspicion has now been cleared.'[99]

However, Hughes, confidently if pessimistically, expected history to repeat itself, not least because of the claims of the 'SIGINT Centre'. His history, he noted, was 'not the occasion to discuss the rights and wrongs of the post-war Signal Intelligence scheme'. However, he imagined that 'the Director of the SIGINT Centre' would soon be 'irked' by the Services, and 'begin to wonder why he should share the secrets of his trade with serving officers.' Given what Bletchley was writing about the armed forces, this was a reasonable interpretation.[100]

Hughes's history was more than naval *amour propre*. Bletchley's own analysis confirmed his account of how signals officers had been treated, and the potentially disastrous consequences.[101] In the same month Hughes delivered his history, the man who sat next to him in the Admiralty, Commander W.G.S. Tighe, delivered his own sobering report on B-Dienst's penetration of British signals. Only three copies of the Tighe Report were made, 'but the Report was considered of so disturbing and important a nature that it was widely distributed in "High Places" in the Admiralty.'[102]

In brief, the capture of German documents and the interrogation of personnel revealed that the Nazi-era Kriegsmarine had an almost total grasp of British naval codes. They had used this mastery to break into British ciphers from mid-1938 onwards. As with Bletchley, B-Dienst lost its access at times, but until the end of 1943 it had an excellent record in breaking back in. What the British had done to the Germans, the Germans had done to the British. Both thrived in the same conditions: the failure of intelligence and signals officers to communicate effectively with one another.[103]

The difference between Britain and Germany was that, on a broader level, Britain had found ways to co-ordinate its intelligence efforts. In 1944 and 1945, the fulcrum of co-ordination, the Joint Intelligence Committee, certainly received plenty of attention. It formed the third important strand of the intelligence history of 1945.[104]

The men who 'wrote up' the JIC were Victor Cavendish-Bentinck and Denis Capel-Dunn.[105] Since Cavendish-Bentinck and Capel-Dunn were also playing such an important role in shaping the Bland Report, the JIC version was inevitably entwined with the SIS version. The genius of Capel-Dunn was in providing a plausible overarching framework for interpreting the role of intelligence in the Second World War. He also formalized the portentous phrase 'the intelligence machine'.[106]

The perverse effect of this construction was that, in the emerging history of 1945, the JIC served as the proxy for armed-forces intelligence, thus ensuring that the actual armed-forces intelligence effort got little attention. Areas in which the armed forces were dominant players, most notably prisoner-of-war intelligence and photographic intelligence, were labelled as diminishing assets, with little future relevance.[107]

When they began to discuss how to write the history of the JIC, Cavendish-Bentinck and Capel-Dunn necessarily put a great deal of thought and calculation into how they might present themselves, and their role, to best effect. Their first thought was that they needed to get out from under military tutelage altogether, becoming a civilian-controlled organization.

Capel-Dunn, however, intuited that this would be an unwise manoeuvre: in any reorganization of the state at the end of the war, the Chiefs of Staff, with their enormous and growing prestige in fields other than intelligence, were bound to survive. The JIC was much safer as a cuckoo in the military nest.[108]

The armed forces themselves played a significant role in their exclusion from the main joint intelligence narrative. In August 1942, as part of his plans for the NID history, John Godfrey had suggested to the then-Secretary of the JIC that he should write a history of his own organization, so that everyone else could understand what it did. The attempt to piece together the history of the JIC revealed that there was a paucity of relevant documents and some shaky memories. At that time Denis Capel-Dunn had been assistant secretary to the committee.[109] Charles Morgan returned to the charge with Capel-Dunn in March 1944 for the second edition of *Naval Intelligence*. Capel-Dunn said that the naval interest in history had prompted him to create sound historical records to underpin his work on the future of the JIC.[110]

Godfrey was one of the early boosters of the JIC, not least because it seemed to serve NID's interests: given the 'DNI's predominant influence in Inter-Service Intelligence organisation it would be bad policy for him to initiate any action which might weaken Inter-Service collaboration.'[111] In the Rushbrooke years, doubts surfaced, not least because, once Godfrey departed, Cavendish-Bentinck began to act as a 'headmaster,' treating the new DNI and his deputies as recalcitrant schoolboys. In these latter years, NID came to believe that Cavendish-Bentinck and Capel-Dunn were too ready to bend intelligence reports to fit in with the preconceptions of their superiors. It was, the head of NID 17 observed, 'a dismal tale of orthodox logic being allowed to displace intelligence pointers.'[112] However, such doubts never fully displaced the Godfrey-centric view of history and remained *sotto voce*.[113]

F.H.N. Davidson was the Director of Military Intelligence between November 1940 and February 1944. He too had seen the miserable failure of early war attempts at joint intelligence and was thus an admirer both of the philosophy and the work of the JIC: 'Modern war,' he wrote in October 1943, 'is no longer an affair of small professional armies … from a series of independent, overlapping, and often conflicting, intelligence agencies before this war we have already made great strides in combined intelligence and, by the very nature of modern war, no other sort of intelligence can fit the bill.' He believed that the JIC should co-ordinate many combined intelligence functions, including signal intelligence.[114]

Davidson's own historical concerns were altogether more parochial. His abiding passion was the army's Intelligence Corps. The corps had first been formed in the First World War, disbanded in 1919, and reconstituted in 1939. Davidson was determined that it should become a permanent fixture in the army's order of battle. 'If we are to safeguard the Corps' interests in the future, it is very necessary that we should build up a record of its history in the present,' he decreed. The problem was that there were no real Intelligence Corps units, merely detachments in other units. Davidson's solution was to 'try and start some system by which we can keep a trace of the more important happenings in connection with the Intelligence Corps.' He asked 'for the co-operation of all officers serving in senior I appointments.'[115] As he prepared to leave London to become the army's intelligence representative in Washington, Davidson made a personal pilgrimage to enlist officers to the cause.[116]

Tellingly, the military intelligence officer who was keenest on writing military intelligence history found himself blocked at every point by the JIC. Dudley Clarke's main interest was in giving the 'Wavell Model' – devolved General Staff Intelligence, operating at theatre level – due credit. Clarke had been one of the intelligence officers summoned by Wavell to the Middle East in 1941, in his case to set up A Force controlling deception operations.

As Clarke put it to the JIC, this means of conducting the intelligence war was 'wholly British in conception, the idea of one of the great British war leaders (Field Marshal Wavell), developed entirely by British staff and subsequently shared whole-heartedly with our Allies.' Wavell had subsequently set up a similar organization in the Far East, GSI (d), under Peter Fleming. It was crucial for everyone to realize that General Staff Intelligence was not 'a collection of "Blimps"'.[117]

As the focus of the war shifted to North-West Europe in 1943, London and the main operational theatre became coterminous. The Chiefs of Staff set up their own London Controlling Section to do the same job as A Force and GSI (d). Clarke had ambitious plans to tell this story, including not only an internal history but also a popular public history, and even documentary films. This overreach made him easy to refuse.[118] He was told to confine himself to his account of A Force.[119]

As for the RAF, Air Vice-Marshal Inglis, ACAS (I), said that his ambition was to offload as many intelligence responsibilities to joint intelligence as he could get away with in order to concentrate on '"Air" matters of purely operational importance to the air force.'[120] He also wanted to get Air Intelligence out of the history business and hand everything over to the Air Historical Branch, so that it could write conventional operational histories. His successor, Thomas Elmhirst, said that the 'historical work' of ACAS (I) would end in August 1945.[121]

That is not to say that there were not some very keen intelligence historians in the RAF. The most energetic was the chief of air force prisoner-of-war interrogation, Assistant Director of Intelligence (k), Group Captain Denys Felkin. Felkin had started amassing material for a history as early as 1943, not least because he was sceptical of the secular trend toward joint intelligence.[122] In August 1943, ADI (k) had been given the responsibility not only for prisoner-of-war intelligence but also for captured-document intelligence. From June 1944, documents began flooding into their London offices. Felkin was thus sitting on top of a gold mine of sources in 1945.[123]

In 1939, the armed forces had, without any top-down push, created a joint interrogation intelligence agency, the Combined Services Detailed Interrogation Centre (CSDIC).[124] Military Intelligence, in the form of MI19, ran CSDIC.[125]

The head of CSDIC throughout the war was an army officer, Thomas Kendrick. Kendrick was neither a regular nor a wartime recruit, however. He had previously featured in the Bland Report as the hapless Passport Control Officer arrested by the Germans in Vienna in 1938. In addition to running CSDIC, Kendrick moonlighted as part of the SIS team that ran an interrogation camp near Aldershot – for but one prisoner, the Deputy Führer, Rudolf Hess, who had parachuted into Scotland in May 1941.[126] Kendrick returned to SIS when CSDIC closed its doors in November 1945.[127]

British prisoner-of-war intelligence had been one of the great intelligence success stories of the war.[128] Victor Cavendish-Bentinck wrote that it was by far the most effective military intelligence agency of the war, and 'one of the most valuable sources of intelligence'.[129] In order to carry out effective interrogation, the military had recruited exactly the kind of people that the Bland Report had suggested were needed in civilian intelligence agencies – good linguists, who were well educated, empathetic, ruthless 'men of the world'.[130]

However, Felkin himself concluded that joint intelligence bodies had developed a tendency to collect and hoard intelligence for the sake of so doing. This was a poor way of doing intelligence. 'The time factor is all important,' Felkin wrote, 'since in a fast moving war much information that is intelligence on one day becomes history on the next.' The key was to break the prisoner very quickly through direct interrogation. Hidden microphones and stool pigeons were overrated by CSDIC, in Felkin's view. The key to good intelligence was writing it up quickly and getting it out to those who could use it: ADI (k) had direct telephone and teleprinter links to the other sections of ACAS (I) and to every RAF Command. About two hundred copies of each ADI (k) report were distributed. The primary role of intelligence services, Felkin believed, was to save British lives.[131] He most certainly did not adopt the Capel-Dunn view that, with the end of world war, prisoner intelligence would fade away, since 'interrogation is concerned with the eternal fallibility of human nature.'[132]

Felkin's views were coherent with those of the RAF as a whole.[133] Sir Orme Sargent, the second-ranking official in the Foreign Office, had ruled that RAF intelligence nostrums should be ignored: 'I do not understand the mentality of people who reason in this fashion,' Sargent wrote in July 1944. 'I am sure the FO should do all they can to prevent this reasoning from being accepted as the basis of British Foreign Policy.'[134]

When Capel-Dunn came to write up his findings on joint intelligence, he argued that the armed forces could not be trusted to deliver intelligence of the kind required. The reasons were twofold. First, history suggested that the military could not be trusted to give intelligence or intelligence officers a high enough priority: 'Before the present war,' he observed, 'the Intelligence Branches were not much favoured parts of the Staff in any of the three fighting Services. Indeed it would be foolish to pretend that even now, in the sixth year of the war, intelligence has not many critics.'

Second, the history of military intelligence agencies demonstrated that they could only flourish in the conditions of total war. However effective CSDIC, for instance, might be, it was sustained by a constant flow of prisoners. 'It is hard,' Capel-Dunn wrote, 'to see much scope for such an organisation in peace time.' He recommended that interrogation should be handed over to SIS and MI5.[135]

Capel-Dunn produced a clever construct. It articulated with both the Bland Report and the Findlater Stewart inquiry.[136] Its characterization of military intelligence officers had resonance with those very officers: they felt underappreciated by their own services.[137] John Sinclair, Davidson's successor as DMI, was tapped up to become deputy chief of SIS, with the expectation that this would lead to him becoming C.[138] The head of G-2, Supreme Headquarters Allied Expeditionary Force (SHAEF), the British's army's most prominent intelligence officer, Kenneth Strong, decided to jump ship for a career first as head of the Political Warfare Executive and then of the Joint Intelligence Bureau. Major-General Geoffrey Vickers VC, the head of the Enemy Branch of the Ministry of Economic Warfare, resigned his commission in October 1944 when his organization was transferred to the Foreign Office.[139] In 1945, the army's senior intelligence officers were planning their careers as heads of civilian intelligence agencies.[140]

The fourth strand of intelligence history, that of the Special Operations Executive, was, in turn, a product of the preceding JIC strand. The SOE was another intelligence agency that fitted all too well into the JIC version, as a military organization that would have to be euthanized. It was a highly militarized – although, as it vehemently insisted, not military – intelligence agency.

Set up in July 1940 as the result of the merger of three existing organizations – Military Intelligence's 'Research' section, MI (R); SIS's D Section; and a Foreign Office/Ministry of Information black propaganda unit known as Electra House – SOE, like Bletchley Park, took on its mature form only after 1942. The black propaganda elements had been spun back out to create the civilian Political Warfare Executive. The SOE as it existed in 1944–45 was what had been known as SO2 in 1940–41.

The status of SOE, and in particular the history of His Majesty's Commission in the organization, was a very sore point. Early in its development, SOE had decided that it wanted all its British military members to be officers. However, the term 'commissioned officer' had covered a range of possibilities. Some officers were army officers seconded to SOE, while some early intakes of able-bodied young men had joined as civilians, and then been conscripted and sent back to SOE. A third group, the 'pseudo officers', had been commissioned merely for being in SOE. To make things worse, these officers had not only wangled themselves higher and higher ranks, they had negotiated special salary packages that gave them pay far in excess of their titular rank. Those who had joined before April 1941 were also paid tax free: this was known as SOE's 'venal period'. None of this had been particularly secret, and indeed questions were asked in the House of Commons about these practices.[141]

By 1944, SOE's military members – essentially the whole organization – were overwhelmingly other ranks. However, the proportion of officers remained very high. The HQ staff in London and overseas was made up entirely of officers. Its head – CD – Major-General Colin Gubbins was the genuine military article. The director of operations, Eric Mockler-Ferryman, had been Kenneth Strong's predecessor as G-2, AFHQ, for Eisenhower. Even Gerald Templer, wounded as a divisional commander in Italy, did a stint in SOE. Templer would go on to be Director of Military Intelligence after the war. In 1945, military commanders in the field maintained that not only was SOE a useful 'special forces' outfit, it was a better *intelligence* agency than SIS.[142]

The 1945 history dealt a double blow to SOE. In its militarized form it could be lumped in with military intelligence agencies such as CSDIC as a highly effective hostilities-only organization whose saliency would wither with peace. In its politicized form it could be portrayed as venal, ineffective, and dangerous.[143]

The members of SOE were not unaware of how others regarded them. Their defensiveness spawned the apologia that was the SOE version of history. As a result, SOE articulated the clearest vision of 'secret history'. One of its assistant directors, James Hanbury-Williams, had identified their audience as 'the limited "outside public"'. This 'limited outside public' was not 'the public'. Rather it was those who had an awareness of the activities of specific intelligence agencies, but were not themselves 'in intelligence'. He was thinking of ministers, civil servants, and parliamentarians.[144]

The successive ministers of Economic Warfare who had responsibility for SOE, Hugh Dalton and Top Selborne, made it a practice to circulate 'secret histories' of what they regarded as particularly successful operations, beginning with the overthrow of the Yugoslav government in the spring of 1941.[145] The two best-known examples of this genre were 'Inside Greece' of 1943 and 'Heavy Water' of 1944.

'Inside Greece' was the history of SOE's attempt to find a Greek resistance. In September 1942, Brigadier Eddie Myers had been parachuted into Greece. Myers was one of the 'real officers' in SOE. A Royal Engineer, he had been specifically recruited because he was the only senior officer anyone could find who was both a trained parachutist and skilled at blowing up very large structures. Myers needed these qualities because he was expected to act as an intelligence officer, finding out what was actually happening 'inside Greece'; a subversive, encouraging the creation of a Greek resistance movement; and a saboteur.

In November 1942, Myers, having stitched together some resistance groups, blew up the Gorgopotamus Viaduct that carried the main railway line from northern Greece to Athens. The blowing of the Gorgopotamus Viaduct had been the first significant act of anti-German resistance anywhere in Occupied Europe. Before Gorgopotamus, resistance had mainly been jaw-jaw rather than war-war.

In June 1943, Myers repeated the trick when he blew up the other main north-south viaduct, the Asopus. The Asopus Viaduct was attacked not by the Greek resistance but by Myers's small British band acting alone in a tale of 'endurance, sheer "guts" and determination'.

Myers himself embodied the intelligence, political, and military identities of SOE. He built an airstrip and he was exfiltrated back to Cairo in August 1943, where he was justifiably fêted as a hero. However, he brought with him a Greek resistance delegation, dominated by Communists, thus roiling a sea of troubles.[146]

'Heavy Water' was the history of intelligence agencies against atomic weapons.[147] In between the Gorgopotamus operation and the Asopus operation, in February 1943, at the opposite end of Europe, SOE had blown up part of the Norsk Hydro facility at Vemork, where the Germans were manufacturing 'heavy water' as part of their atomic bomb programme. A year later, the remnants of the same party blew up the ferry transporting the remaining stores of heavy water to Germany. In the Vemork case, the SOE operatives were all Norwegians, and the attacks were organized in close co-operation with the military intelligence agency of the Norwegian government-in-exile – FO.IV – and the Norwegian resistance organization, Milorg.[148]

If any operation made a cast-iron case for what were becoming known as 'special forces', Vemork was surely that case. The SOE had, after all, saved western civilization. That was most certainly the argument made over the summer of 1945. A fortnight after the end of the war in Europe, the *Daily Express* published a story from its Stockholm correspondent, entitled 'Secret Army Fought Nazi Atom Bomb'. This was two months before the first atom bomb, the Allies' super-secret super-weapon, was even tested. A subsequent investigation found that the Norwegians in Oslo had given the journalist the full story on the day the war in Europe ended.[149]

The publication of the Vemork story did not provoke any kind of secrecy drive. When the Allies used the first atom bomb on Hiroshima, the news headlines concentrated not on Japan but on Norway. On the evening of 6 August 1945, both the prime minister, by then Clement Attlee, and his predecessor, Winston Churchill, issued statements on the history of atomic weapons. The *Daily Mail* headline summed up the prime ministerial statements as 'Spies, RAF, commandos in Battle of Wits.' Attlee's statement identified 'the intelligence service', and he said that 'the possession of these powers by the Germans at any time might have altered the result of the war.' Churchill gave the exact date of the SOE attack – February 1943 – and suggested that we 'beat the Germans by a few months.'[150]

In the wake of these statements, SOE sought, and was given, permission to provide a version of the 1944 history to the BBC.[151] Eric Welsh, the head of atomic intelligence, did remark, ungenerously, that the tale had 'already been told *ad nauseam* by the Norwegians', and questioned whether it was '*really* necessary' for SOE to tell it again, 'for the purpose of personal aggrandisement?' The answer was, plainly, yes.[152] None of these accounts spelled out the brand 'Special Operations Executive', but it was common knowledge in the 'limited outside public'. The SOE historians expected everyone they contacted to know about Vemork, since it had been 'already fully described in the press and radio'.[153]

The SOE was well used to writing its own version of history by the time its leadership took the formal decision to push ahead with a range of *histories* in August 1944. These histories were conceived by an organization that was very aware of the 'limited outside public', in the knowledge that it now had to sell itself in order to prosper.

Unfortunately for SOE, others beat it to the punch. The bulk of SOE historical writing occurred in a very concentrated period of the autumn of 1945, not least because its authors now knew that their organization was doomed and they wanted to get as much down on the record as possible. As Harry Sporborg, chief of staff to CD, remarked, acidly, 'like the Bourbons, everyone has "learnt nothing and forgotten nothing".'[154]

The Bland Report had got to SOE as early as April 1944. The Foreign Office and SIS barely needed to discuss the line they would take, since everyone agreed. 'Covert action' was a very useful tool of secret service. The idea should be retained in SIS, but SOE should be dispensed with as soon as the war ended. In order to bolster the historical case, Loxley arranged to take the testimony of Rex Leeper, the Foreign Office official whom Eddie Myers had denounced in his Greek history.[155] Leeper viewed Myers as a dangerous fool. Myers saw Leeper as an effete egomaniac. In October 1943, Leeper managed to have Myers disbarred from any further work in Greece.[156]

The SOE histories would be completed immediately after the Foreign Office and SIS finally unmasked their guns. As ever, Victor Cavendish-Bentinck was at the heart of this exercise, playing SOE and the military along until his bosses were ready to act.[157] Gubbins could do little other than react with fury when Cavendish-Bentinck finally told him he, Cavendish-Bentinck, had always been working the JIC toward abolishing SOE.[158]

The SOE history that had the most immediate impact in the autumn of 1945 was the so-called 'popular version'.[159] In the summer of 1944, Gubbins and his advisers had envisioned two versions of SOE history: the 'detailed version' and a 'popular version' that would cherry-pick the highlights. They wanted the 'popular version' to have a widespread, perhaps even a public, release. To this end they had commissioned Lionel Hale, well-known scripter of such plays as *The Mocking Bird: An Extravagance in Three Acts* and *She Passed Through Lorraine: A Comedy in Three Acts*. Hale was a familiar voice on the wartime BBC.

Hale's theme was that SOE had fulfilled the mission that it was given in 1940: it had organized a political and military resistance to the Nazi occupation of Europe from Athens to Oslo. He quoted Eisenhower's chief of staff, Walter Bedell Smith, as saying that 'without the organisation, material,

4.4. Lionel Hale. Playwright, popular broadcaster, and the first historian of SOE.

and training which SOE supplied "Resistance" would have been of no military value and in some countries might not have existed at all.' Such resistance had made four major contributions to the defeat of Germany: industrial sabotage, illustrated by Vemork; sabotage of lines of communication, as with Gorgopotamus and Asopus; direct support of regular forces; and shaping the post-occupation political settlement.[160] Hale's version of SOE's history had staying power, not least because it continued to be circulated after January 1946 when SIS took over SOE and made it once more its own D organization.[161]

Hale drew the distinction between 'clandestine organisations in cells' and 'para-military or guerrilla organisations'. By concentrating on the latter, he was able to smooth over the tribulations of the former. However, the final leg of the SOE version of history concentrated on those very tribulations.

The core lesson drawn from history by the Bland Report had been that 'penetrating enemy service' lay at the core of all intelligence work. It was held that such penetrations were excruciatingly difficult and required long-term planning and serious resources.[162] However, the history of SOE demonstrated that the despised Germans – although ineffective at spying on Britain – had been very effective at penetrating enemy service.

In one sense, the history of the penetration of SOE formed the first element of the fifth strand of intelligence history, the MI5 version. In the autumn of 1944, the director general of MI5 said that his organization's most pressing task was accumulating information 'regarding German penetration of British Intelligence organisations'.[163]

In writing the history of penetration, MI5 – and specifically MI5 B Division – tended to hold the whip hand.[164] Their evidence came from two main sources: captured German documents and the interrogation of German intelligence officials.

When the invasion of Europe was being planned, SIS insisted that it would provide SHAEF with its Special Counter Intelligence units – SCI – and an SIS 'War Room' in London that would co-ordinate their operations. Special counter-intelligence was an SIS operation under military cover, albeit one commanded by Dick White, an officer seconded by MI5 as its 'Brigadier'.

By the autumn of 1944, however, Kenneth Strong, G-2 SHAEF, had concluded that SIS was not doing a very good job, and demanded that the War

Room should be re-organized to collate and analyse information on the Nazi deep state for the benefit of military counter-intelligence officers.[165]

The MI5 B Division officer Tar Robertson had been appointed head of a new SHAEF War Room, with MI5 and SIS now staffing the reformed War Room equally, with the balance of its numbers made up by American OSS officers and representatives from the French intelligence agency, DSDOC. The War Room's stated aim was to forensically pick apart the Reichssicherheitshauptamt.[166] War Room reports, based on an increasing flood of documents and interrogations, were distributed widely.[167] 'With,' Robertson wrote, 'the increasing success of CI staffs in capturing and accounting for the significant members of GIS [the German Intelligence Service], the War Room's knowledge of GIS became in all essentials complete.' Robertson wrote a history of the War Room before it finally closed its doors in November 1945.[168]

MI5 also controlled the intelligence output of Camp 020, set up in 1940 under the command of Robin 'Tin Eye' Stephens to interrogate suspected spies. Its product was analysed by a section of B Division under the direction of Buster Milmo. In the summer of 1945, senior German intelligence officers captured by the Allies were transferred from the Continent to Camp 020 for detailed interrogation. They included Ernst Kaltenbrunner, the head of the RSHA, Heinz Jost, head of RSHA VI until 1941, and his successor, Walther Schellenberg, who held the post until the end of the war.[169] The results were circulated as Camp 020 'Yellow Perils'. The deputy commandant of Camp 020 wrote a history of the operation in late 1945.[170]

The investigation into the German intelligence service homed in on the activities of Abwehr III Feind (Enemy). When Abwehr had disintegrated under the pressure of Himmler's rival RSHA, Abwehr III F had survived as RSHA Amt VI Z. Most of the personnel involved in penetration operations, however, had dispersed into the Mil. Amt's paramilitary FAK, attached to field armies. The FAK continued to run penetration operations and 'had so much material available about allied intelligence services that they were nearly always well-informed about the developments of resistance movements in France, Holland and Belgium.'[171]

The German captives also included Hermann Giskes, former head of Ast-Niederlande III F, who arrived at Camp 020 in June 1945.[172] Giskes had joined the Abwehr in 1938, having been recruited by Major Feldmann, the head of Ast-Hamburg III F. Feldmann went on to lead Ast-Frankreich III F in Paris. Feldmann himself was captured in early September 1945 and was duly interrogated, as was the III F officer who ran the penetration operations in Paris on a day-to-day basis, Hugo Bleicher.[173]

By the time the War Room began writing the history of the Abwehr and RSHA VI, it was clear that Ast-Niederlande and Ast-Frankreich III F had specialized in sophisticated penetration operations. In 1945 the British were able to ask their officers about these operations in person. The SOE cases lay at the heart of the investigation. In the autumn of 1943, two Dutch agents of SOE N Section had escaped from the custody of the RSHA's police force, the SIPO, in Holland. When they got back to England, they claimed that the Dutch Resistance was little more than a German front organization.[174] The men were treated with grave suspicion and imprisoned in Brixton, leading to an Anglo-Dutch diplomatic incident.[175]

In April 1944, however, Hermann Giskes sent a taunting message to the head of N Section, Seymour Bingham: 'Thank you for your long mutual cooperation. In case you should come to the Continent I shall receive you with the same as your agents.'[176]

In February 1944, Henri Déricourt, a French agent of SOE Section F, was denounced by other members of the resistance as a German penetration agent,[177] and by the beginning of 1945, additional suspicion had fallen on Nicholas Boddington, a British F Section officer, who operated undercover in Paris in 1943.[178] Boddington was cleared of treachery, but the investigators discovered that the deputy head of the resistance group with whom he was operating in Paris had indeed been an Abwehr III F agent. The 'Abwehr got everything,' Guy Liddell, the head of MI5 B Division, noted.[179]

Paris itself fell to Allied troops in August 1944. Among the documents captured in the headquarters of the Abwehr was a 160-page report by another British SOE officer, Ronald Seth, originally parachuted into Estonia during 1942. The report outlined Seth's penetration work in Paris on behalf of the Abwehr. A few weeks later Seth himself was captured, and claimed to have 'turned' in order to save his own life.[180]

Each of these cases descended into acrimonious arguments about who had betrayed whom. These arguments continued for decades. However, in 1945 no one doubted the overarching conclusion that the Germans had been running successful penetration operations. The disagreement was whether

SOE had been an effective organization that accepted some degree of penetration as the inevitable consequence of doing business in hostile environments, or whether it had been a compromised intelligence agency whose other activities were merely cover for the risk to which it had exposed the entire British intelligence machine.[181]

However, as the investigatory work continued, it became clear that, in the overall history of penetration, SOE was a red herring. The SOE had been created in July 1940. Both Abwehr III F and the SD were running penetration operations long before. The road led straight back via Venlo. By the time Giskes had joined the Abwehr in 1938, Feldmann's 'main pre-occupation was the breaking down of the English Secret Service Organisation in Holland.' There was also a shadow organization directly answering to III F in Berlin, run by Richard Protze, known as Stelle P. An old naval friend of Admiral Canaris, Protze had been the architect of the whole III F service, serving as its head in Berlin between 1929 and 1938.[182]

Feldmann and Protze had done an excellent job in penetrating the SIS Passport Control Office in The Hague. A British employee, Jack Hooper, was wholly their man. Feldmann recruited Hooper in 1937;[183] Giskes had been his case officer in 1939. MI5 did not have far to go to find Mr Hooper, since he was by then a highly regarded officer in B Division, which he had joined after leaving SIS.[184] There was no evidence that Hooper was active after he returned to London: his German handlers had no means of contacting him. Giskes, however, continued to run penetration operations into SIS networks in Holland as late as 1944.[185] Hooper was quietly 'let go' by MI5 in September 1945.[186]

To make entirely sure that they got III F technique and terminology straight, MI5 re-interrogated their captives on that very point. The Germans explained that they had drawn a strict distinction between two kinds of counter-espionage agents. A GV-Mann was a German agent who gained the confidence of the enemy and passed them false or censored information – *spielmaterial*, or, as the British would say, 'chicken food'. An E. Mann was a much more dangerous beast – a German agent who penetrated enemy service and passed back material without the knowledge of the enemy. By the middle of 1945, the history of German penetration operations had been thoroughly written up.[187]

In turn, the British had their own history of penetrating German service. The MI5 version of history rested heavily on the success of these deception agents. From the middle of the war, counter-espionage had 'seemed of little account' in comparison with the 'preparation of the deception' to cover British amphibious operations, pre-eminently D-Day.[188]

By far the most influential history in shaping this understanding of counter-intelligence was that written by J.C. Masterman. 'J.C.' already had to hand the case histories prepared by his colleagues in B Division, most notably 'the GARBO Case', authored by Juan Pujol-Garcia's case officer, Tommy Harris.[189] For 'connoisseurs' of deception agents, the GARBO case was 'the most highly developed example of their art', 'interesting alike for the illustrations it gives of all the many sides of the work, for the skill and ingenuity with which it was controlled by its case officer and for the efficiency with which all possible advantages were squeezed from it.' The Lisbon-based Pujol-Garcia was the most successful purveyor of D-Day disinformation.[190]

Masterman, the history don, did the job of writing history well, and he did it swiftly. He was helped by a number of other factors. First, he worked in close collaboration with Ewen Montagu of NID 12. Montagu wrote the parallel history of the W Board, the high-level body that oversaw the release of deception material.[191] Masterman and Montagu cross-referenced each other's histories and made sure that they tallied in both conclusion and detail. Montagu wrote the naval section of Masterman's history for him. Masterman, unusually, drifted off his assigned topic – double agents – to pay special tribute to Montagu's Operation *Mincemeat*, which, he admitted, had not involved any double agents – merely the corpse of a British vagrant.[192] Masterman was allowed to present a preliminary version of his history, in the form of a lecture, to the final gathering of the W Board in August 1945.[193]

Both Masterman and Montagu were slighting of military intelligence, as opposed to intelligence operations carried out for the benefit of the military. From the beginning of 1944, Masterman wrote, 'all our activities were swallowed up in the one absorbing interest of the grand strategic deception for the Normany invasion.'[194] Montagu argued that deception-agent operations had to be kept out of military hands, because 'it had a high "gossip" value: it would have been too great a temptation to trust to senior officers.' Keeping

4.5. J.C. Masterman. Oxford history don, MI5 officer, and the historian of double-agent operations in the Second World War.

the military at arm's length 'was the greatest single factor in enabling double-agent work to achieve its success.'[195]

Nevertheless, Masterman's history was very nuanced. Although celebratory in tone, it clearly drew on the forensic opposition research done in the past year. There was a cornucopia of evidence, unlikely ever again to be replicated. This material demonstrated that it was very unwise to rely on the history of counter-espionage when writing the history of penetration of service.

The Germans had been at a disadvantage since the war began. The Abwehr had been feeble in not creating a pre-war espionage network in the UK, but this was on a par with SIS, which had not established any networks in Germany. Both services had individual spies in each other's countries. When the Abwehr had tried to insert agents into Britain from the autumn of 1940, they had suffered predictable disaster. The Germans had had 'a geographically small target,' which 'restricted the channels through which agents could be introduced.' Conversely, 'the situation favoured the British'. They knew that there was only 'one target for German Intelligence to aim at'. Once the initial fear of a huge network already in place dissipated, it was the 'obvious conclusion' that the enemy 'would attempt to infiltrate agents as ordinary travellers.' The only flights from Europe to England from June 1940 took off from Lisbon and Stockholm. The British had merely to crimp a 'narrow bottle-neck'.[196]

The Abwehr effort in 1940–41 had been on a small scale and fairly easily contained. During the course of the war, the Abwehr sent their 'agents' in Britain £85,000 in pay and support. In one operation later in the war, RSHA VI had paid the valet of the British ambassador in Istanbul £88,000 to photograph his employer's papers.[197]

Masterman wrote down the 'simple proposition that in time of war espionage in an enemy country is doomed to failure because the dice are hopelessly loaded against the spy.'[198] 'It would be agreeable,' he continued, 'to be able to accept the simple explanation that we were very clever and the Germans very stupid, and consequently we gained on the swings and roundabouts as well.' 'But,' Masterman concluded, 'that argument won't hold water at all.' As the deceivers themselves fully realized, they only looked like masterminds compared to other intelligence services because of Bletchley Park.[199]

Leaving aside the unique advantage that British deceivers enjoyed, which, Masterman said, had gone 'a little to our heads', the 'evidence' demonstrated that the Abwehr:

> were at least our equals in all the arts connected with espionage and counter-espionage. They had studied the subject over a long period; after some early clumsy improvisations they settled down to train agents carefully; they certainly handled many of them with admirable psychological understanding; they supported them loyally and rewarded them adequately; in short there is no reason whatever to attribute our success and German failure to our superior wisdom or our greater ability or our better practical handling of agents.[200]

Although Masterman's warnings about not allowing a false view of history to breed overconfidence were absolutely clear, he weakened his technical case by arguing for a moral history of the intelligence war.[201] Masterman saw British intelligence success as primarily a moral triumph. It had demonstrated the 'integrity of all officers and other persons concerned in the UK from the top to the bottom.' The double agents had been a rum bunch – they were, 'after all', foreigners, 'who had been in touch with the enemy' – but the Brits were sound.[202]

The history of deception was coeval with Findlater Stewart's inquiry into MI5. Stewart had been a member of the W Board and commented extensively on Masterman's presentation of his findings. More than that, he emerged as a very prominent character in Masterman and Montagu's histories. In contrast to the relative neglect of the military, it could indeed be argued that Stewart featured rather disproportionately in the histories. From the spring of 1941 onward, Stewart's Home Defence Executive (HDE) had been in charge of attempts to divert the Luftwaffe away from British cities.[203] He had used the MI5 double-agent network to put over 'dangerous stuff', accurate information that alerted the Luftwaffe to genuine military installations that they might attack, or indeed strategically unimportant factories in less densely populated areas.[204] This work had reached a new peak of activity in 1944, in response to the V-weapon attacks. Stewart claimed 'that thousands and thousands of lives were saved by the removal of the mean point of impact outside London.'[205] John Drew, Stewart's deputy at the HDE, who had run the V-weapon deception operation, was in charge of drafting the historical sections of the Findlater Stewart Report.[206]

The main problem that Findlater Stewart addressed was that Britain ran two large counter-espionage agencies in the UK throughout the war. The head of the Security Executive, Duff Cooper, had pointed out the absurdity of this system in 1943. It was redundant having SIS Section V and MI5 B Division doing the same job, and constantly at cross-purposes. Why not amalgamate them?[207] Churchill had shot down Cooper – but it was a difficult question to ignore.[208]

Stewart had to operate within clear tramlines. His inquiry was designed as a lineal successor to that of Nevile Bland: he could hardly challenge his predecessor's recent conclusions about SIS.[209] Stewart was told not to gratuitously offend the War Office or the Home Office, while effectively ignoring them.[210] Military intelligence was most definitely to be kept out the picture, for 'under modern conditions security has ceased to be primarily a Service problem.'[211]

Both Stewart's formal remit and his actual room for manoeuvre placed the focus on investigating MI5, and doing something to or about it. The historical capital that the MI5 version had created within government was therefore important. The Foreign Office architects of the Findlater Stewart inquiry believed, after all, that MI5 was no good. Its officers were little men, with 'no imagination' and 'no variety of personal contact.'[212]

The history of deception was used to neutralize such attacks. The cut-and-thrust of deception and penetration agents, the matching of wits with a dangerous enemy, was quite different from searching under furniture in dingy bedsits. The future of MI5 depended in large part on how decision-makers viewed the recent history of B Division's ambitious deception operations.[213]

There were three ways that MI5 was able to mobilize its version of history effectively. First, and most straightforwardly, they were able to demonstrate how useful B Division had been. Second, they were able to demonstrate how problematic the 'Cowgill Regime' in SIS Section V had been.[214] Third, and least expectedly, they were able to harness the JIC version to their advantage. The Capel-Dunn Report had cleared the ground by constantly portraying military intelligence as having to be overseen, guided, and corralled.[215]

In private, some MI5 officers felt that the army was quite competent at security.[216] Findlater Stewart preferred the official MI5 version. His first act was to kill any debate. He was not going to argue the toss about 'the need in these times for the kind of work done by MI5'. The 'security history' of Britain since the inter-war period left no room for 'any doubts about the need for secret means to counter underground attempts to penetrate our military secrets.' The history of the SIS V-MI5 B clash was an 'embarrassment'. Stewart put down the squabbling to the 'three-mile limit', the pre–First World War convention that the 'home secret service bureau' would confine itself to home waters. This Edwardian conceit had been rendered nonsensical by the wartime scientific revolution and its 'harvest of "counter-intelligence"'; MI5 should now be allowed to operate 'in defence of the realm' on a truly worldwide scale.[217]

The intelligence history written in 1945 had its own particular texture. There was certainly plenty of it. It was raw, ragged, and rough round the edges, but it captured the thoughts of the British state as it reflected on its wartime experience. The historical writing carried out within the state was complex, the work of different individuals with different personal objectives. For some it was a 'lessons learned' exercise, for others an act of memorialization, for others history was mainly the means for burnishing a personal reputation. However, despite these complexities, the history was not particularly fractured. There was a great deal of overlap between different history projects. A reasonably coherent narrative and analysis of intelligence emerged.

This interpretation of contemporary history was an important factor in the construction of the British state. The overriding conclusion was that the 'intelligence machine' must lie at the heart of the state. Of course, there were dissenting voices. Certain senior military commanders believed that intelligence officers were getting a little above themselves. In the public sphere, and, marginally, in the private, there were qualms about creating a 'Gestapo'. However, there was no convincing counter-narrative to the emerging consensus. Although politicians and civil servants were willing to challenge the competence of the 'intelligence machine', few now dismissed it. They wanted intelligence to work.

Very few of the intelligence histories were written in the belief that they would remain truly secret. The main debate in 1945 was about how much to say in public. By the middle of the year, the mood was against too much revelation. The aftermath of the First World War in this, as in so many other things, was cited as the way one should not do things. History was to be 'semi-secret', aimed directly, or more likely indirectly, at the limited public sphere. The intelligence agencies wanted Westminster and Whitehall to know about them, their deeds, and their mystique.

The soldiers, however, remained almost voiceless. The DMI and GSI were not even secret organizations. Although soldiers made a lot of noise on many intelligence issues, they did very little to articulate what intelligence in war was for, and how it was actually used to achieve victory.

5

The History Boys
History from the 1940s

In November 1949, the intelligence machine was consulted for the umpteenth time about its view on the publication of wartime histories. For the umpteenth time the representatives of intelligence organizations, wearily, 'maintained their view that they were always averse to the publication of secret matters'. Yes, it was 'quite true that any amount of material has been published,' but the trick was to avoid saying anything authoritative.[1]

On such an argument, fringe players had been relatively easy to squash, ignore, or manipulate. In January 1946, Eddie Chapman delivered his memoirs to the left-wing publisher Victor Gollancz, having already published a version in France.[2] Chapman was already an exotic presence in the secret histories. He was the only Abwehr agent to parachute into England on two separate missions. He was the only British double-cross agent trusted enough to have been deliberately sent back to Germany to penetrate the Abwehr. Chapman was certainly a deserter, a criminal, and a traitor, but his handlers viewed him with a kind of affectionate amazement.

At same time, the journalist Sydney Firmin delivered a manuscript to his publishers for an instant history of British wartime intelligence. Firmin, it was acknowledged, had done a good job, based on genuine sources; MI5 suspected that those sources worked in Special Branch. Firmin also engaged in some intelligent speculation 'about cryptography and the use of machines for that purpose'.[3]

Firmin and Chapman were taken as a pair. Chapman was prosecuted under the Official Secrets Act: Firmin was given further 'off the record' briefings and told to go ahead and publish his findings. His juiciest story involved the arrest of the head of the Free French navy, Emile Muselier, in

1940. Muselier had been a drug user and a sexual experimenter, but not a spy.[4] The scandal had long since passed, many people knew about it already, and Muselier, having fallen out with de Gaulle, was no longer a figure of any account.[5]

Some cases struck closer to home. One of the two protagonists of 'the famous Venlo Incident', Richard Payne Best, was outraged that no one had shown the least interest in his story when he was liberated from Sachsenhausen. In 1946 he wrote a personal history of his captivity.[6] It was eventually published in 1950.[7] Stewart Menzies had hoped that Best would be 'now happily forgotten'. He had no desire for Venlo to re-emerge into the 'limelight'. Unhappily for Menzies, the Dutch government was still interested in Venlo, not least because one of its own intelligence officers was killed during the incident.[8]

Trials were a hazard that needed to be minimized. In the summer of 1947, two trials got entangled with the secret history itself. Two years previously, 'Tin Eye' Stephens, the wartime commandant of Camp 020, had transplanted his operation to Germany, under joint MI5 and MI19 auspices, where it was known as CSDIC, Bad Nenndorf. In Germany he was much better placed to interrogate any prisoners who fell into the hands of the British forces of occupation. He also brooded mightily on what he saw as the shortcomings of the history of wartime Camp 020. He fulminated to London that it was 'uneven, it does not cover the ground and it is tedious reading.'[9]

Almost as their last act as they left MI5, David Petrie and his deputy, Jasper Harker, agreed to allow Stephens to rewrite the history. They reassured him that Camp 020 had been of 'such vital importance to the organisation that it is essential that any future DG, who may have to staff a similar show, should have the full benefit of all your experience both as regards the set up and practical administration.'[10]

Stephens wrote a new history of Camp 020 – or as he called it, with heavy-handed humour, 'a digest of Ham' – in collaboration with his assistant commandant at both 020 and Bad Nenndorf, Major Short. Camp 020 had been based at Ham House. Stephens and Short finished work in January 1947: the result was more than twice as long as the previous effort, and no better for its length.[11] The new 'digest' was mainly a monument to Stephens's ego, although he appeared only as 'the editor', an anonymous 'regular officer of the Security Service', who 'himself must surely be interrogated one day.'[12]

5.1. The Case That Would Not Die: Venlo. Dutch reconstruction of the Venlo Incident, November 1939, staged in 1948.

It is doubtful if he thought that questioning would be by British army lawyers a few months hence. Sadly, for all concerned, the winter of 1946–47 was the hunger winter across Europe. Some of Stephens's prisoners at Bad Nenndorf died, others had to have limbs amputated for frostbite, because buckets of freezing water were thrown over them and the windows of their cells were deliberately smashed.

In the history, Stephens had written that 'the responsibility is from first to last in the Commandant'. The 'ideal arrangement' was for the commandant 'to interrogate with the whole weight of the establishment in support.' There was no point in being 'precious' about interrogation, 'the bitter, uncompromising approach' was the best: and, 'as with a man, so with a woman – no quarter.'[13] The star witness against Stephens was his co-author, Major Short.[14]

In June 1947 the army arrested Stephens. The first thought of MI5 in London was to cut him loose. Had not Stephens berated them during the war for wearing military uniforms as cover, while he was a properly commissioned officer? When he started writing the history, Stephens had been an MI5 officer, but before he finished, he had transferred onto the payroll of the Intelligence Division of the British Control Commission in Germany.[15]

According to MI5, the introduction to the history of 020 was therefore misleading, the author was no longer, as he claimed, 'a regular officer of the Security Service'. Stephens's former colleagues did not want their history sullied by Stephens's present: their 'only fear is that people will say that this is how Camp 020 got their information during the war.'[16]

The solution MI5 found to their Stephens problem was to pay for a sharp lawyer, in theory for his benefit, but in reality 'someone there who could unofficially look after our interests.'[17] The lawyer was Dick Butler, the wartime personal assistant to the Director-General of MI5.[18]

The case was further complicated, for those who feared reputational damage to British intelligence, by being coeval with the start of another set of trials in Germany that put another of the great British wartime interrogators in court. In their history of Ham House, Stephens and Short had stressed that interrogation, like British intelligence as a whole, had become the 'machine, the system, the network, call it what you will.'[19] At the heart of the machine was Camp 020, CSDIC, and the Prisoner of War Interrogation Section (PWIS), which had been run by a man very much after Stephens's own heart, Lieutenant-Colonel Alexander Scotland of the Intelligence Corps. Better known as 'the London Cage', PWIS had acted as the army's screening camp for filtering PoWs for transfer to CSDIC.[20]

As Stephens was placed under arrest, Scotland arrived in Hamburg to testify at the German army trials. The defence strategy was to attack the London Cage, and Scotland personally, in the witness box, for obtaining confessions or witness statements by means of torture.[21]

Butler's defence for Stephens was that, *pace* his own words, the commandant was not responsible for what went on in an interrogation camp. In the event, this worked. He was acquitted at court martial. Stephens was re-employed by MI5 and sent to West Africa, while Short was cold-shouldered as a man without caste.[22] The list of defence witnesses that Butler assembled, Lord Swinton, Duff Cooper, Sir David Petrie, and Dick White, had helped, as did intense negotiation between MI5 and the DMI.[23] None of this success came without hard work on the historical record, in face of 'dangerous gossip' and 'sticking mud'.[24] A core goal of the defence had been to establish that no torture had taken place at Camp 020: if anything had gone wrong, it had gone wrong on the German wild frontier.

Although the court martial took place in camera, it did not shield Bad Nenndorf from the prying eyes of Labour MPs, and thus of senior ministers who had to defend British conduct in parliament. It became a point of honour for Labour MPs, and for many journalists, to refer specifically to MI5 by name in public: Bad Nenndorf was described as an 'MI5 Camp'.[25] The leading members of the Labour government, Attlee, Bevin, and Herbert Morrison, were not altogether willing to believe the protestations of innocence made by the intelligence machine. They all knew people who had been mistreated for their political beliefs.[26]

Accordingly, the now well-established line that MI5 had been in chaos in the early part of the war because of under-resourcing, had to be deployed by the senior leaders of MI5. Britain in 1940 had been as much a wild frontier as Germany in 1947. Once regular systems were put in place, everything was done as it should be.[27] The portions of Jack Curry's history of MI5 that dealt with internment were shared with the official historian working on that subject, to illustrate how sensitive MI5 had been.[28]

The MI5 account given to Attlee by Guy Liddell was that 'in this country physical violence was not a weapon the interrogator would wish or be permitted to use.' However, 'it would be idle to pretend that an interrogating officer does not, in a large percentage of cases which he handles, put pressure – and often severe and continuous pressure – upon his subject before he can achieve or hope to achieve any result … it will, more often than not, be founded on fear – fear for himself, fear for someone else.'[29] The political line ministers took was 'that appalling stupiditys [sic] have been committed in the past, but that the Labour Government are going to see that we are properly supervised.'[30]

The press did not necessarily buy that line. In August 1945, orders had been issued to prevent journalists getting hold of documents on intelligence operations in liberated countries.[31] From that point might be dated the rise of the 'insurgent' history of intelligence created by frustrated reporters. Harry Chapman Pincher, the dean of troublemakers, started work at the *Daily Express* in September 1945. His first scoop even derived from an official history – the American study of the Manhattan Project – a pre-publication copy of which was shown to him by a contact at the department of Tube Alloys.[32]

The first post-war budget revealed that the Secret Vote during the war amounted to fifty-two million pounds; Britain's wartime atomic research had cost one-thirtieth as much.[33] If it was legitimate to investigate atomic weapons, it was reasonable to ask about intelligence. Neither could this eye-watering sum be written off simply to the cost of fighting a total war. The first post-war Secret Vote was two-and-a-half million pounds. In real terms it was thus six times higher than the peak of the post–First World War Secret Vote.[34]

Members of the intelligence great and good also punctuated the five years after the war with public lectures about British intelligence. Their motivations were various and several: personal grievance at having lost a bureaucratic battle; a sense that they or their former colleagues had been unfairly traduced; a desire to dispense wisdom; and, above all, in explicit terms, the fear that the Attlee government had not got a proper 'grip' on the Cold War. History could provide both a warning and a guide for the future.

In February 1947, R.V. Jones, former ADI (Science), gave a long public lecture on scientific intelligence.[35] The lecture was published in August 1948, just as a secret inquiry by Sir Douglas Evill criticized the post-war conduct of scientific intelligence in terms remarkably similar to those used by Jones. In February 1948, Colin Gubbins, former CD of SOE, lectured on the wartime support for subversive movements in territory controlled by a repressive alien power.[36] In January 1950, Sir Robert Bruce Lockhart, former 'British Agent' and former Director-General of the Political Warfare Executive, lectured on how to conduct political warfare.[37]

In the spring of 1945, Churchill's wartime government had decided that there would be an official military history of the war. It was not until November 1946, however, that the Attlee government actually announced the plan for the official history and appointed an overall editor, J.R.M. Butler. Butler then had to go about assembling a team, 'consisting partly of academic historians, most of whom had some Service experience, and partly of retired officers of the regular forces'.

Just as after the First World War, it was imagined that the Royal Navy and the Royal Air Force would want to commission shorter, more 'popular', histories, and indeed this proved to be the case. The army was not to have its own history; rather its actions would be recorded in a series of campaign histories.

The First World War official history had not actually been finished by the time Butler was appointed to write the history of the Second World War, which was plainly ridiculous. Nevertheless, even the 'streamlined' Butler history was clearly going to be a very long-drawn-out project. In the event, relatively little was published before the late 1950s, by which time the historians – some of whom had had no great aptitude for their task – were beginning to retire, and pointed questions were being asked in parliament.[38]

In the view of the leaders of most intelligence departments, Butler could hardly take long enough. They regarded him, and the editors of other historical series, such as Michael Postan for the 'home front', with some unease. The overall cabinet decision seemed unchallengeable, but the devil remained in the detail. In particular, Bletchley's 1945 scramble to 'CONTROL THE DOCUMENTS' meant that, at best, official historians were going to receive highly curated intelligence documents, which they could not use, except inasmuch as they 'prevented error'.[39]

The challenge, such as it was, to the control the intelligence services had over their own history arrived at the beginning of 1948. Sir Winston Churchill, leader of His Majesty's Opposition, former prime minister, and author of best-selling works of history, claimed that 'he would find it difficult to complete his book' – the second volume of *The History of the Second World War* – 'without including at some point or other statements which implied that we were able to break the codes and cyphers of enemy powers.' In his own commercial interest, Churchill argued that it should be entirely permissible to talk about intelligence. There was only one 'real secret': the '*extent*' to which Britain read German and Japanese cyphers.[40]

The government response was predictably dismissive.[41] The SIS, MI5, and GCHQ combined to argue that Churchill could not be allowed to get away with his 'naughtiness'. They simply reiterated the statements made in 1945. First, it could not 'be reasonably expected that the many thousands who were in the secret during the war would continue to be as guarded as they have been enjoined to be if … Churchill had given the secret away.' Second, 'no possible excuse must be given to the Germans or the Japanese to explain away their complete defeat by force of arms. Knowledge this source of information was available to us would provide such an excuse.' This was why the official historians were able to write only about 'force of arms'. They were allowed to know about intelligence merely 'to frame their histories' of 'force of arms'.[42]

As Churchill rightly pointed out, albeit for pecuniary motives, it was impossible to write good history under such conditions. The secretary of the cabinet, Sir Edward Bridges, took his point and arranged for a degree of flexibility with Stewart Menzies and Edward Travis: on occasion it would be permissible to admit that British intelligence had decoded a message, even to reproduce parts of that message, as long as such references were infrequent and made no mention of machine enciphering or machine decryption. Frequency rather than fact had, of course, been Churchill's original point.[43]

What spooked gatekeepers, such as Menzies, Travis, and Liddell, was published history, meant for the masses and Russians. No one doubted that each intelligence organization – with the partial exception of SIS – would cheerfully pursue the writing of its own 'classified' or 'cabinet histories'.

Just as the intelligence machine consistently tried to crimp public revelations about its history, it equally consistently maintained that the writing of classified histories was desirable. Indeed, the model had already been established for it by the Foreign Office. The Foreign Office was determined to stand aside from any official history movement, and instead produce a classified history of their conduct of British diplomacy. In its early years, the history did not shy away from the 'missing dimension'. The wartime history of the Venlo Incident had been compiled with a view to passing it to the official historian. It was not until September 1948 that the Foreign Office got cold feet and started pulling intelligence history out of diplomatic history.[44]

Nearly every civilian intelligence organization of note was afforded a classified history, including defunct organizations that no longer possessed any political capital, and about which very few now cared.[45]

Some of the secret histories ran into problems of one kind or another. Jack Curry's history of MI5 was supposed to be ready before Sir Percy Sillitoe walked into St James's Street as the new director-general of the Security

Service on 1 May 1946.[46] It was, but it was also unwieldy and turgid. Whether Sillitoe ever read a word is doubtful, but in any case, he disliked both Curry and his history. Curry's history was to be 'kept for instructional purposes for officers joining us or going out to Stations abroad.' Curry himself was demoted, went sick, and was constructively dismissed.[47]

David Garnett's history of the Political Warfare Executive, completed in February 1947, with the encouragement and support of Sir Kenneth Strong, then charged with winding up PWE, was regarded as scurrilous. William Mackenzie's SIS-sponsored history of SOE enjoyed a clearer run, apart from a serious fire in the archives of SOE's main office in Baker Street. An Oxford don, Mackenzie was one of the most talented of the secret historians, and delivered the history in September 1948. His work was greeted with approbation, but then got caught up in the backwash from Gubbins's attempts to propagate the achievements of wartime SOE.[48]

By far the biggest damp squib was Frank Birch. The historians of NID warned Birch that writing the history of Bletchley Park would be a quite different beast to the history of Room 40, 'the decoding done by a small group of Cryptographers, known as OB40, was but a trickle compared to the rush of Special during 1939–45, nor was there the full and elaborate collation with other sources of intelligence.'[49] Birch, however, did not listen. He was intent on tackling the task in much the same way as he had in 1919. As a result, his progress was as slow as that of any of the public-facing official historians. The history was still unfinished when Birch died in 1956. The rambling final result, stitched together by his assistants, made very poor reading.

However, the relative failure of the 'cabinet' histories of intelligence, both as viable histories and useful policy documents, was not the whole story. The most important point to bear in mind is that none of the 'cabinet' historians were revisionists. All they were doing was reinforcing the historical consensus created in the 'versions' of 1945.

Bill Mackenzie wrote that 'practically every section of SOE before its dissolution produced a narrative of its work. These vary enormously in quality and in the number of references they give, but they are all in a sense primary sources, as they were generally written by junior officers who had been actively engaged in the section's work: most of them were also checked by senior officials.' Mackenzie's version followed the 1945 histories very closely. He was full and long where there had been a good previous history, terse and uninformative when that had not been the case.[50]

The collective power of this recently generated historical memory was more important than the fate of any specific history. When MI5 decided to shelve the Curry history, they did not shelve what they regarded as the lessons of history. Guy Liddell, now deputy director-general, Harry Allen, the wartime deputy director of Military Intelligence, and Dick White, the new director of B Division, instead wrote an alternative short guide to the development of counter-intelligence, for distribution to senior military officers and civil servants.[51] Liddell 'thought it was of the greatest importance that they should understand exactly what the scope of this office was and what it had been doing during the war.'[52] The guide was based on various contributions they had written for Curry's history, as well as the history itself.[53]

In March 1946, Clement Attlee and his inner core of cabinet ministers accepted the Findlater Stewart Report. The ministers did not have much choice, since Attlee opened the meeting by saying 'that there would be general agreement with the basic assumption in Sir Findlater Stewart's Report that some organisation must remain in being in peace adequate in experience and numbers to detect attempts to penetrate our defence organisation.'[54] Attlee then promulgated a directive instructing MI5 to 'keep the Prime Minister constantly informed' about the 'security of the State'.[55]

MI5 wanted as many people as possible to understand how they had reached this exalted state through their wartime exertions. The starting point for their guide was the assumption that everyone in Whitehall knew about 'those Intelligence people'; but that they now needed to understand the true organization of the intelligence machine.[56]

Liddell also took the guide on the road, hoping to convince sceptics in the military and the police. The line he took with Sillitoe's former colleagues in the Scottish police was that, 'frankly', MI5 had been poor in 1939 and 1940. This was 'through no fault of their own': they had been understaffed and had no money. It was therefore important to lay aside any experiences from the decade from 1931 to 1941 and to concentrate on the history of 'the subsequent years and the present situation.'[57]

Meanwhile, for all his shortcomings, Frank Birch was playing a considerable role in stimulating the historical efforts of others. Since GCHQ controlled the most important cache of original sources, official historians of various stripes had to deal with Birch. His fingerprints were all over the history of NID, naval affairs being his own personal interest and specialization. Birch's attempt at a comprehensive history of intelligence history, with Bletchley always at its core, led him to accumulate the histories of other intelligence organizations as they were written. In the specific field of signal intelligence, he enabled – sometimes even commissioned – histories to fill in major gaps.

The army had written virtually nothing about signal intelligence in 1945, but it had two long histories contributed on its behalf in 1948 and 1950. These histories took the Bletchley line that Birch required, rather than the more military view that the army might have desired. The 1948 history of military signal intelligence pointed out that War Office interception, based first in Chatham, then at Beaumanor, had not even been an army unit until October 1943. The personnel of WOYG – War Office Y Group – had been deliberately kept out of the army, and only the senior people were put in uniform in 1943.

Beaumanor, like Bletchley, looked like a military camp only because the majority of its personnel, after mid-war expansion, were uniformed ATS women. As in the First World War, the War Office had demonstrated its skill in mobilizing civilian expertise, but this was a very different thing to 'Army Y', confined to units in the field.[58] By the time of D-Day, WOYG was making nearly half of all British intercepts.[59]

The 1950 history of military signal intelligence was written in the hope that it 'may prove of value to GC&CS and to the War Office as a book of reference in the sorry event of our finding ourselves engaged in another World War in the future.' It was, however, very much the GC&CS version of military signal intelligence, rather than the army version. In passing, it noted that there was very little evidence that GC&CS was interested in military signal intelligence at the beginning of the Second World War: all the evidence came from War Office documents and interviews with army officers. But 1942 had been the caesura. 'Anyone with experience of what happened in 1939–1945 who ponders these questions in future will see,' the historians of military signal intelligence concluded, that 'success by the cryptanalysts is likely to necessitate, as in 1940–45, a central cryptanalytical organisation … The necessities are obvious now after the expansion of 1942–45. They were not so clear in 1940.'

According to the history of military signal intelligence, military signal intelligence had been invented at Bletchley in 1942. By April 1946, its final manifestation, which retained the name No. 4 Intelligence School, was wholly a Bletchley/Eastcote-controlled unit, albeit manned by service personnel.[60]

The most secretive of the post-war secret services, the Diplomatic Wireless Service, established by the merger of Radio Security Service and SIS Section VIII to ensure that 'black chamber' interception would never again be beholden to the military, wrote up a history of the Radio Security Service, drawing on Birch's material.[61]

The history offered a great deal of insight into counter-intelligence.[62] It pointed out that nothing had been done about illicit wireless intercepts, certainly not by any civilian agency, whether SIS, MI5, or GC&CS, until the summer of 1939, when the army set up the RSS. Trevor-Roper had cracked the Abwehr hand cyphers, and GC&CS had somewhat belatedly set up ISOS, a 'messy little corner' on the outskirts of Bletchley.[63] The 'messy little corner' had given the civilian agencies their edge in the intelligence war.[64]

The history of special operations was hardly forgotten either. The deputy head of SIS, John Sinclair, used Lionel Hale's history of SOE as the basis for a lecture tour around military and civil-service colleges.[65] Sinclair preached the importance of special operations and resistance movements as the basis for SIS's fabled 'twenty-eight thousand agents'. With some grumbling, the intelligence machine had granted permission for limited public revelation about SOE.[66]

Before David Garnett delivered his history of PWE, one of the most sensitive issues faced by the Attlee government was the question of whether to repurpose the Political Warfare Executive as an anti-Soviet agency, what Attlee described as the 'British Comintern'.[67] That was why Kenneth Strong asked Garnett to include a pithy summary of lessons emerging from his history in an introduction.[68]

After the history had been delivered, the interest in political warfare recrudesced. In spring 1948, the Foreign Office disinterred the idea, and this time convinced Ernest Bevin, the Foreign Secretary, to sign off on the creation of a new political warfare agency.[69] Bevin worried that 'we are letting loose forces difficult to control'. His personal memory was that PWE had not been 'too successful in the War.'[70]

This was not the story told around Whitehall. The Foreign Office announced that their new Information Research Department (IRD) 'was equipped to do what the Political Warfare Executive and the Ministry of Information had done during the war, that is to say, to plan, to guide, and to produce the material for, the whole field of political warfare.'[71]

They brought in a consultant, Dallas Brooks, to model the IRD on 'that which served the needs of the Political Warfare Executive during the war.'[72] Brooks featured prominently in Garnett's history of SOE.[73] He had started out in Electra House in 1939, transferred with it to SO1 in 1940, and was one of the key players in establishing PWE in 1941. He was head of its Military Wing, handling Ultra and SIS, and deputy director, until 1944.[74]

It might be thought that the history of the Second World War would present an opportunity for those who had actually fought the war to explain their own activities. That was not to be the case. Although the armed forces and their leaders devoted considerable attention to recent history, they were rarely in charge of intelligence history and, even when it fell within their ambit, they failed to pull together much in the way of coherent analysis or narrative.

When Eric Mockler-Ferryman embarked on the history of wartime military intelligence in 1947, he was hampered both by his narrow brief and a lack of evidence. Since the 'history of the war' was by that stage being written elsewhere, his task was to write an administrative history of the Directorate of Military Intelligence. Very little had changed since Major Potts wrote the history of the DMI after the Great War. Mockler-Ferryman found only two documents waiting for him in the War Office: the War Diary of the Directorate of Military Intelligence, put in its final form in April 1946, and the history of MI19.[75]

Mockler-Ferryman relied instead on his own memory – he had been Alan Brooke's head of intelligence at GHQ Home Forces and then Eisenhower's G-2 at AFHQ – and the documents and histories that he could recover from civilian agencies. He found MI5 the most helpful. He hardly tackled his task with alacrity: it took him five years to finish what should have been a relatively straightforward project. The final result was barely more than a heavily annotated version of the War Diary. In this regard,

Mockler-Ferryman compared unfavourably to Major Potts. At the end, he returned with relief to his true love – Scouting – and barely looked back.

Mockler-Ferryman regarded the engine-room of the DMI to be MI14, set up initially under the command of Kenneth Strong in May 1940.[76] It was MI14 that had provided the daily 'I Notes' delivered to the director each morning at 09:15. The DMI, first Davidson, then Sinclair, in turn briefed Sir Alan Brooke, the CIGS, every day. The 'I Notes' thus underpinned the titanic struggles about operations and strategy that Brooke recorded in his own diary. They also formed the basis of the War Office position at the Joint Intelligence Committee.[77]

Initially, the history of MI14 was nowhere to be found in the War Office. It had to be recovered from the history team at Bletchley, for whom it had been written.[78] The main role of MI14, the history explained, was Order of Battle Intelligence (OOB). Order of Battle Intelligence was not particularly glamorous: it involved sifting through endless minutiae to reveal the strength, organization, and deployment of the enemy as it changed on a day-to-day basis. However, it was the basis of all good military intelligence. Without a good grasp of the Order of Battle, planning operations became treacherous, as the Germans learnt to their cost. An examination of German OOB intelligence had revealed that, in 1942, Fremde Heere West was quite the equal of MI14 in Order of Battle intelligence, whereas, by 1944, it was leagues behind.

In 1945, MI14 was asked to assess how important Ultra from Bletchley was to their endeavours. The short answer: very. Their longer answer was somewhat more nuanced. In the vital year of 1944 – upon which the history concentrated – Ultra had arrived in MI14 hourly via the teleprinter from Bletchley. The typescript batches of decrypts were sent up to London once per day. Ultra provided up-to-date intelligence on the state of the German armed forces. 'For appreciation of enemy strategy and intentions and for day-to-day tactics Ultra was invaluable,' MI14 concluded. The daily 'I Notes' essentially consisted of Ultra decrypts, with additional MI14 comment.

However, the bulk of Ultra intelligence was far from overwhelming, and MI14 used other sources for accumulating their intelligence on the German armed forces. By this late stage in the war, SIS reports – CX intelligence – actually outweighed Ultra. The reports SIS was sucking in from the Allied intelligence services meant that up to 150 lengthy papers arrived in MI14 each day. The quality of these reports from 'on the ground' was extremely variable, and as a result they required much more analysis to extract intelligence than the pithier decrypts.

At the same time, MI14 dealt with the daily 'sitreps' from British forces in the field, most notably G-2, 21st Army Group.[79] The final source of intelligence was the prisoner-of-war reports from CSDIC. On the whole, MI14 remarked, 'for long-term appreciations of Axis war potential Ultra was not one of our most profitable sources. Some of the information that it did produce was very valuable, in particular on the question of tank production, but its main value was not in this sphere.'[80] The DDMI in 1946, Brigadier Hirsch, himself a former head of MI14, insisted that the MI14 history contain the statement that 'altho' Ultra was of immense value it always needed handling with great care.'[81]

There were some outlets for the military-intelligence history of the war other than Mockler-Ferryman's project. In late 1945, officers of the Joint Intelligence Staff produced the first draft of their detailed analysis of 'why Germany lost'. The JIS was a small and tight-knit team, comprising about twenty officers. They had started work in March 1945, but had picked up speed from May 1945, when even more documents and interrogation reports started flooding in. The first draft of their history was completed in October 1945, in order to form the basis for the cross-examination of Generaloberst Jodl, one of the defendants at Nuremberg.

In early 1946, while the JIS was awaiting the outcome of the trials before finalizing the history, two of the seven-man army team peeled off to write the parallel history of the JIS's use of Ultra. Unlike MI14, the JIS had not received decrypts from Bletchley. Instead they had received the 'I Notes', while their naval counterparts got the 'Oranges' from NID 12.

The Directorate of Military Intelligence had proved to be the best intelligence agency for accurately estimating German production and supply. The investigation into the German documents had confirmed how good this intelligence was.[82]

However, the most direct translation of intelligence into operations had occurred in the naval war.[83] 'The knowledge obtained about U-boat activities was probably of greater value than anything else,' Laurence Kirwan and George Waterfield wrote, 'enabling us to route shipping away from U-boats as a result of messages received perhaps only a few hours before a convoy sailed, or while it was en route.'

The JIS officers were much more ambivalent about Ultra's usefulness in military operations and reproduced the analysis of its pitfalls produced by Bill Williams, the head of intelligence at 21st Army Group.[84] Of course, no one would ever wish to do without Ultra: it was fantastic intelligence. In Ewen Montagu's phrase, however, Ultra was a 'drug of addiction'. When intelligence staffs were on Ultra, they took insufficient trouble to sift intelligence. It was simply not worth the time to do meticulous intelligence work. If something was marked 'Ultra', it immediately got all recipients excited to the point of placing 'too much emphasis' on the latest decrypt. The comedown from the Ultra high was dreadful: a shortage of Ultra intelligence could very rapidly become an obsession. Kirwan and Waterfield even lamented that the very term 'Ultra' had ever been introduced.[85]

The JIS team returned to their history of German defeat in the summer of 1946, and the history was formally submitted in September 1946. By this stage, the authors already had an eye on their wider readership: they deliberately included 'a mass of technical information which we considered would be of use to future historians'.

The first phase of the Nuremberg Trials ended in October 1946, and it was only then that the Chiefs of Staff approved the wide circulation of the JIS's history. The Chiefs insisted, however, on a 'health warning' being attached to the JIS findings: they 'should not be considered as authoritative histories, nor as complete or balanced'. 'It may well be,' the Chiefs continued, 'that the official histories when compiled may show that there are errors and omissions' in the work of the JIS. Their work 'should be considered purely as illustrations ... orientated from the German point of view.' The final text of the history thus specifically included the self-deprecating remark that a 'final assessment ... must be left to the historians'.

Nevertheless, the JIS's tone remained lapidary. One criticism of the history made by the Chiefs – that its authors were too reliant on the German point of view – was rather unfair, given their intervening work on the British side. The JIS history was the first attempt at a sustained historical analysis from both sides of the hill. It was bound to be an explosive text, since it skilfully upended many pet theories and conspiratorial stories.

It did so in two main ways. First, it put intelligence in its proper operational context. Second, and perhaps even more dangerously, it used a dissection of German intelligence to show what a good intelligence system should look like.[86]

The JIS concluded that intelligence had been a very useful, but ultimately not a war-winning tool. It was Allied materiel superiority that had won the war. 'Up to the middle of 1942,' the JIS wrote, 'the military strength of the German Army was such that it was not vitally dependent on intelligence. The result of the battles would have been much the same if the intelligence services had been bad or good. After the summer of 1944, equally no amount of efficiency in intelligence work could have made any appreciable difference to the result, or perhaps even to the duration of the war, as allied strength was overwhelming.'

In both the battle of the Atlantic, and the series of successful amphibious operations that the Allies launched against the Axis in North Africa, Sicily, Italy, Normandy, and southern France, however, intelligence had saved lives, many, many thousands, perhaps hundreds of thousands of lives. The history did not attempt to quantify, it merely talked of 'consequences of extreme gravity': 'allied casualties might have been incomparably higher than they were, though no doubt allied superiority would have eventually caused Germany's defeat.'

Many of these lives were saved because, fortunately for the Allies, German military intelligence was poorly run just at the point it could have caused most damage. Each of the amphibious landings was fraught with risk, but 'the Abwehr's major failure during 1942–44 was its inability to provide its share of the information on which reasonable forecasts of allied strategic intentions could be made.' This failure hampered specific operations against the landings. Perhaps more importantly, it created a climate of 'strategic uncertainty' that deepened Germany's inability to devise a coherent defensive strategy, despite its possession of 'interior lines of communication'.

The German intelligence system had not failed because the officers of the Abwehr and the RSHA were corrupt and ineffective hacks, although many of them were just that. In a universalizing analysis, the JIS pointed out that 'all intelligence services depend largely for their success upon the quality of the higher personnel they employ; in addition to their technical abilities, their staffs must be capable of objective and disinterested appreciation of events and be as free as possible from political or social bias.'

In different ways, the Abwehr and the SD had fallen far short of that ideal. The Abwehr had been staffed by service personnel, with the addition of 'volunteer reservists' from business and the professions. The regular Abwehr officers were second-raters who had failed in regular service. The reservists were often able, but also unscrupulous and disillusioned. The SD had 'recruited largely from members of the *petit bourgeois* lower middle class, which,' the JIS historians remarked rather pointedly, 'in all countries is the least cosmopolitan, the most conventional and the most narrow minded.'

German intelligence had not failed because the Abwehr and the RSHA were often at one another's throats, although they were. It had not failed because all Abwehr officers were incompetent: some of them, especially in Amt III, were highly competent. They had demonstrated that 'better information was in fact obtained by the use of penetrating agents than by the use of direct informers.' The Abwehr had most certainly not failed because it was staffed by 'superficially charming' anti-Nazis, who sabotaged their own efforts. Many senior members of the Abwehr were implicated in the July 1944 plot to overthrow Hitler, but ineffectiveness had predated disloyalty. A 'uniform record of failure', to predict Allied amphibious operations, the JIS noted, 'was the prime cause of the collapse of the *Abwehr*'.

German intelligence had failed because the military high command of the Wehrmacht was an incompetent handler of intelligence. 'The responsibility for failing to appreciate Allied intentions lies most heavily on the Planning Staff of the OKW [Wehrmachtführungsstab], who had many other sources of intelligence at their disposal and should not have relied on secret intelligence alone,' the JIS concluded. The high command had lacked 'any inter-service staff for the co-ordination and appreciation of intelligence. Both Keitel and Jodl have stated that no organisation comparable with the allied joint intelligence machinery was ever formed. Operational intelligence was supplied by each of the service ministries and by the *Amt Abwehr* direct to the planning staff of the *OKW* where it was inadequately co-ordinated.'

Striking rather uncomfortably close to home for some, the history painted a stark picture of what self-serving intelligence agencies looked like: 'uncontrolled by any organisation for collating the intelligence requirements of the service and other ministries in time of war, for assessing priorities and for evaluating the general significance of intelligence received from sources, both overt and secret, the *Abwehr* and the *SD* alike were free to concentrate on whatever objectives suited their directors or were easiest to attain, and they were not subject to criticism except on particular issues.'

The best intelligence history of the Second World War was unsparing both of ill-controlled intelligence services and service intelligence organs devoted to the support of service operations staffs.

Another history of military intelligence history in the war, proved equally unsparing of service intelligence. The history of military deception, after Dudley Clarke was shut down, lay in the hands of the army officers writing the history of the D-Day deception operations. As the Joint Intelligence Staff had already established, it was this operation that saw the greatest opportunity for the Germans to inflict a bloodbath on the Allies. D-Day might not have been the riskiest amphibious operation of the war, but it was by far the largest.[87]

Roger Fleetwood-Hesketh and his brother, Cuthbert, were nothing if not thorough in their investigation. Cuthbert Hesketh interrogated the former Oberbefehlshaber West, Feldmarschall von Runstedt, and his chief of staff, von Blumentritt, and then made the pilgrimage to Nuremberg to interrogate Generaloberst Jodl and General Keitel.[88] The Hesketh based much of their analysis on the careful assemblage of the Lageberichten West, the daily OKH situation reports. They also had excellent access to decrypts, of which the Blue Jackets proved most revealing.[89]

The Hesketh' close analysis paralleled that of the Joint Intelligence Staff on much the same evidence base: the Germans had been bad at co-ordinating their intelligence. The Hesketh paid particular attention to Oberst Krummacher, the plainly inadequate Abwehr liaison officer at OKW. Krummacher had fed 'chicken food' to Jodl, and thus to Hitler, on a regular basis, with no check on his work.

One aspect of intelligence that the Hesketh' focus on Krummacher's files revealed, was that the Abwehr and the RSHA had supplied very few reports from British deception agents to OKW. Most secret intelligence had been provided by Paul Fidrmuc's network, operating from Lisbon, and Karl

Krämer's network from Stockholm. The Hesketh dismissed both Fidrmuc and Krämer as fraudsters.

The argument that deception agents had scored a tactical coup over the Germans, rested on the Hesketh' account of the few days after D-Day, when OB-West and OKW had been indecisive about the commitment of reserves to Normandy. During those days, Krummacher had provably passed a number of messages from MI5-controlled agents to Jodl. However, as both the Hesketh and the JIS historians had made clear, the real claims for deception rested much more firmly on OOB denial, a long-term process that created an inevitable, constant, and debilitating 'fear of the unknown'.[90]

The Hesketh also told the story of D-Day deception operations from the point of view of a particular military staff outfit, Ops. B. Ops. B had been Eisenhower's own strategic deception section at SHAEF. However, the Hesketh proved no friends to armed-forces intelligence. Their history took pains to run down military deception in general and the role of the Controlling Section of the Chiefs of Staff in London, in particular.

The Hesketh history effectively reprised Masterman's 1945 history of double-cross. Military intelligence work was best left in the hands of a specialized civilian agency. As they pointed out – and its name indicated – Ops. B was not a military intelligence section, but part of the operations staff of SHAEF, G-3 rather than G-2.

It was a source of enduring regret to Roger Hesketh that his historical efforts did not enjoy a wider distribution. After all, the Soviets were already in possession of all the crucial information about D-Day deception operations.[91] John Bevan, the Controlling Officer, Deception, had personally gone to Moscow in 1944 to explain the extent and purpose of British deception operations. By the end of the war, the Germans understood that they had been deceived, and Jodl had issued a detailed report on the matter, of which the Russians were known to possess a copy.[92] When Hesketh finished writing his 'magnum opus' in 1949, it was sent only to MI5, SIS, and the Future Planning Section of the Ministry of Defence. There were plenty of other copies printed, but they were 'kept for distribution as and when the occasion arose.'[93]

On the other hand, and long before Hesketh finished his history, its findings were being promulgated around Whitehall and beyond. Hesketh's conclusions were a gift to MI5, which had already accrued the benefit of the attention lavished on Masterman.

When Gerald Templer became DMI in the spring of 1946, he found that the Masterman history was one of the few documents his predecessor, Freddie de Guingand, had left in his safe.[94] It was easy to convince Templer that the history of deception should be spread around army officers destined for senior command and staff positions.[95]

In October 1946, Guy Liddell, the deputy director general of MI5, gave a lecture to the students of the Imperial Defence College that 'took the lid off completely'. In the chair was Field Marshal Lord Slim, widely – and accurately – tipped as the next Chief of the Imperial General Staff. Liddell's theme was how MI5 had gained control of the German Intelligence Service in Britain, not only for the sake of security but also for the 'turning over of our DA organisation for the purpose of deception'. He was able to explain the effects in full because the Hesketh's had 'ultimately checked against enemy intelligence reports and the statements of Keitel, Jodl and Runstedt.' The purpose of this 'lid blowing' exercise was to demonstrate the repeated successes of MI5, as, without the Hesketh's' evidence, 'many might regard them as too fantastic to be believed.' Deception proved how wrong they had been, especially in the armed forces, who had belittled MI5 as creepy secret policemen. With the Hesketh evidence in hand, Liddell urged his audience to disregard the sceptical attitudes of their seniors and do what MI5 told them, no questions asked.[96]

When Liddell briefed William Hayter, the incoming chairman of the JIC, on the history of wartime deception, he felt able to claim that 'the Service Intelligence Branches … had only been co-opted in order that we might impress upon them the value of the work we were doing and the necessity of keeping our agents alive with "Chicken food".'[97]

By the summer of 1947, when Air Chief Marshal Sir Douglas Evill was commissioned to investigate British intelligence on the Soviet Union, historical investigators had already concluded that the main problem could not be bad secret services *per se*, but a failure to understand the process of intelligence. That failure was most likely to come from the armed forces. The Germans had had multiple intelligence services, and those services assembled information. Malformed intelligence services became a serious problem only because the controlling brain was rotten. Evill commented that there was not much point in his digging too far into history, because the intelligence machine was 'going to adhere to the general framework of our existing intelligence organisation', whatever he said.[98]

He was forbidden from investigating the secret civilian-intelligence agencies, although he was quite capable of expressing an opinion. That opinion was that, since the war, British secret intelligence had proved ineffective at providing anything useful for national defence. In 1944 Nevile Bland had asked the Service intelligence directors what they would need in the future. They replied, unanimously, that above all they needed technically sophisticated intelligence on new weapons. That was exactly what they had not received since the end of the war. Evill pointed out that SIS and MI5 were 'large organisations deployed in the field', but the intelligence they provided for 'the defence of the realm' was 'so seriously backward' that 'the effect of the evidence obtained during this review as to the state of defence intelligence is very disturbing.'[99]

The only intelligence agency whose history Evill thought worthwhile delving into was one of which he had personal wartime experience.[100] The air marshal visited the Central Interpretation Unit – now known as JAPIC – at RAF Medmenham – and pronounced himself horrified by its decline from its wartime glory. A few specialists were working in the ruins of a once-great endeavour. In this case, Evill argued, history mattered, because JAPIC held all the German wartime photographs of Eastern Europe and the Soviet Union, but had not even managed to catalogue them. Evill recommended that the RAF's Photographic Unit and the inter-service Central Interpretation Unit should be resurrected.[101]

Returning to his strict brief, Evill concluded that parts of the intelligence brain had similarly rotted since 1945. The collection of intelligence about new weapons, such as missiles and atomic weapons, might be poor, but the analysis of the intelligence that came in was, if anything, worse. When the dust had settled on the 1945 reforms, Britain had been left with two committees, one for technical and one for scientific intelligence, with the 'absence of any effective authority'. Atomic intelligence was not even part of the remit of the service intelligence: it had remained hived off in a small unit of the Ministry of Supply's Department of Atomic Energy. One of Evill's witnesses claimed that, between them, scientific, technical, and atomic intelligence, had 'not contributed a single worthwhile bit of intelligence.'[102]

The Evill Report, despite its expressed lack of scope to interrogate the past, did have an impact on intelligence history. In the intense debate about the report that echoed around Whitehall, Eric Longley-Cooke, the Director of Naval Intelligence, repeatedly referred to the naval history to make his points.[103]

The long-running naval-intelligence history project changed direction in the wake of Evill. In 1946, John Godfrey had set himself the task of producing a series of supplements to the Morgan history. When he wrote the first supplement in January 1947, he imagined that his audience would be a Director of Naval Intelligence, '15 years hence'.

The early supplements recorded the names and addresses of reputable 'consultants', such as Ian Fleming. Godfrey was at pains to stress that the NID had thrived because of its ability quickly to commission civilian talent. Intelligence, especially high-pressure operational intelligence, 'called primarily for moral courage and intellectual integrity. It needed a quality of breadth of mind and knowledge of the world, of human personality, of the mentality of men in high command, and how to handle equals, juniors and seniors. It needed a well trained mind able to work on evidence as the criminal lawyer, the archaeologist or the zoologist work.'[104]

In the wake of Evill, however, Godfrey came to believe that his idea of a closely held NID supplementary history series was 'too dogmatic'. He became even more concerned to 'sell' the NID version of history on the broadest front possible. He took care to visit other intelligence agencies and let them know what the Royal Navy was cooking up.[105] Intelligence, Godfrey argued, had to get its story out independently of its supposed political masters. Politicians could be trusted to say either too much or not enough, as it suited them. He had little time either for Churchill or for A.V. Alexander, the wartime First Lord of the Admiralty, now the Minister of Defence.[106]

The 'most potentially dangerous person is one who is highly placed partially or wholly in the know', who had access to the most spectacular items, 'but whose indoctrination is insufficient to restrain his indiscretion.' The most spectacular 'breaks' came from those at 'the very top'. The most likely 'guilty men', in Godfrey's view, would be Churchill and Alexander. Churchill had a list of indiscretions stretching back to the First World War. Alexander had refused to sign the 'need to know' book in the Second World War, and had been unable to keep quiet about the role of Ultra, even when an entire Admiralty Board of Enquiry had been nobbled to cover up for Bletchley.[107] Alexander was an idiot; Churchill was something worse, a twister. Godfrey wrote a dissection of how Churchill, as First Lord of the Admiralty, had made up estimates of German U-Boat numbers to suit his own political advantage.[108]

In his end-of-project reflection, Godfrey wrote that the real enemies of intelligence were 'wishful thinkers'. 'The fact that, during World War II, so much A1 information existed, encouraged wishful thinkers to discredit, belittle, or frown on whole groups of intelligence which, although not absolutely A1, were of a very high order of authenticity. It seemed to the author of these monographs that [they] would make it more difficult for wishfully minded people to have their own way in the future.' In the main, the 'wishful thinkers' had been, and would be, politicians.

The whole purpose of the great naval history project was to stave off 'wishful thinking'. It drove home the conclusion, again and again, that intelligence had to work constantly to increase its prestige. Intelligence had to sell itself: 'an intelligence officer must, "advertise his commodity".' In particular, it was not 'the business of Naval Intelligence to shroud itself in mystery and then prophesy the future.' Godfrey subsequently made these points publicly in 'The Naval Intelligence Officer', published in the *Naval Review* of 1951.[109]

However, Godfrey described himself as having been a 'wishful thinker' when it had come to SIS: he reproached himself for standing up for them too strongly. His officers had told him that SIS intelligence was 'worthless, and frequently so evidently worthless as to provoke laughter.' The SIS officers had been 'muddle-headed and incompetent' and 'enjoyed mystery' for its own sake. They did little more than attempt 'to find out odd bits of information, to attempt to prove a preconceived theory.'

He had, he admitted, been misled by his personal liking for successive Cs, Sinclair then Menzies: 'they were both so kind, patient, and receptive and put up with a lot of outspoken criticism without umbrage. I feel personally greatly indebted to them both.' In retrospect it was clear that Sinclair, 'although a remarkable man, can have been no good at choosing a staff, judging by his "Naval specimens".'

Godfrey felt he had made a bad mistake in backing Menzies as Sinclair's successor. The SIS had needed a 'man of stronger and more decisive personality'. Menzies undoubtedly had 'charm' and 'nimbleness of mind', but he was much better at 'political than naval intelligence'. Claude Dansey, the power behind the throne, had been 'negative, critical, sceptical and unconstructive'.

Menzies now pretended that he had always been a champion of GC&CS, but this was simply false. He had not really been interested in it, and had very little to do with the cryptologists under Sinclair. Through no virtue of his own, GC&CS had 'saved his bacon (and probably does today)'. 'I have a feeling,' Godfrey concluded in his *mea culpa*, 'that history is going to repeat itself, that it would be wise for NID to take a continual personal interest in the internal economy of that organisation.'[110]

Some officers in NID went further. They described John Godfrey as having been a useful idiot for Stewart Menzies.[111] There was no point in his repenting after the event. The DNI had been the instrument of his own downfall. Godfrey had let what was 'incomparably his most important source of intelligence' get out of his own control: it was no use pretending anything other than that the head of GC&CS/GCHQ was essentially in charge of naval intelligence.[112] As DNI, Godfrey had 'weakened his own position perhaps beyond remedy.' 'I do not know,' an NID contributor to the history wrote, 'to what extent this betrayal (for it is no less) is appreciated in NID generally.'[113]

Not that historical matters were necessarily sweetness and light over at Eastcote Manor: Frank Birch was tackling his task of reconstructing the history of British signal intelligence with painful slowness. As a result, when the leadership of what had been formally designated GCHQ on 1 November 1948 needed and wanted their history, it was nowhere to be found. Instead, Eric Jones, the incoming deputy director of GCHQ, turned to another old Room 40 hand, Nigel de Grey, to write a quick historical review suitable for current needs. De Grey obliged by reprising much of the 1945 GC&CS version of history, in which he had a hand as the then–deputy director of Bletchley Park.

De Grey had been robust in 1945 in arguing that Bletchley was the entirety of British intelligence, with all other intelligence services little more than puffing auxiliaries.

He was equally robust in the summer of 1949. De Grey reserved his real venom for the Signals directorates of the three Services, whom he accused of welching on an agreement to place interception wholly under the direction of GC&CS. This was, perhaps, a little unfair. The GC&CS had certainly attempted to railroad the Services into such an arrangement in 1945. In doing so, however, they had only convinced them that armed-forces intelligence would be signing its own death warrant by handing over any more control to Bletchley.

De Grey said that he would not review the role of Menzies as director-general of wartime GC&CS and still, in 1949, of GCHQ. However, he then went on to conclude that C had been, and was, a very bad boss for code-breaking. 'It was a mistake,' de Grey wrote, 'to interpose SIS between the Ministries, Service or civil, and GC&CS.' There was no point in it, save possibly some obscure and long-since-forgotten loose thinking about security. 'Experience of war,' had demonstrated to de Grey 'that direct reporting to user was the safest and cleanest method, for both sides.'[114]

'In writing this history,' de Grey remarked to Jones, he had been ineluctably drawn to the conclusion that GCHQ was something entirely different from GC&CS. There was little point in Birch attempting to describe continuities in intricate detail, for that was to suggest that GC&CS had in some way prepared for what Bletchley had become.

Pre-war GC&CS had been a black chamber that had made little or no real effort to prepare to take on the military communications system of a major power. The GCHQ's *raison d'être* was to take on the military communications system of a superpower, while keeping their hand in and their Foreign Office paymasters happy by doing black-chamber work. He estimated the proper balance to be 75:25.[115]

The real lesson of the Second World War was that the Intelligence Centre had to take over the whole intelligence machine: 'GCHQ should not hesitate to pursue any course that may lead to better signal intelligence and better use of it, whatever the theoretical objections,' de Grey advised. Ignoring or outmanoeuvring the Services was how they had organized Hut 6 to consistently break Enigma, Hut 3 doing the state's most important military and air intelligence work, and the Naval Section 'running the naval war'.

An enormous amount of time had been wasted during the war by 'pandering' to the Services. The directors of Bletchley had to dress up the personnel of Hut 3 'in the appropriate uniform, even though their knowledge were no greater than civilians.'

'GC&CS policy' had 'veered between initially preferring civilians lest the Services demand too great a say in the conduct of GC&CS and later urging the Services to provide more people.' 'No Ministry showed much acumen in recruiting suitable high-grade staff,' de Grey wrote dismissively. The de Grey history was everything that the armed forces might have feared.[116]

By the end of the 1940s, the history of the intelligence machine was well established. As in the post–First World War period, there had been plenty of 'noise' about intelligence. It was clear that the machine was bigger and more powerful than it had been after the First World War.

There was a settled and coherent view of the machine available to those with any access to Whitehall, Westminster, the West End, or Fleet Street: the 'limited outside public'. The 'settled view' of the history of the British intelligence machine, as it existed in 1949, was not that different to the one many intelligence historians hold to this day.

The 'settled view' boiled down to five propositions underpinned by extensive historical investigation. First, Britain had developed an 'intelligence machine' during the Second World War. Britain did not have an intelligence machine before the war, it should have existed before the war, and it should now be a permanent feature of the British state.

The genius of the British system, made obvious by comparison with the German system, was to co-ordinate the machine through a series of interlocking committees, with overlapping membership. The intelligence machine thus comprised intelligence organizations, ministries, agencies, and committees.

It was possible to chart the evolution of the intelligence machine over the previous decade. That evolution was complex and confusing, but it made reasonable sense. The very act of charting its own evolution became a core feature of the machine at work.

Second, in order to maintain a well-functioning intelligence machine, it had to be embedded in a field of intelligence. In the Second World War, the field of intelligence established readily recognizable boundaries. The most obvious boundary was between the 'indoctrinated' – about Bletchley Park – and everyone else. One could be an intelligence officer without being 'indoctrinated', but an intelligence officer was only of any importance if he had been indoctrinated. Therefore, indoctrination was a key signifier of the inner circle. For an individual, the negotiation over his indoctrination was the defining moment of his career in intelligence.[117]

Third, 'indoctrination' had become such an important issue because of the rise of signal intelligence. Before the Second World War, cryptography was a specialized and marginal activity. During the Second World War, signal intelligence became the core of all intelligence work: surveillance of rivals and enemies, domestic and foreign, should be a permanent feature of the British state.

Fourth, the intelligence machine should be run by civilians and dominated by civilian organizations. The Second World War provided no evidence of military competence in intelligence. Good military intelligence officers had merely been civilians in uniform. Having a commission, being an officer as well as an intelligence officer, was beside the point. At most, a uniform was a prop or a cover. Further than this, the war had demonstrated that the best intelligence officers were educated men, who looked, thought, and acted very much like their peers in the civilian civil service. The intelligence machine should seek out, recruit, and promote such men. There was little point in relying on dodgy businessmen, ex-policemen, or ex-soldiers.

Fifth, last but significant, special operations became a signature part of the British intelligence toolkit during the Second World War. Special operations had generated much of the bad blood within the intelligence machine. Within the confines of a properly constituted intelligence machine, however, special operations, the techniques of political warfare, subversion, and direct action were well worth maintaining in the intelligence repertoire.[118]

Because so much effort had gone into writing down this settled view, it seemed a plausible and defensible view of the history of the Second World

War. The various authors were confident that they had offered an accurate picture of the past decade. The historians admitted that the evidence for the years before 1938 was patchy. The history of those years rested more on personal recollection than on historical documents. Because there had not been a machine, it had not kept a machine's records. The old days comprised the intelligence dark ages, a land of myth as much of history, to which dangerous nostrums and practices could be ascribed. Its heroes were those who had seen the need for a machine when others pooh-poohed even the idea.

The 'settled view' had much to recommend it. It did, however, suffer from two notable blind spots. It was not very convincing in assessing effectiveness, except inasmuch that it demonstrated that the Germans had got it wrong. As a result, there was persistent surprise when the British intelligence machine proved to be ineffective.[119] As Sir Gerald Templer, the DMI who became 'the Tiger of Malaya', pointed out in the 1950s, every time a new crisis arose, Britain was unprepared. The men on the spot had to start from scratch, learning how to do intelligence work anew. The major challenge and the solution usually fell on army officers and policemen, the very groups written out of the 'settled view'.[120]

Even more spectacularly, and in the full glare of public revelation, the settled view was demonstrated to have committed the historical sin of omission. The historians had done an excellent job of analysing how the heart of intelligence was counter-intelligence, and of establishing that at the heart of counter-intelligence lay penetration of service. But they had specifically been commissioned to write a history of the Second World War. Each had devoted a section to intelligence relations with the Soviet Union, but these sections had been tucked away at the back of the histories. There, they concentrated on the repeated failure to secure fruitful intelligence relations with the Russians after June 1941.

It was only at the end of the 1940s that revisionism began in earnest. Then it emerged that Britain's intelligence history had been on a par with Germany's: a tale of woe. The failure of British intelligence had not been a failure to establish intelligence collaboration with the Soviet Union: it had been the hostile penetration of British service by the Soviets. The Germans had failed to protect themselves: so too had the British.

6

Look Back in Anger
History from the 1950s

Until the beginning of 1950, the history of British intelligence had only intermittently been about the Soviet Union. Overwhelmingly, the history written between 1917 and 1949 had been about Britain's response to the existential threat of Germany. This is not to say that the British intelligence machine had been uninterested in the Soviet Union. Since September 1945, it had been formally identified as Britain's most important intelligence target.[1] It had become the 'ultimate objective'.[2]

However, the state had not reflected at any length about the history of the Anglo-Soviet intelligence rivalry. The histories of the Second World War each gave some attention to Anglo-Soviet intelligence relations, but the accounts had been cursory. This fact was sometimes occluded by the obsessions of special-interest groups. For example, the Zinoviev Letter of 1924 remained the historical touchstone for some Labour politicians, while an over-emphasis on the Soviet Union also proved beguiling to later generations of historians, writing their history in or after the Cold War. To many, for good reason, the Soviet history had been the true history of British intelligence.[3]

The genuine history of British intelligence as it stood, after much effort, at the end of the 1940s, did contain some material that proved germane to the histories written after 1950. The idea of stealing a super weapon, for instance, reached back to the First World War. The Germans had made efforts to steal advanced British weapons technology, and at least one high-profile case had come to public trial by 1918.[4] Commentary on the intelligence cases of the late 1920s had centred on the ability of spies to steal aircraft technology from the private companies that were then on the leading edge of technical development. Jack Curry's 1946 history of MI5 outlined various German and Soviet attempts to penetrate British state arsenals. Curry himself had been as much an expert on the Soviet intelligence services as he became on the GIS.[5]

The development of super-weapons was a long-running staple of spy fiction. For example, Eric Ambler's first novel, *The Dark Frontier*, published in 1936, had revolved around an attempt to produce atomic weapons. Its hero was a British nuclear physicist. The Soviet intelligence services featured repeatedly in Ambler's pre-war novels, albeit as noble figures working to disrupt the transfer of super-weapons to right-wing dictators.[6]

The post-war secret historians had devoted some attention to atomic weapons. They devoted a great deal more to ballistic missiles. The history of the V2 programme had been one of the dominant strands of intelligence history. The interest in the history of V2 far outweighed its military significance. Instead it served as useful shorthand through which historians could exemplify the quickening pace of technological development, allowing them to establish that the world of 1944–45 was very different from that of 1939–40.[7]

Equally, the secret historians and their readers had lavished attention on penetration of service as a key professional concern. In this element of the wartime story, the histories of German and Soviet intelligence were explicitly intertwined. Soviet intelligence had visibly been at work in the same space as German, and many personnel, from agents to intelligence officers, personally interacted with their British opposite numbers. 'Russian penetration in … the Low Countries,' for instance, 'was,' the British and Germans agreed, 'widespread, and on a high level.'[8]

The Venlo Incident, by 1950 probably the best-known case of penetration of British service, had a Soviet angle. In 1946, Roger Hollis, the head of MI5's F Division, and Kim Philby, the head of Section R.5 of SIS, returned to the history of the case.[9] The Dutch had finally interrogated the head of the Stelle P organization in Holland, K. zur See Protze.[10] Protze pointed out that his men had posed as Russian intelligence agents because British officials seemed keen to sell information to the Soviets.[11] The histories of the 1940s highlighted such complexities. The penetration agent was known and feared.[12]

However, such was not the main focus of intelligence history as written to 1949. The joint efforts of many historians had fastened on three streams of interpretation of British intelligence. First, the British were deceivers rather than penetrators. Second, British penetration of service was achieved by technological rather than human means. Third, secret service was an ineffective activity, certainly when it came to military intelligence.

The fact remained, however, that Britain had developed a military super-weapon, and their intelligence services allowed that weapon to be stolen from under their noses. They had no real inkling of what was happening until after the Soviet Union succeeded in detonating its own atomic bomb in August 1949.

During the same period, the British intelligence services had themselves developed an intelligence super-weapon – machine decryption. They allowed the fruits of that intelligence revolution to be stolen from under their noses too. The intelligence machine had no real inkling of what had happened until the Americans helped them to work it out.

Soviet agents were then detected in nearly all current and historical intelligence agencies: SIS, MI5, GC&CS, DMI, and SOE. By any measure, it was a testament to the woeful incompetence of the men who had run intelligence and had then commissioned its histories.

There was inevitably a re-evaluation. Notably, however, the settled version of history proved remarkably resilient in the face of new revelations. History proved to be an essential form of capital. The intelligence services were able to rely on three decades of writing about their successes to ride out contemporary commentary about their palpable failure.

The official re-evaluation of British intelligence in light of its failures emerged in staccato beats. The first, Fuchs, was crystallized in the Brook Report of March 1951. The second, Maclean and Burgess, was captured in the Cadogan Report of November 1951. The final, Philby, was written up by Cedric Cliffe, the civil servant who had served as the draughtsman for the Brook Report.

Taken as a whole, the investigations of the 1950s marked the failure of intelligence history. The events proved too raw for historical method, even at the deepest levels of government secrecy. The lack of a visible ending, and thus the pressure of current work and the dearth of sure evidence, combined to produce a kind of anti-history, an attempt to avoid serious conclusions even within the secret world. Having read the Cadogan Report, compiled by a former permanent under-secretary of the Foreign Office, the current permanent under-secretary of the Foreign Office told his senior diplomats that, 'I am glad to say that the Committee did not find anything radically wrong.'[13]

This crippled infant of official history was born into a world now populated by iconoclastic purveyors of conspiratorial stories. They comprised the journalists employed by popular newspapers in 1945, who realized that there was a real story in British intelligence. There was enough interest to support the creation of a specialized subscription newsletter, in the form of *Intelligence Digest*.[14]

The journalists flourished because there was money in intelligence stories, and current and former intelligence officers – including C – were consistently willing to brief them. Benefits on offer ranged from payment to the use of villas in the south of France.[15] Some of the press briefings were official, some were officially tolerated; most were conversations in a club or pub.[16]

When MI5 discovered that some of the press contacts upon whom they were 'planting' stories were also being used by SIS to publish derogatory stories about MI5, John Drew, the head of the Future Planning Section in the Ministry of Defence and the author of parts of the Findlater Stewart and Brook reports, remarked that leaking true stories about MI5's incompetence was a good way of disguising false stories. In fact, MI5 had become its own chicken food.[17] The result was that the serious history of the 1930s and 1940s had to await the historians of the twenty-first century. Unlike some of the earlier histories, those of the 1950s cannot be profitably read, except as evidence of delusion.

In April 1950, the prime minister, Clement Attlee, told Norman Brook, the secretary of the cabinet, to carry out a thorough review of the intelligence services. By the time he summoned Brook, Attlee had already discussed the need for such an inquiry with Lord Bridges, Brook's predecessor and former boss, who was then permanent secretary of the Treasury, as well as Lord Swinton.

6.1. Sir Norman Brook. Cabinet Secretary, and author of the Brook Report on Britain's intelligence services.

In talking to Bridges and Swinton, Attlee was reaching back into their collective wartime past. The inclusion of Swinton was notable, since he was a partisan Tory peer.[18] The history of his Security Executive, which had been created to bring order to failing intelligence services, but which had expired, unmourned, in 1945, was once more deemed highly relevant.[19] In March 1950, the *Daily Telegraph* reported that the prime minister personally oversaw MI5 and was revisiting the history of the Security Executive.[20]

In his instructions to Brook, Attlee expressed an interest in the further integration of intelligence. However, Attlee's real interest was in having the cabinet secretary examine how his government had agreed to transform the peacetime funding of intelligence, without asking whether the historic apportionment of money had been based on any rational logic. Attlee wanted to know if he was getting real value for money.[21] Technically, Brook was to investigate all organizations involved in the intelligence machine. But it was clear to him that Attlee wished him to flush out information on SIS and MI5.[22]

Although the prime minister and the cabinet secretary couched their conversation in terms of pounds, shillings, and pence, both of them were aware that something had gone very badly wrong. In February 1950, the police arrested Klaus Fuchs, a senior nuclear physicist working for the Ministry of Supply's Atomic Energy Research Establishment at Harwell. Harwell's primary task was to develop and build a British A-bomb. That information was secret. What was not secret was that the Soviet Union was ahead of Britain in atomic weapons, the Soviets having tested their first A-bomb in August 1949.

Fuchs went on trial in March 1950. The case itself was straightforward: on 24 January 1950, Fuchs had confessed to an MI5 officer 'that from 1942 to February 1949 he was active as a Soviet agent and had given the Russians everything he could, including details about the manufacture of the atomic bomb.'[23] The real trial – 'the onslaught' – was not of Fuchs but of Britain's intelligence machine, and the prosecutors were, in the main, journalists.[24]

In February 1950, the American FBI started feeding both US and also British journalists stories about the incompetence of British intelligence. The Fuchs case was not the only such story in the news. In January 1950, the *Daily Express* reported the history of 'Cicero', the RSHA's wartime penetration of the British Embassy in Istanbul.[25]

LONDON LAUGHS: By LEE

"Baint much good us being so 'ush 'ush, now they're telling all they chatterboxes about it."

6.2. London Laughs. The press did not think much of atomic security in July 1948, well before the intelligence services realized that important members of the A-bomb development team were Soviet agents.

Attlee and Brook also knew, although the press was yet to learn, that a second physicist at Harwell, Bruno Pontecorvo, was already suspected of being a second Soviet agent within the British A-bomb project. Unlike Fuchs, Pontecorvo had not confessed: he was quietly sacked and found an academic position at the University of Liverpool.[26]

In parallel with Brook, but feeding into his inquiry, Attlee set a Treasury civil servant, John Winnifrith, to work on finding out why aliens and Communists had been allowed into the most secret parts of the British state with seemingly reckless abandon.[27]

The very nature of the Fuchs and Pontecorvo cases was historical. To find out what had happened, British investigators had to follow a breadcrumb trail backward into the past, trying to discover when, how, and by whom the British nuclear project had been penetrated. That historical investigation started some time before Fuchs confessed, but it only moved to the heart of affairs once Attlee commissioned Brook and Winnifrith to find out what had been going on. The prime minister was predisposed to believe that something very sinister was afoot. In March 1948, Attlee was behind his own government's decision to 'purge' Communists working in sensitive positions, both in government and in private industry.[28]

Brook's task was framed, and complicated, by the fact that the prime minister himself was an historical actor. He told Brook, 'I doubt if there has ever been (at any rate for very many years) an enquiry which took all the organisations in question under its purview.' Attlee had joined the government on the day in 1940 that Lord Hankey delivered his second report on the British intelligence services. He had told Churchill that he thought those inquiries had been poor.[29]

Five years later, Attlee took a much more public role in the history of Soviet penetration of the atomic bomb programme. In 1945, as the newly elected prime minister, he had little choice but to personally negotiate with President Truman and the Canadian prime minister, Mackenzie King, about the previous great revelation of Soviet espionage. On 15 November 1945, Attlee, Truman, and King gathered in Washington to declare that they were not willing to share the secrets of nuclear technology with other powers. The meeting was overshadowed by their knowledge that the British had managed to introduce a Soviet agent into the Manhattan Project.[30]

According to the history of events with which the prime minister went to Washington, on 7 September 1945, a GRU cipher clerk at the Soviet Union's embassy in Ottawa, Igor Gouzenko, had presented himself, out of the blue, to the Royal Canadian Mounted Police, asking for asylum in return for an account of Soviet intelligence operations in Canada. Gouzenko brought with him a cache of documents that he had removed from the embassy.

The documents confirmed the existence of a sixteen-agent Soviet network in Canada. The Soviet spies were targeted less on the Canadians *per se* than on Canada's allies. There was, for instance, a Soviet agent in the British High Commission in Ottawa. Gouzenko also named a British nuclear physicist working on the A-bomb, Alan Nunn May, as a Soviet agent. The Canadians immediately shared their intelligence windfall with London. Nunn May was due to return from wartime service to take up a job in London. Attlee gave his personal permission for Nunn May to be allowed to return to the UK rather than being arrested by the Canadians.[31]

The American and Canadian press had not been willing to accept their leaders' careful handling of Soviet espionage. As a means of relieving the pressure on his government, Mackenzie King announced, in February 1946, that he was setting up a Royal Commission to investigate Soviet espionage. Since the evidence was easily to hand, the Royal Commission managed to report within a month. The reports and the supporting evidence were published in July 1946.

Despite the speed of its inquiry, the Royal Commission did a thorough job. The publication of the documents, and their reporting in the press in Canada, the US, and Britain, meant that in the summer of 1946 any well-read person could have had an understanding of 'Russian methods of penetration' barely less sophisticated than that of senior politicians, or indeed the intelligence services themselves.[32] Woundingly, that indeed was the view of Harold Caccia, then chairman of the Joint Intelligence Committee.[33]

Once more signal intelligence restored the intelligence machine's advantage over the 'the limited "outside public"'. In 1947, the US Armed Forces Signals Agency, known from its location as Arlington Hall, started a determined attempt to decrypt messages sent by Soviet officials in New York to Moscow in the latter years of the Second World War. These messages had been intercepted but not deciphered.

Some of the three hundred or so staff working on the project had spent the war at Bletchley Park. They informed their former colleagues in Britain what they were up to, and British cryptanalysts made similar but less-well-resourced efforts against wartime Soviet transmissions. The project was codenamed VENONA by the Americans, and GLINT by the British. In November 1947, the project began to report some tentative progress on the 'Russian BJS'. Of particular note to the British was 'that a Government document, supplied by us to the Australians had leaked almost *in toto*'. This was 'disquieting, since so much of our information is going in that direction and experimental work on rockets'.[34]

It was only in August 1949, however, that a 'serious atomic case' was cracked. In 1944 a British scientist on the Manhattan Project had been giving atomic secrets to Soviet intelligence, which transmitted them to Moscow.[35] The project teams identified Klaus Fuchs in September 1949. It was only at that point that MI5 went back to the original Gouzenko dossier and confirmed that Fuchs's name had been present.[36] The leadership of MI5 concluded, gloomily, that 'it was our experience that when Ministers found themselves in difficulties of this sort they were inclined to say that the Intelligence Services had let them down unless they were allowed to tell the House of the facts. In this case such a course would be impossible.'[37]

The real impossibility was in admitting to VENONA/GLINT. It demonstrated the continuing scale of British signal intelligence. The project relied on the fact that Britain and America had signed an open-ended signal intelligence agreement in March 1946, the central premise of which was that the two countries would not spy on each other, but they would spy on everyone else, enemy, neutral, ally, and share the results.[38] The fear at MI5 was that their political masters would sacrifice the human-intelligence services in order to protect GCHQ.[39]

In January 1950, the senior officers of MI5 agreed that their first priority should be to work out a defence of their own conduct. This defence amounted to the contention that, in 1942, Churchill and Lord Beaverbrook, then and in 1950 the owner of the *Daily Express*, had been eager to share everything with the Russians, and that the only black mark against Fuchs's name was that he had been a member of an anti-Nazi youth movement.

MI5 claimed that there were, 'certainly now and to a large extent at the time other projects of equal, if not greater, secrecy and importance than the atomic bomb'.[40]

As a result of this desire to sidestep their historical responsibility for Fuchs, MI5's briefing of Attlee was not as full and accurate as it might have been.[41] Percy Sillitoe, the director-general, remarked that he probably deserved to be sacked for the rubbish that reached the prime minister's desk. 'Further research' revealed that MI5 had collected rather more information on Fuchs than they had shared with the prime minister. Indeed, a number of the responsible MI5 officers had written minutes during the 1940s specifically concluding that Fuchs was a Soviet spy.[42] It was hardly surprising that Attlee should turn to another quarter for a history of British security.[43]

Brook started by reading the Bland, Findlater Stewart, and Evill reports. He therefore had a launching pad of three major investigations into British intelligence carried out between 1944 and 1947.[44] He appointed two assistants to devil out further details: John Drew, who had done the same job for Findlater Stewart, and Cedric Cliffe from the Cabinet Office, who had once been Lord Swinton's private secretary.

Brook himself was no disinterested actor. As he made clear in his interviews, he was an 'old Home Office man'.[45] The Home Office bitterly resented its effective extrusion from the intelligence machine, a grievance that it had been nursing since the 1920s. No one currently inside the machine thought that the Home Office would improve anything about British intelligence, but Brook was determined to impose Home Office control on MI5, whatever any of his sources might advise.

Brook had been deputy cabinet secretary during the war and was now cabinet secretary: he believed in the British civil service and regarded its permanent secretaries as the ultimate examples of a superior breed.[46] He was determined also to give them control over the intelligence machine.[47]

Brook's first observation was that everyone needed to stop harping on about the past. The Second World War was done and gone. Britain could not hope to replicate what it had then. In the war, the intelligence services had been staffed by 'intelligent people (university dons and the like)': in peace they were much stupider, and the state just had to live with that fact.[48]

Brook discovered that GCHQ had succeeded in recruiting no new high-grade cryptographers since 1945, by regular methods at least. Men with the requisite brains and intelligence could have better and better-paid careers outside the secret world. The high-grade GCHQ cryptanalysts were hold-overs from the Bletchley Park days.[49]

The Brook Report was formally delivered in March 1951. Brook, however, had reached all his important conclusions by October 1950. Indeed, he had reached many of those conclusions before the outbreak of the Korean War on 25 June 1950. Although the Brook Report got caught up with the short-term panic over Korea, it remained, as billed, a product of the Fuchs case.[50] Attlee and his senior ministers would sign off on the report on 5 June 1951, after the disappearance of the British diplomats Guy Burgess and Donald Maclean, but two days before that disappearance became public knowledge.[51]

Brook's first port of call had been the Treasury. The bedrock of the Brook Report was hard-headed analysis of how much Britain had been spending on its intelligence services, and which of them had been getting the money.[52] Brook understood that the Secret Vote and the intelligence budget were two very different things.[53] His method was to establish how much the Treasury was paying out, and compare that figure with the amount the intelligence agencies thought they had been spending.[54] In broad terms, Brook's team calculated that the current Secret Vote was three million pounds, but the real intelligence budget was closer to ten million pounds.[55]

Brook took 1938 as his base year. The most obvious feature of historical intelligence expenditure was that it had fluctuated wildly over the previous twelve years as a result of fighting a world war. The 1938 baseline for the Secret Vote had been four hundred thousand pounds; it had peaked in 1943 at over fifteen million pounds, bottomed out in 1946 at one-and-three-quarter million, and had since climbed to the aforementioned figure of three million.

The historic figures for non–Secret Vote expenditure on intelligence services proved irrecoverable – although the figure was plainly large. Using the three-and-a-third multiplier calculated from the more-recent figures, Brook calculated that Britain had spent about fifty million pounds in a year on intelligence services at their most expensive.[56]

The real analysis was, of course, in the details. By combining the various open votes and the Secret Vote, Brook was able to reveal the relative wealth of each intelligence service. In terms of budget, the ranking of British intelligence agencies was: SIS, GCHQ, the Directorate of Military Intelligence, the Assistant Chief of the Air Staff for Intelligence, MI5, the Naval Intelligence Division, the Joint Intelligence Bureau, and the Directorate of Scientific Intelligence.

This ranking did not necessarily bear out the assumption that Brook or his readers would have originally made, given that the Director of Scientific Intelligence was the most persistent participant in the Brook review. In the public sphere, politicians gave most attention to MI5. Former members of the Directorate of Naval Intelligence, influenced by their former chief, John Godfrey, were determined to publicize the achievements of that agency.[57]

It was possible to rearrange the budget figures by activity rather than agency. Besides their intelligence divisions, the Services were maintaining large and separate Y services. If the Service interception services were counted together with GCHQ, then signal intelligence was the major intelligence activity. If the Service signal-intelligence departments and their intelligence divisions were counted together, armed-forces intelligence became by far the largest intelligence organization of the British state.[58]

Brook was reassured by these figures. He started the main part of his inquiry believing that historical distribution of the intelligence budget had been about right. The role of SIS as Britain's best-funded intelligence agency might seem a little ridiculous, but there were historical reasons why this was so, and the preponderance of spending was heading in the right direction.[59] He concluded that 90 per cent of useful intelligence came from signal intelligence, while conceding that he had been kind in allocating 10 per cent to SIS: the consumers of intelligence had told him that 'their estimate was in fact far less generous than mine.'[60] To some in intelligence, Brook's questioning seemed unnecessarily severe, but he was, in fact, a relatively complacent paymaster.[61]

Accusations of complacency were levelled most vocally by the representative of the Chiefs of Staff in Washington, Sir William Elliot, who said that Brook had ducked his main challenge. He had failed to acknowledge that civilian intelligence agencies had historically been, and remained, useless – 'except in the notable exceptions where we apply highly scientific methods'. For his trouble, Sir William, the future Chief of the Air Staff and Britain's first Chief of the Defence Staff, was barred from seeing reports on Burgess and Maclean because he was 'unreliable'.[62]

The first intelligence agency that Brook subjected to extended scrutiny after he had established the budget ranking, was the fifth most important. In MI5, the team of Guy Liddell and Dick White had always insisted that history was important.[63] Since 1945, the deputy director general and the head of B Division had regularly delivered lectures on the history of MI5, both within Whitehall and to chosen audiences in other organizations.[64] They thought they had a good story to tell, and that as a result of their long preparation 'it could quite easily be done.'[65]

The MI5 history of anti-Soviet espionage since 1945 amounted to the calculation that ten spies had been detected, seven of whom had been active before the end of the Second World War.[66] The state had, by one means or another, moved fifty-six Communists away from sensitive work: this figure compared to a total of sixty-five thousand people classified as being involved in such work.[67] Very few of those definitely known to have been spies had been members of the Communist Party.[68]

Although MI5 assumed the Soviet embassy in Kensington Gardens to have been the hub of all serious intelligence activity in Britain since 1941, 'there is no actual evidence'.[69] The obvious question – which Brook posed – was why MI5 had chosen to concentrate so much of its counter-espionage effort on the Communist Party when those known to have spied for Russia were rarely members of the party. The section of B Division that monitored the party had twenty-nine officers: the section that worked on the Soviets had only nine officers.[70]

The answer came in two parts. First, the prime minister had ordered MI5 to carry out 'The Purge' in 1948: inevitably this had been manpower intensive. In any given week there were thirty detailed Purge investigations in train.[71]

Second, the Communist Party was the sea in which Soviet spies swam. Investigations tended to show that even the 'cleanest' skin may have been tainted by communism in the past; operational necessity sometimes forced agents to rely on Communists for aid or communications. Rather more uncomfortably, MI5 admitted that they had come to rely on investigations of

Communists because they had gathered so little intelligence on the Soviets. Their 'study of Soviet espionage,' had, 'not succeeded in elucidating the up-to-date organisation.' If they were 'compelled by political pressure' to devote more resources to the physical surveillance of Soviet officials, this would largely be 'eye-wash.'[72] Their only really valuable intelligence had come from the VENONA/GLINT programme.[73] They 'could think of no way of improving our knowledge of Russian intelligence activities that was not already being pursued.'[74]

During the course of the inquiry, the MI5 briefers were anxious lest Brook should not believe their version of history. They need not have worried: he did. As it turned out, Brook heartily approved of any or all crackdowns on Communists. In fact, MI5 even feared they might have laid it on a bit thick.[75] Brook argued that the 'first duty of a Security Service was to counter subversive activities by Communists.'[76] He believed that 'the business about MI5 dealing with defence is rather rot'. The contemporary threat was that the Soviet Union was 'trying to subvert other countries from within'.[77]

Brook and MI5 saw eye-to-eye on the Fuchs case. Liddell and White argued that 'Fuchs was not discovered earlier because he was "lost among his scientific colleagues"'.[78] The Communist Party was a known and controllable phenomenon. The real problem was the all too numerous 'intellectual Marxists' that had infected every part of the nation and the state.[79]

After Brook had finished his interviews with the leadership of MI5, but before he wrote up his conclusions, Bruno Pontecorvo, the second British atomic scientist suspected of spying for the Soviet Union, disappeared. Pontecorvo's defection made a mockery of MI5's contention that they did not wish to be lumbered with any more 'Watchers'.[80]

The Pontecorvo case nevertheless amply confirmed the loathing of 'intellectual Marxists' shared by both Brook and the Security Service.[81] Marxist ideas, Brook wrote, 'evidently have a strong appeal to a certain type of intellectual; and scientists and artists, in particular, seem to be specially susceptible to them. It is significant that it was in this class that Fuchs and Pontecorvo were found.'[82]

By the time Pontecorvo disappeared, Brook had already turned his attention to SIS. The history that fascinated him was how SIS had transformed itself from collection of shady ne'er-do-wells into a group of bureaucrats, without any appreciable improvement in its performance. He concluded that SIS officers had been transformed into mere administrators. 'There is, to me,' Brook remarked, 'something faintly ridiculous about the system of engaging spies by Civil Service Commission Selection Boards.'[83]

Even those SIS officers sent overseas – and the majority were to be found in London – were not agent-runners. The old model of letting a 'big man' or 'unofficial agent' do all the work had ossified 'to avoid compromising the cover of the SIS officer as a member of the Embassy or Legation staff.' From 'reading between the lines' of the Bland Report and talking to officials who had dealt with SIS in the Second World War, Brook realized that some order had had to be imposed on chaos. Sinbad Sinclair had brought some 'military discipline' with him from the DMI. But what had happened was beyond a joke. The SIS had become 'respectable' and had lost any 'vigour, initiative and enterprise' it had once possessed. Brook longed for some 'buccaneering spirit'. The past now seemed rose-tinted.[84]

Stewart Menzies was the person most aggrieved by the Brook inquiry. Brook affected to believe that Menzies was cavilling over his choice of words. Yet from the day he became C in 1939, Menzies had had to suborn or rebut inquirers who came close to learning about the history of SIS. He was not about to break the habit of a professional lifetime. He took it ill that he had been told to make his intelligence service look more like the civil service in 1944, had done so, and was now being mocked for doing so. Menzies fell back on the argument that a civilian such as Brook could not possibly know about the secret world from his seven interrogative days in SIS's headquarters at Broadway Buildings.

Menzies ended mysteriously by declaring that all the key SIS achievements of the post-war years had been centred in Vienna. Those who needed to know about these triumphs – specifically the DMI, the DNI, and ACAS (I) – already knew about them. They were too secret to share with Brook.[85]

Since 1947 Vienna had been the site of an 'expanded' SIS station, staffed by five officers and headed by one of the new 'university men'.[86] The city was under military occupation, and divided into British, Russian, American, and French zones. The 'university man' station head had worked out that he could tap into the landlines of the Soviet occupation forces by tunnelling under the city from the British zone. Because the work of tunnelling was

"Never seem to run into such a thing as a BEAUTIFUL spy these days."

Daily Express, May 11th, 1954

6.3. Beautiful Spies. MI5 was subject to public naming and shaming by 1954.

labour intensive and difficult to conceal, SIS had to work in close collaboration with military intelligence. The results were regarded as so startlingly good that a much larger project for Berlin was planned.[87]

Despite Menzies's reluctance to go into written detail about the Vienna tunnel, there was an historical account of a different kind on the table when Brook arrived at Broadway to carry out his tour of inspection. The year 1949 marked the nadir of SIS-MI5 relations. At issue was the conclusion of the 1945 Findlater Stewart Report that the 'Defence of the Realm' meant not the 'defence of the UK' but the defence of the formal and informal empire. The implication was that, in collaboration with armed-forces intelligence, MI5 would work throughout the globe.

The further implication of Findlater Stewart was that the counter-espionage, services MI5 B Division and SIS Section R.5, should be merged into a single organization, potentially as part of either SIS or MI5. To stop the two agencies trying to dismember each other, Lord Bridges had put an eighteen-month moratorium on further discussion. This had not stopped the issue poisoning personal relationships.[88]

In an attempt to calm tempers, Percy Sillitoe and Stewart Menzies had, in late 1948, established a working party to draw up a written 'concordat' to regulate demarcation disputes. In terms of historical accuracy, matters had not started well. The SIS arrived at the first meeting armed with a 'Charter' that they claimed enshrined their right to control all espionage outside Britain. This was the latest in a long range of such charters, stretching back to the Nicolson Minute of 1915. At best, the charters were simply documents signed by the Foreign Office, at worst they were made up for the needs of the moment. The MI5 negotiators had pointed this out: they had asked to see the proof that, at some time in the past, the 'charter' had been approved by anybody of authority in the state. Predictably, no such proof was forthcoming. The two services, Guy Liddell wrote, were like a 'set of Orientals bargaining over a carpet'.[89]

The acridity of their exchanges hid, however, the essential agreement between SIS and MI5 about the nature of intelligence, which they had reached in July 1949. Both sides were driven by the fact that long custom and practice dictated that they needed one another: 'the only people who could understand these matters were SIS and ourselves,' Liddell wrote in response to one of his own officers who wanted to pursue SIS's fake charters to the nth degree.[90]

The two services had a joint interest in preventing any 'inexpert working parties' from probing into the affairs of the civilian intelligence. Thanks to Klaus Fuchs, they did get an 'inexpert working party', but at least the concordat was firmly in place before Brook could interfere.[91] 'I am glad to be able to report,' Brook reassured Attlee, 'that relations between these two organisations are today more harmonious than they have been for many years past.'[92]

The SIS told Brook that 'the collection of' counter-espionage was now, 'clearly demarcated between Commonwealth and Foreign countries.' Both SIS and MI5 had a legitimate need to collect counter-intelligence. Both agencies needed to analyse their own counter-intelligence themselves.

Since its formation in 1945 by the merger of the former Sections V and IX, the purpose of SIS Section R.5 had been 'to satisfy themselves that their own organisation was not being penetrated, and that any agents they were employing were not in fact double agents who were working for the enemy.'[93] Menzies assured Brook that the information R.5 had been amassing would soon bear other fruit. They were now in the process of analysing that intelligence. In 1951 they might even be in a position to begin thinking about penetrating Russian and Soviet-bloc intelligence services.[94]

However, it emerged that penetration and counter-penetration had not been the primary concern of SIS since the war. The Foreign Office remained committed to their historical view that their large and well-funded intelligence portfolio was not there to play spy games with the Soviets, much less to steal military secrets. It existed to give the Foreign Office early warning of the political gambits of other powers and to help it outmanoeuvre others to Britain's advantage.[95]

As William Strang, the recently appointed permanent under-secretary of the Foreign Office, put it to Brook, 'diplomatic intelligence is different in character from military intelligence'.[96] Like his predecessors, Strang presided over a formidable intelligence empire, of which SIS was but part, and none of which he intended to have constrained in any way.

Whereas SIS took up the lion's share of the Secret Vote, the Foreign Office also provided the budget for GCHQ and the Diplomatic Wireless Service. The three were interwoven. In August 1945, C had been confirmed as director-general of SIGINT, thus maintaining his – and thus the Foreign Office's – control over signal intelligence. In 1947 the Foreign Office had created the Diplomatic Wireless Service as a merger of SIS Section VIII and the Radio Security Service. The new director of communications at the Foreign Office, Richard Gambier-Parry, who had been head of the VIII-RSS operation since 1941 as a full-time SIS officer, remained in charge as a part-time SIS officer. He controlled the interception of diplomatic communications, and DWS also carried out electronic intelligence operations from within British embassies. Foreign Office communications were essentially SIS communications, and vice versa.[97]

When Brook gave credit to SIS officers as the wartime begetters of signal intelligence techniques in use in 1950, he was thinking of Gambier-Parry, Section VIII, RSS, and DWS, not the general run of SIS officers.[98] He labelled the latter pig-ignorant of how intelligence was actually collected by the British state.[99]

Strang's intelligence empire put him on a potential collision course with Brook. However, unlike his predecessors, Strang also had a serious structural problem with SIS. The solution to that problem made Brook and Strang allies. Because the Passport Control Office cover had been abandoned in the wake of the Bland Report – it was now used only in closely allied countries – nearly all SIS officers operated under Foreign Office cover. The trouble was that there were actually more SIS officers than core members of the Foreign Service. In 1950 there were 267 SIS officers operating under cover.[100] Strang put the number of 'key posts' in the Foreign Service, at 125.[101] The British Foreign Office was thus in danger of becoming similar to the foreign ministries of the Soviet satellites: a shell for intelligence, with a boutique diplomatic service attached.[102]

Strang was 'disturbed' by the nature of the SIS cuckoo he had inherited: 'there was, for instance, no man with University training among its leading officers.' 'By custom', the appointment of C, and his two direct subordinates, had been 'referred' to the permanent under-secretary. However, this was scant consolation, since the only actual examples of the appointment of C had occurred in 1923, when Sinclair replaced Cumming, and 1939, when Menzies had stepped into Sinclair's shoes. The last PUS to be 'consulted' was Cadogan, who had approved John Sinclair's appointment as vice-chief in 1945.

By definition, only two of the seven relevant permanent under-secretaries had had a hand in appointing a C: Strang was likely to be the third, as Menzies approached retirement age. He asked his fellow PUSS to give him the authority to control the appointment of the ten most-senior officers in SIS: to this they readily assented. Strang's Foreign Office might be little more than the host body for a parasitical infestation, but at least it would have some degree of control over its 'friends'.[103]

Because Brook was willing to probe only so far, the main practical focus of his report fell not on the biggest and best-funded intelligence service with a well-developed track record, but on the smallest, most recent, and least well funded. The Directorate of Scientific Intelligence had been set up only in 1949. Since the DSI had such a short history, Brook's historical investigation was narrowed even further to the status of a former air-force intelligence unit left over from the war. That intelligence unit comprised three officers.

At the beginning of the Second World War, most service intelligence officers had believed that they would get the bulk of their signal intelligence from finding the source and destination of signals. Deciphering signals would be an occasional bonus. This assumption had been falsified by events. Not only had the British enjoyed great success in decryption; in addition, direction location and the like had yielded few useful insights. As a result, signal intelligence had become synonymous with the deciphering of words.

When Bletchley Park had come to review the history of their achievements, some code breakers maintained that they should evince little interest in the cul-de-sac of non-verbal communications. The alternative school, led by Gordon Welchman, argued that, instead, Bletchley should play up whatever successes traffic analysis had enjoyed, not least to keep it out of the hands of the armed services.

Throughout the war, experiments had continued with alternative techniques. One line of inquiry had been into the emissions of enemy electronic devices, such as radar, navigation aids, or guided-weapon controls. Air Intelligence's Assistant Director (Science), R.V. Jones, was a particular champion of such work. At his behest, ACAS (I) had set up a small 'noise listening' unit.

The so-called Overseas Party still existed; it was still run by the men who had created it during the war, though it had been transferred from the RAF to the civilian Directorate of Scientific Intelligence in 1949. It currently resided in Germany, where it was trying to make sense of Russian radar arrays. The director of scientific intelligence claimed that it was this unit that qualified him as the head of a full-blown intelligence agency, with the ability to both collect and analyse intelligence. The Overseas Party was making enough progress to re-ignite the hope that what the British in 1950 called 'noise listening', and would later be commonly referred to as electronic intelligence, would one day rival signal intelligence in importance.[104]

The Brook team took against the director of scientific intelligence, Bertie Blount, always referred to dismissively as 'Dr Blount'. Blount made the mistake of believing what he was told by his political masters. He had been recruited in 1949 by A.V. Alexander on the premise that British scientific intelligence since the war had been a disaster. As a result, in his attempt to create a functioning scientific intelligence agency, Blount had picked fights with both Edward Travis of GCHQ and Eric Welsh of the Atomic Energy Intelligence Unit of the Ministry of Supply, who, like Richard Gambier-Parry, remained a part-time SIS officer.[105] In effect, Blount's shiny new corvette had taken on Stewart Menzies's barnacled Dreadnought.

History declared *nolo contendere*. As Brook's figures showed, SIS was the most-costly intelligence agency, and signal intelligence was the most costly intelligence activity: the DSI was but a tiny speck in comparison. Brook recommended that electronic intelligence should be transferred to the 'Intelligence Centre' at GCHQ. To no one's regret or discomfort, Bertie Blount announced his resignation. In passing, Brook's investigator did note that, thanks to this bickering, Britain had had no electronic intelligence capability in the Korean War zone, where it might actually have been useful to British forces.[106]

Although the actual intelligence controversy over the summer of 1951 was centred on the control of electronic intelligence, very few people were interested in that particular field. Government ministers and intelligence mandarins had a much more pressing matter with which to deal.

On 7 June 1951, the British press started reporting that Guy Burgess and Donald Maclean had disappeared. The journalists were getting their information primarily from press briefings in the United States, supplemented by their sources around Whitehall. The Attlee government endured an 'embarrassing' barrage of scorn in the House of Commons while trying to explain what had happened and what it meant.[107]

Attlee's immediate response was to commission yet another internal review. It was chaired by the former permanent under-secretary of the Foreign Office, Sir Alec Cadogan, sitting with Sir Norman Brook, author of the Brook Report, and Sir Nevile Bland, author of the Bland Report. By this point, these men were truly pickled in intelligence history. The chances of them seeing anything new, or bringing any particular insight to bear on the matter, was approximately nil. In any case, their remit was stiflingly narrow: did the history of Burgess and Maclean demonstrate any shortcomings in Foreign Office security? Implicit in this brief was the question for which the Cadogan Report later became notorious: should homosexuals as well as communists be purged from government service?[108]

The Burgess and Maclean case had a long history but a short gestation. The history with which the Cadogan inquiry engaged was the history of an Anglo-American investigation into Soviet agents operating in Britain and America. They were interested in when, and to whom, certain findings of this investigation had been revealed. By definition, as they acknowledged, they could not know the 'real history' of what had happened, since the key to that 'real history' lay, unreachably, in Moscow, not in London or New York.[109]

In brief, the 'real history' was as follows.[110] In May 1934 Stalin had undertaken one of his frequent re-organizations of Soviet intelligence. He had subordinated the Razvedupr, the intelligence directorate of the Red Army, to the INO, the foreign-intelligence service of the NKVD. The head of the INO, Artur Artuzov, had thus additionally become deputy head of military intelligence. The combined forces of the two intelligence agencies had created a critical mass for a decent effort in London.

Between 1934 and 1937, under Artuzov's leadership, Soviet intelligence enjoyed what would later come to be seen as a golden age in Britain. Artuzov was committed to long-term penetration operations based on the recruitment of agents and their *subsequent* placement in areas where they could steal intelligence for the Soviet Union.

The new policy was run in parallel to, but separately from, the recruitment of agents in place – people who already had sensitive jobs but could be suborned. The combined Russian intelligence service had continued to run bribery operations. In the early 1930s, they controlled Ernest Oldham, a debt-ridden alcoholic in the cipher section of the Foreign Office. Oldham committed suicide, but not before talent-spotting his successor, another debt-ridden drinker, John King, whom the Soviets recruited in 1935. King was discovered and imprisoned in 1939. The latter case was well-known to the Cadogan Committee.

The Soviets had also continued to run traditional ideological operations, recruiting communist workers to the cause. The best known such case was the Woolwich Arsenal Case, in which a Soviet spy ring in the state artillery arsenal had been broken up in 1938.[111]

The overall key to Artuzov's tactics was the use of 'illegals', intelligence officers not operating under the cover of official Soviet organs. He had sent a small team, led by Arnold Deutsch, from Vienna to London to explore new lines of attack. For the first few months, more-senior INO officers, Ignace Reiss and Alexander Orlov, supervised Deutsch.

Between 1934 and 1937, Deutsch recruited a string of seventeen English agents of the new type. His first recruit, in July 1934, was Kim Philby, who had already been spotted by Deutsch's old boss in Vienna, Tivadar Mály. One of Philby's first tasks was to talent spot those among his Communist contemporaries at Cambridge who would make good agents. Deutsch recruited Guy Burgess in December 1934, Donald Maclean in February 1935, Anthony Blunt in January 1937, and John Cairncross in May 1937.

Reports by the NKVD claimed that Deutsch had a string of up to seventeen agents, although no definitive list has ever been established. The Cambridge Five could easily have been the Cambridge Dozen. Possibly the most effective of the bunch was the 'MI14 agent'. Between 1943 and 1945, he passed a constant stream of Ultra to his Soviet controller.[112]

The most established star was Donald Maclean. Immediately after he was recruited, he joined the Foreign Office. In 1936 he started passing high-grade intelligence to his handler. Mály, serving temporarily as INO *rezident* in London, ordered that Maclean should be hived off from the rest: he was now a high-value agent-in-place, the others mere aspirants.

The golden age of Soviet recruitment ended in 1937. Stalin had another change of heart. Artuzov was sacked and executed. Mály was recalled to Moscow and executed. Ignace Reiss fled, but was found murdered in a ditch in Switzerland. In July 1938. Alexander Orlov defected. So too did the Razvedupr's *rezident* in the Netherlands, Walter Krivitsky. The intertwining of the INO and the Razvedupr under Artuzov had given Krivitsky many insights into what had gone on. He shared this intelligence with his American hosts, the FBI. In early 1940, they instructed him to share the information with the British too. Upon his return from London to Washington, an NKVD assassin murdered Krivitsky.[113]

In 1938, Deutsch was ordered to mothball his London operation and return to Moscow. He left his team behind, but there was no longer an illegal hub in Britain, and the legal *rezidentura* was reduced to the one INO officer who had escaped the purge. In March 1940, even that officer was withdrawn, leaving 'the seventeen' as self-tasking agents. They continued to report to Moscow via Communist Party channels.

In 1939, Stalin appointed Pavel Fitin as head of foreign intelligence in the NKVD. Three years after Artuzov's death, a competent professional was back in charge. Fitin remained in command throughout the war, even as the NKVD metamorphosed first into the NKGB and then the MGB. The legal *rezidentura* in London was re-established in November 1940, and rapidly expanded. By the time the Nazi-Soviet alliance ended in June 1941, the residency was running sixty agents. London was now acknowledged by Moscow as the most valuable source for Soviet intelligence.

In 1940, Kim Philby joined SIS and Anthony Blunt joined MI5. In August 1941, SIS and MI5 agreed that Anthony Blunt should go down to Bletchley Park on a regular basis to make notes on any useful counter-intelligence material that was coming in from the decryption of Abwehr signals, thus giving the Soviets full access to British counter-espionage signal intelligence.[114]

In September 1941, Lord Hankey appointed John Cairncross as his private secretary to help with his investigation into the potential for building an atomic bomb. Cairncross passed the atomic reports to the London *rezidentura*. In August 1942, Cairncross was transferred to Bletchley Park and began transferring Ultra decrypts. The Razvedupr also had an agent passing BJS from Bletchley.

The end-of-year report for the London *rezidentura* in 1943 noted that a further twenty agents had been successfully recruited. The original core group established by Deutsch was, however, still paying 'high dividends'. Returns were very strong in all fields of intelligence: military, political, economic, and scientific. And scientific intelligence was particularly good on the 'the uranium problem'. Fitin calculated that, although the practical work on atomic weapons had shifted to the US and Canada, the richest haul of atomic intelligence still emanated from London.

In his 1945 review, Fitin wrote that London had 'managed not only to sustain the high level of operational work achieved but also to guarantee the delivery of important documentary material on all questions of interest to the Centre.' The London *rezidentura* had produced and was continuing to produce 'the most valuable political intelligence information, and also data on work carried out in Great Britain on the creation of the atomic bomb.'

Gouzenko's defection caused a second period of upheaval for the British apparatus. In Moscow, Stalin undertook another of his disruptions of the intelligence services. In May 1946, the NKGB had become the MGB. In December 1946, Pavel Fitin was sacked as head of foreign intelligence.[115]

A year after the creation of the MGB, Stalin ordered an even more ambitious reform: MGB foreign intelligence was merged once more with military intelligence, known since 1942 as the GRU, under the title of the KI. The Committee of Information was supposedly a single super-agency: in reality the MGB and the GRU fought like rats in a sack. The experiment was terminated in January 1949, when the GRU was re-established as a separate agency. The KI soldiered on, now comprising only the former foreign intelligence arm of the MGB. The KI was re-united with the MGB in November 1951, as chance would have it only one day after the Cadogan Report was finalized.

In London, changes were afoot too. Anthony Blunt ended his wartime service with MI5 in September 1945, although he remained a familiar figure in Leconfield House.[116] Guy Burgess joined the Foreign Office, but he too remained a familiar figure in the intelligence world. The day the Fuchs case broke, Burgess and Guy Liddell were participating in a 'good' interdepartmental conference about next steps against Russia.[117]

The super-agent Donald Maclean sailed on with seeming serenity. Not only was he passing excellent political intelligence, he also played an important role in Anglo-American atomic diplomacy. Maclean was thus in a position to supply important intelligence about supplies of fissile material and the bomb construction programme to his handlers.

In July 1948, John Cairncross was given responsibility within the Treasury for overseeing the budgets of the armed forces, and began passing accurate information on the strength of British armed forces to his Soviet handler. This was at a period in which Britain was trying to convince the Soviet Union that its armed strength was greater than it truly was.[118]

The Gouzenko post-mortem in Moscow had made Soviet intelligence officers in London much more circumspect and fitful in communicating with their agents in place. After the hiatus of 1946, however, the London *rezidentura* had re-asserted a firm grip over its British agents. In June 1949, SIS and the CIA had signed an agreement for joint action. It specified that they would 'collaborate on a joint basis in one specific operation … [as a] forerunner of other joint understandings.'[119] The specific operation was the overthrow of the government of Albania. In July 1949, the London KI *rezidentura* sent a complete set of plans for the Albanian operation to Moscow. As a result, Albania was a fiasco: the in-country agents were all doubled, and the *émigrés* that were sent in to raise the revolution were all captured.[120]

At the moment when the Fuchs case broke, the Russian intelligence services were running a highly effective agent network based in London. This network was large: it was not confined to the Cambridge group. With regard specifically to that group, Anthony Blunt was out of intelligence but active in subtle misdirection. Guy Burgess was first secretary of the British Embassy in Washington. Kim Philby was SIS representative in Washington. Donald Maclean was head of the North American Department of the Foreign Office. John Cairncross was still in the Treasury.

However, running long-term penetration operations was highly stressful. In January 1947, Kim Philby wrapped up his term of office as head of SIS Section R.5, and left London to become head of station in Istanbul. The iron grip the Cambridge spies had hitherto held over British counterintelligence had thus loosened.

Although, on the whole, the London *rezidentura* had proved a competent agent handler, the chaos, suspicion, and purges in Moscow meant that the Soviets had seemingly arbitrarily abandoned their agents at various stages in their careers, most notably in 1938 and 1946.[121] These stresses were eventually manifested in the Tangier incident of October 1949 and the Cairo incident of May 1950. Both Guy Burgess and Donald Maclean suffered alcoholic nervous breakdowns, leading them to spew verbal abuse in public. Both were re-assigned within the Foreign Office, for conduct unbecoming of British diplomats.

Thus, when the Cadogan team came to write the history of what had just happened, the personalities and foibles of Burgess and Maclean loomed large. The question was whether anyone could be blamed for failing to spot that the Foreign Office had been employing alcoholics who engaged in illegal sexual behaviour and denounced British foreign policy at the top of their voices in public places? There was also the question of who was the 'ringleader'. Because no one doubted that that 'little skunk' Guy Burgess was a long-time degenerate, tolerated because of his quickness of mind and amusing antics, there was a tendency in 1951 to think of him as the corruptor who had led others down the path to treachery.[122]

As Cadogan explained his team's historical practice, 'since it was the disappearance of Mr Maclean and Mr Burgess which gave rise to the appointment of our Committee, it is appropriate that we should first describe the events leading up to the disappearance of these two officials and give a summary of their careers, before dealing with the main substance of our enquiry.' It was the history of Maclean and Burgess that comprised the top-secret portions of the Cadogan Report, and that history concentrated strictly on a joint biography, nothing wider. The conclusions and recommendations were widely disseminated.

The history contained in the report, for what it was worth, worked backwards towards its origin story. On 7 June 1951, the disappearance of two British diplomats, believed to be Soviet spies, had been splashed all over the national press. On 28 May 1951, various agencies had awoken to the fact that they had left Britain. Subsequent inquiry showed that they had left by ferry on 25 May 1951.

Guy Burgess had arrived back in Britain as recently as 7 May 1951. He had been flown back in drunken disgrace from Washington. In April 1951, Donald Maclean had been definitively identified as a Soviet spy, based on decrypts supplied by Arlington Hall. On 23 April 1951, MI5 Watchers had been set on Maclean. They had observed nothing of significance, apart from the fact that he was in frequent touch with Guy Burgess.

Both Burgess and Maclean had been vetted in 1948 and had passed. However, once their disappearance had become public knowledge, some of their former colleagues had come forward to say they that they had known since the 1930s that one or both had been dodgy. Both were 'out' homosexuals, although Maclean subsequently married a woman. Burgess had been a Communist at Cambridge in 1932 and 1933, and had openly kept up his friendly contact with other Communists until 1939.[123]

It would have been hard to find people who knew more about the history of intelligence in 1951 than Alec Cadogan, Norman Brook, and Nevile Bland, or the committee's main advisers, Dick White and John Winnifrith. They certainly knew enough to understand that they were involved in act of almost medieval casuistry, carefully setting down factual information as precisely as they might, without any regard to any kind of broader truth.

At least the disappearance of Burgess and Maclean and the arrest and trial of Klaus Fuchs provided punctuation marks, clear points of closure from which history might be traced backwards. By the time Cadogan and Co. finished their work, however, the story had already travelled beyond such points of historical vantage.

On the same day that the Cadogan Committee was appointed in July 1951, SIS and MI5 agreed that they would have to look seriously at Kim Philby and Anthony Blunt as Soviet agents.[124] Once intelligence officers began poring over the old files with new eyes, the prospect seemed 'blacker' by the day.[125] By the time Cadogan came to report, the civilian intelligence agencies had concluded that all their previous views must be revised: there was no such thing as a 'youthful indiscretion'.[126]

The present was messy, with no fixed point. Churchill, the incoming prime minister, was briefed that 'all the evidence amounted to was a chain of circumstances which pointed to Philby's guilt.'[127] A few days later, SIS announced, however, that it no longer believed that Philby was a Soviet agent.[128] Philby's friends had rallied round. Anyone who might wish to write history was caught in the slipstream of events.[129]

This was amply illustrated by the attempt to write a history of what had happened to British intelligence. In 1955, Norman Brook's former assistant Cedric Cliffe, by this time an officer in MI5's D Directorate – as the counter-espionage division, B, had been rechristened – tried to synthesize everything that had been learnt about the Russian intelligence service's secret war against Britain.[130]

The difference between the 1951 investigation and the 1955 history was striking. In 1951, a team under the secretary of the cabinet had proceeded with Olympian serenity. Each element of intelligence had been measured and held to judgement. The most senior intelligence officers were obliged to account for their actions, both in person and on paper. They had to endure pointed criticism, before being given a clean bill of health.

Brook was still secretary of the cabinet in 1955, but his contemporary and former assistant Cliffe was now a relatively junior MI5 officer. Ronnie Reed, the D officer in charge of 'historic cases', proved Cliffe's most constant guide. James Robertson, the head of D Directorate, had himself previously been the officer in charge of 'historic' cases.[131] But beyond MI5 D Directorate, no one really was any help to Cliffe.

As a result, Cedric Cliffe's history was no Olympian judgement, but rather a ragged and incomplete survey, without political sanction. The history was flawed by incomplete information, the political necessity of not using information that was deemed incendiary, faulty historical method, and doubtful logic.

Some of those flaws were personal to the author. Cliffe may have been the brightest civil servant of his generation – he had beaten Norman Brook in the entrance exam – but he was much more interested in his musical hobbies than in Whitehall. More significantly, he exemplified the inability of his generation (he and Brook had entered the home civil service in the late 1920s) to deal dispassionately with the intelligence history of the 1930s.

Some historical characters had shuffled off the stage. Stewart Menzies, Edward Travis, Percy Sillitoe, and Guy Liddell had all retired in 1952 and 1953. However, the force of continuity was much stronger than that of change. John Sinclair, Eric Jones, and Dick White had all stepped up from within their agencies to become heads of SIS, GCHQ, and MI5 respectively. Kenneth Strong was head of the JIB throughout, as was Richard Gambier-Parry of the Diplomatic Wireless Service. Bertie Blount had gone in 1952, but his successor as DSI was a familiar figure, R.V. Jones.

Cliffe began work, in a very low-key fashion, in the spring of 1955. By the time he finished, a year later, the Burgess-Maclean case had sprung back into public view. In September 1955, the Eden government issued an official public account of what had happened. At root, the 1955 White Paper was the Cadogan Report. However, the facts had been cavalierly altered in the interest of the perceived need of protecting sources and blushes. Line for line, the Burgess-Maclean White Paper was the most deliberately error-strewn command paper released to that date, 'an insult to the intelligence of the country'.[132]

Notably the Home Secretary attempted to defend the White Paper, not by talking about the 1930s, when the Soviet agents had been recruited, or the 1950s, when they had been discovered, but about the history of British intelligence in the Second World War. Gil Lloyd George claimed that 'there is one fact I can disclose viz., the achievement of our Security Service in counter-espionage during the war. We now know from captured German records that the number of intelligence agents operating against the United Kingdom during the war was 201. And the number detected and arrested by our security service was 200.'[133]

No one in the alt-intelligence history movement believed a word of what they were being told. A settled view of British intelligence history was impossible in such circumstances.[134] Nevertheless, the history that Cliffe was writing suddenly had some potential wider usefulness. His work 'was originally planned as a manual for new officers' joining D Directorate. It couldn't be for the Americans, 'since it reveals an alarming number of known spies walking about as free men.' It could not go to the Commonwealth for the same reason. It could not go to SIS, since they refused to believe that Kim Philby was a Soviet agent. In fact, Cliffe believed, his history should not ever be seen outside MI5 Head Office.[135] However, because of the excoriation of MI5 in the press, the history did see relatively wide distribution within the intelligence machine, albeit with one key alteration: all references to Kim Philby and Anthony Blunt were removed. Thereafter it was sent to Washington, Canberra, Singapore, and Nicosia, shared with SIS London, and distributed to all officers of D.[136]

Apart from self-censorship, the most obvious weakness of the 'Survey of Russian Espionage' was its approach to historical causality. Cliffe divided the survey into two parts: a history of the years 1935 to 1955 and an analysis of all the counter-espionage cases on file. He said that he chose 1935 as an 'arbitrary' start date, because it was twenty years before 1955, and because the Italian invasion of Abyssinia in October 1935 had marked the start of the 'pre-war' era. However, as the history itself made clear, the Italian invasion of Abyssinia was an event of passing irrelevance with regard to Soviet intelligence operations in Britain. Even Cliffe conceded that there was, in fact, 'no logical reason' for starting the history in 1935.[137]

Second, Cliffe attempted to link Soviet operations, and their success in recruiting British agents, with supposed 'waves' in world affairs affecting 'the fluctuating value of Russian stock on the English market.' Again, none of the evidence presented in the second section of the survey accorded with the 'wave' thesis of the first. Soviet intelligence had gone through waves, but those waves had had little to do with the ups-and-downs of Anglo-Soviet diplomatic relations, as opposed to the upheavals in Stalin's rule. The history of the agents revealed that, once recruited, they stuck with their Soviet masters, whatever was happening in the short term. Cliffe also introduced a binary divide into his analysis. Those agents recruited before 22 June 1941 were 'fools and criminals': those recruited after June 1941 were 'intelligent and conscientious people'.[138]

Any reader would have finished the first half of the history thoroughly confused as to motivation, method, and chronology. As Cliffe wrote, 'the main story should in theory divide itself into three sections corresponding roughly to the pre-war days of suspicion of Russia, the wartime honeymoon and the post-war period of disillusionment. Unfortunately it does not always work out so neatly as this in practice.'[139]

The second half of the survey was more firmly grounded in reality, at least as MI5 understood it by 1955. Cliffe organized the individual cases into five networks.

The first historical grouping of Soviet agents that Cliffe identified was the Mály *équipe*. Cliffe correctly argued that 1937 was the high point in the creation of this circuit. He also understood that in the mid-1930s the Razvedupr and INO operations in London had been intertwined, with lines of control switching between the two organizations.

In 1955, most of the useable information on the 1930s was still derived from Krivitsky's 1940 testimony. Cliffe identified Krivitsky as his main source and described him as 'an extremely trustworthy witness'.[140] Krivitsky's testimony had been disinterred in April 1951 because it was regarded as particularly pertinent to the live investigation of Donald Maclean. Krivitsky's credibility was instantly reinforced by the confirmation of Maclean as a long-time Soviet agent.[141]

Since Krivitsky had a Razvedupr perspective and collaborated most closely with Mály, it was Mály's name, rather than that of Deutsch, Orlov, or Reiss that became the tag for the London operations. However, Cliffe made clear that there had been a chain of 'illegals' operating in the UK, most unidentified.

In identifying the Mály circuit as comprising at least eleven agents, Cliffe also failed to draw out the difference between the different types of agent. Thus, the Mály string as presented by Cliffe contained Donald Maclean. It also contained Edith Tudor-Hart, Arnold Deutsch's communications specialist. However, Cliffe also lumped in Percy Glading, the CPGB organizer of the spy ring in Woolwich Arsenal, and John King, the corrupt Foreign Office cipher clerk who was run as a separate paid agent. For want of a better place to put him, Cliffe also included Wilfred Macartney, the 'Admirable

Crichton of roguery', the former member of 'Club Med' who had been convicted as a Razvedupr spy in 1928 and had popped up in unwanted places ever since.[142]

Cliffe's second grouping was the Rote Kapelle. Rote Kapelle was the name the Gestapo gave to their operations against RIS circuits in Germany, France, Belgium, Holland, and Switzerland in 1941 and 1942. Both the investigating officers and their documents had fallen into British hands in 1945. Indeed, some of the members of the group itself had passed through British hands in 1945. The best known was Alexander Foote, whose *Handbook for Spies* Cliffe described as 'interesting and readable'. In 1955, Foote was making his living as a London newspaper commentator on Soviet intelligence.[143]

The name Rote Kapelle had come also to be applied to the Soviet circuit as it had affected Britain. The key figure was a Razvedupr representative in Paris, Henri Robinson, who maintained an illegal *rezident* – not always the same person – in Britain between 1930 and 1940. The 'illegal' had in turn run a German 'cut-out'. The 'cut-out' acted as courier to two British diplomats who worked in the Washington Embassy at the same time as Donald Maclean. Despite what was said in the Cadogan Report, the Foreign Office had a known penetration problem long before the Burgess and Maclean case.[144]

The two most notable UK-based agents of the 'illegal' were two technicians, employed at the time of their recruitment in 1935 at the Royal Aircraft Establishment, Farnborough. They had been identified after the war on the basis of the German evidence, but no action was taken because one was still working usefully on classified weapons and the other was a Labour MP.[145]

The Rote Kapelle case left some intriguing loose ends. One of the agents run by Robinson's 'illegal' had been codenamed ELLI. This 'female' GRU agent remained of interest, 'since,' Cliffe recorded, 'it has been alleged that she was in some way connected with the British intelligence services.'[146] Indeed, ELLI was the questing beast for spy hunters.[147] The GRU defector Gouzenko had also mentioned 'the agent known as ELLI who is alleged to hold some high position in British Intelligence.'[148]

In addition, one Razvedupr agent in the War Office in London had been run not by the 'illegal', but by a 'legal' in the Soviet trade delegation. He made 'tantalising allusions', 'to somebody on the "security side" of the War Office who might inform the Russians ... if [his] name appeared in reports of MI5 interviews with him.' The agent 'had always understood that the RIS possessed such a source of information, though he realised that the story might have been merely a bluff intended to boost his morale.'[149]

Cliffe could do little in his survey to throw light on these penetration agents. Later historians have not had much more luck.

The third group was what Cliffe called 'Communists in positions of trust'. That grouping was headed by the names of Klaus Fuchs and Alan Nunn May. Cliffe admitted that he was unsure where to place that group. It was not clear whether they had been recruited in the 1930s, or were his 'intelligent and conscientious people' who had offered themselves to Soviet officials after June 1941. Had Fuchs been sent to England as a Communist agent? Had Nunn May been recruited at Cambridge? Cliffe did not know. He tended to veer toward the opinion that they were indeed 'intelligent and conscientious' rather than fools and criminals.[150]

To this group he added Douglas Springhall, a senior CPGB official who had 'no known' contacts with the RIS before 1942. It was 'not clear' why Springhall had suddenly decided to set up a Soviet spy network. It was not any clearer why Ormond Uren and Joseph Astbury had decided to spy on their intelligence organizations – SOE and GHQ Liaison Regiment respectively. Cliffe could shed little light on why the RAF intelligence officer David Floyd had spied on the British Military Mission in Moscow and then the Foreign Office when he joined it in 1945, or why his friend Arthur Wynn had spied on the Ministry of Fuel and Power.[151]

What was clear was that all these agents had been run by the 'legals' working from the Soviet embassy in London. Cliffe knew this because MI5 had tapped the telephones and ransacked the diplomatic bags of Allied and neutral embassies in wartime London. The Soviets knew it too, since one of the officers in charge of the operation was Anthony Blunt. Blunt's work had been presented to the Joint Intelligence Committee in 1945, and C offered him congratulations by name.[152] Given the Soviet figure of sixty to eighty agents being run by the 'legals', the British tally seemed remarkably small.

When he came to his fourth group, the Maclean and Burgess circuit, Cliffe all but admitted that the historical scheme laid out in the first part of his history made no sense: he found it 'difficult to know exactly where to place Burgess, Maclean and their associates, since their espionage activities extended from right back in the pre-war days, through the shotgun wedding and the honeymoon period with Russia, into the bleak days of the cold war.' Because 'oceans of ink have been spilled' already on the subject, Cliffe's history would concentrate on three things: a chronology, an account of 'how they were employed', and a sketch of their *équipe*.[153]

Cliffe argued that had been no such thing as the 'Burgess-Maclean circle'. They had operated independently. Instead, the two men 'independently left a trail of contacts with intelligence interest which in some cases were duplicated. These contacts were for the most part men of exceptional intellect, enjoying a position in the world which gave them access to classified political information of high importance.'[154]

This analysis was generally nonsense: Burgess and Maclean should have been placed jointly in Cliffe's first group, the 'Mály circuit'. The way in which the spoor had been laid down, however, did make some partial sense of Cliffe's conclusion. Maclean had been hived off early, and treated differently from the others.

Cliffe's 'Cambridge Five' thus looked very different from the later, canonical, version: it was Burgess, Maclean, John Cairncross, James Klugmann, and Harry Smolka. Klugmann had indeed been part of Deutsch's Cambridge recruitment drive. His point of divergence had come in 1939, when he had failed in his attempt to get recruited by SIS. He had penetrated SOE instead. Smolka was linked into the group because he had been passing material to Burgess. He had failed to gain a transfer to military intelligence from the Ministry of Information.

Cliffe's fifth group were those who supposedly had nothing to do with the poisoned wellspring of the 1930s. They were those whom the Soviets had recruited since 1945. Here, Cliffe was able to end his history on an upbeat, 'encouraging' note. The most notable attempt to penetrate a British intelligence agency had been a 'legal' recruiting of David Marshall, an official of the Diplomatic Wireless Service. This certainly suggested that the Soviets knew the importance of Britain's deliberately most obscure intelligence agency.

The Marshall case, Cliffe thought, demonstrated the 'bad work – or perhaps diminishing efficiency – of the [Soviet] security service'. It was the first time that MI5 had been able to identify a Soviet agent by setting the Watchers on a known Soviet intelligence officer.[155] He did not mention that, in 1952, *Intelligence Digest* and *Time* magazine had linked Burgess, Blunt, and Marshall together as members of a homosexual network.[156]

Cliffe's history read like an obscure codicil to a greater whole. His history was ragged. It was hardly surprising that neither Cliffe's colleagues in MI5 nor investigative journalists were convinced by official history. And other historical endeavours were drawing to a similarly ragged conclusion. Historical writing petered out in the mid-1950s because it could do no more.[157]

After 1953 the most striking uses of history appeared not in any further development of historical writing but rather in the public, commercial sphere.

Between 1949 and 1953, Ewen Montagu, the historian of NID 12 and the W Board, had waged a persistent campaign of self-righteous pride and low cunning to be allowed to reveal the history of Operation *Mincemeat*. This was his macabre 1943 brainwave of dumping a corpse in the sea off Spain carrying forged documents for the Spanish to pass on to the Germans. It sometimes appeared that the top officials in the intelligence machine, such as John Drew and Guy Liddell, spent more of their time on the history of *Mincemeat* than on the history of Soviet penetration.[158]

The Man Who Never Was finally was published in September 1953. It would have cost a member of the public ten shillings and sixpence to learn that Britain had had the machinery for deception and that naval intelligence was particularly keen on deception operations, and to receive a detailed account of one such operation from its progenitor. Montagu took the book on tour to the USA in 1954, where he was photographed flourishing a Sherlock Holmes pipe.[159]

As it happened, the long-drawn-out campaign to get *The Man Who Never Was* into print meant that Montagu was beaten to the punch: his former colleague in NID 17, Ian Fleming, dashed off *Casino Royale* in the early months of 1952. The first James Bond novel, also costing 10/6, was published in April 1953. Most of those who purchased the book were public libraries. Bond was a slow-burning success, but truly caught fire with the publication of *From Russia with Love* in 1957.[160]

In the 1950s, Fleming was achingly contemporary: *Casino Royale* was a tale of Russian penetration of the British intelligence machine. James Bond

6.4. Ian Fleming. Intelligence officer, significant figure in, and contributor to, the history of the Naval Intelligence Division, posing with his first novel.

himself, however, was very much a creature of the Second World War. In Fleming's telling, Bond had earned his 00 classification in 1941. His two 'kills' had been a Norwegian 'double' working for the Germans in Stockholm and a Japanese spy targeting British Security Co-ordination in the Rockefeller Centre in New York. The history of British naval intelligence had gone into considerable detail about its two most important intelligence liaison operations of 1941: the collaboration of the British naval attaché in Stockholm with Norwegian *émigré* intelligence, and the mission of the Director of Naval Intelligence, John Godfrey – accompanied by his assistant, Ian Fleming – to New York in 1941.

Montagu and Fleming were plausible because they were known to be former intelligence officers. Their commercial efforts rested squarely on their historical efforts. They had both contributed to, and been major characters in, the history of the Naval Intelligence Division.

The secret history had spawned its own heirs. There was little doubt that the post-war histories, and the inquiries that prompted them, had been an exercise in the management of the limited public sphere by the intelligence machine. What that machine had failed to take fully into account was that intelligence was no longer special. It was now as much part of the known state apparatus as more overtly publicity-hungry government departments.

There is no doubt that the British state made powerful and persistent efforts, both to shape the history of the Second World War and to propagandize its own population as to the right conduct of the Cold War. Yet, in many spheres, post-war British culture was autonomous of the state. Intelligence proved to be one of those spheres.

Conclusion

By the early 1950s, a lot of history had been written about intelligence. It was possible to observe a settled corpus of intelligence history. The history was not limited to any one intelligence agency. Rather, it ranged across the field of intelligence. The authors of the various histories of intelligence interacted with one another, on both a personal and textual level. There were inevitably controversies. However, nearly all intelligence history portrayed the rise of a British intelligence machine as a necessary and welcome response to an external threat.

The histories were written with a view to 'remembering' the bad effects that flowed from neglecting intelligence. They thus comprised both a record of the past and an agenda for the future. It was certainly the case that some individual histories were never completed, barely distributed, stored in cupboards, or simply forgotten. The importance of the historical effort rested less on the fate of particular works than in their collective power over the imagination of policy-makers, opinion formers, and intelligence officers.

It had not always been thus. The historical effort in the wake of the First World War had been quite different. For the most part, what intelligence history that had been written was written as a minor element in the history of military operations. Alternatively, history was held to provide the baseline for technical 'how to do it manuals'. In contrast to other literatures of the First World War, intelligence history yielded very slim pickings.

The First World War literature on intelligence only seems rich from either the longer or broader perspective. Those seeking the origins of modern intelligence have been happy to find a reasonably substantial body of work that could provide 'origin stories' for a particular agency or technique. Compared to some other European countries, notably Germany and France, the amount, quality, and dissemination of the history of intelligence was relatively impressive. However, that is only so when compared to the exiguous effort of others. It tells us little about British culture.[1]

The concept that intelligence history should be written primarily as a contribution to the history of military operations withered during the Second World War. Intelligence history became the history of intelligence for the sake of the intelligence machine. If one were to try and identify the moment when modern intelligence history – and possibly the modern British intelligence machine – was invented, it would be 1942. Its first major historical monument was the history of the Naval Intelligence Division, completed in that year. The NID history became the model for the work of many other intelligence organizations and historians.

The official historians of the 1970s tried to put the clock back by writing intelligence history as a contribution to the history of strategy and operations. In doing so, they acted much like literary critics: determined to tell the writers of the past what they should have been interested in, rather than to record what they *had* been interested in. It is this dissonance that has left generations of readers with a vague feeling of unease when encountering the published official history of British intelligence for the first time. The current generation of official and authorized histories provoke the same feelings of unease.[2]

The primary effect of the actual histories written in the 1940s was to map the field of intelligence. History was much more compelling than internal wiring diagrams. The histories repeatedly returned to the theme of where the boundary between intelligence, politics, and military art began. The histories were histories of intrusion into the intelligence field and invasion repelled by that field.[3] They were histories not so much of professionalism, but of superior judgement. By obsessively recording the histories of intelligence organizations, as they rose and fell within the overall field, the histories described what an intelligence machine looked like and how it should behave.

The most notable absentee from this collective endeavour was the British Army, the largest by far of the armed forces. Military intelligence proved singularly ineffective at writing its own history. This was a notable omission, since it was the army that had a long-standing tradition of official histories. Military intelligence suffered from remaining part of the military field, rather than becoming part of the field of intelligence as it was being defined in the mid-1940s. The army cleaved to the older tradition, abandoned by everyone else, that the history of intelligence should still be subsidiary to the history of military operations.

Military intelligence officers were schooled and socialized into not making expansive claims about themselves. What in other circumstances might have been regarded as laudable modesty, indeed, a prudent necessity for those who proclaimed their activities to be 'secret', generated no cultural capital for military intelligence. In practice, both the wartime and post-war army discovered that, if it wanted any useable military intelligence, it would have to find it for itself. However, such behaviour was now regarded as aberrant, a money-wasting intrusion into the field of real intelligence. The ideal intelligence officer was no longer an actual officer, but, at best, a civilian disguised in a uniform.

It must not be thought that the state wholly controlled the history of British intelligence. Indeed, after both the First and Second World Wars, that history tended to spin out of state control. In the first instance, the purveyors of intelligence history were former operatives and consumers of intelligence, operating in the field of commercial publishing. The post-war Second World War period witnessed the rise of well-informed investigative journalists paid for by the popular press. In some ways, the journalists used the methods of the intelligence agencies against them, gathering intelligence from a network of well-placed informants.

The key difference between the post–First World War and post–Second World War eras was that after the Second World War there was a substantial intelligence machine for the journalists to investigate. That machine now made a significant call on state finances.

The intelligence agencies sometimes expressed horror at the frequency of popular revelations about their history. They were, however, happy to collude with journalists on occasion to broadcast that very history.

More importantly, however, the intelligence history endeavour had aimed to inform what its authors regarded as a vital 'limited public sphere'.

The history of intelligence had to be kept in sight of that 'limited public sphere' if the influence and funding of intelligence agencies was to be maintained at acceptable levels. Since the 'limited public sphere' also intersected with the field of popular journalism, the history of intelligence was necessarily transmitted through that vector.

In light of the genuine history of intelligence history, one might conclude that John le Carré's key character was not George Smiley, but Roddy Martindale, the man who had been a member of wartime secret intelligence committees. Those civilians who had merely 'haunted the fringe' of the intelligence world during the Second World War never tired of boasting of the fact, because of the cachet it now brought.

In the immediate post-war period, intelligence was secret in the sense that the organization of intelligence was kept from the 'common' British subject. However, it was not secret in the sense that an awareness of a powerful 'hidden hand', with distinct characteristics, had permeated the political, military, and administrative elite of the state. According to the 'Intelligence Proverb' Charles Morgan invented for history of naval intelligence, it was 'of great importance not to play ostrich in this matter' by pretending people 'do not know what they in fact know.'[4]

The history of intelligence was devised as a buffer against hard times. Although the intelligence agencies had imagined that those hard times would come in the 1960s, when a new generation had forgotten the Second World War, the history did serve its appointed role in the more unexpected crisis of the 1950s. The history of the war had to be repeatedly deployed as a protective device by the civilian intelligence agencies when their underlying incompetence was revealed to public view.

The secret history served its purpose. Although singed, the intelligence agencies survived the 1950s intact, on the basis of past service and future promise. It was, as le Carré wrote, the 'wartime generation' that still, thirty years on, gave the intelligence agencies their 'flavour of adventure'.

Notes

INTRODUCTION

1 The original phrase, coined by Paul Thompson, writing in 2000, was repurposed for the benefit of intelligence historians in 2015. Andrew Hammond, 'Through a Glass, Darkly: The CIA and Oral History', *History* 100 (2015), 311–26.

2 Jim Beach, 'No Cloaks, No Daggers: The Historiography of British Military Intelligence', in *Intelligence Studies in Britain and the US: Historiography since 1945*, eds. Christopher Moran and Christopher Murphy (Edinburgh: 2013), 202–21.

3 Chistopher Moran and Christopher Murphy, 'Intelligence Studies Now and Then', Moran and Murphy, *Intelligence Studies*, 1–15. In turn, the authors were summing up the findings of the UK Arts and Research Council's project 'Landscapes of Secrecy' at the universities of Warwick and Nottingham. Christopher Moran, 'The Pursuit of Intelligence History: Methods, Sources, and Trajectories in the United Kingdom', *Studies in Intelligence* 55 (2011), 33–55.

4 Adam Sisman, *John le Carré: The Biography* (London: 2015) and Michael Jago, *The Man Who Was George Smiley: The Life of John Bingham* (London: 2013).

5 Joseph Caddell Sr and Joseph Caddell Jr, 'Historical Case Studies in Intelligence Education: Best Practices, Avoidable Pitfalls', *Intelligence and National Security* 32 (2017), 889–904, quotation at 891.

6 Richard Aldrich, 'Strategic Culture as a Constraint: Intelligence Analysis, Memory, and Organizational Learning in the Social Sciences and History', *Intelligence and National Security* 32 (2017), 625–35.

7 Philip Davies, 'Organizational Politics and the Development of Britain's Intelligence Producer/Consumer Interface', *Intelligence and National Security* 10 (1995), 113–32; Philip Davies, 'Intelligence Culture and Intelligence Failure in Britain and the United States', *Cambridge Review of International Affairs* 17 (2004), 495–520; Philip Davies, *Intelligence and Government in Britain and the*

United States: A Comparative Perspective, Vol. 2: *Evolution of the UK Intelligence Community* (Santa Barbara: 2012).

8 Robert Dover and Michael Goodman, eds., preface to *Learning from the Secret Past: Cases in British Intelligence History* (Washington: 2011).

9 Joop van Reijn, 'Intelligence and Strategic Culture: Essays on American and British Praxis since the Second World War', *Intelligence and National Security* 26 (2011), 441–4.

10 Robert Dover and Michael Goodman, 'Lessons Learned: What the History of British Intelligence Can Tell Us About the Future', Dover and Goodman, eds., *Learning from the Secret Past.*

11 Peter Beck, 'Locked in a Dusty Cupboard, Neither Accessible on the Policymakers' Desks nor Cleared for Early Publication: Llewellyn Woodward's Official Diplomatic History of the Second World War', *The English Historical Review* 127 (2012), 1435–70.

12 Peter Jackson, 'Keynote Lecture' in Bernhard Sassmann and Tobias Schmitt, Report on 'Cultures of Intelligence', *Bulletin of the German Historical Institute London* 38 (2018), 35–40.

13 Christopher Andrew, Simon Ball, and Peter Jackson, 'Studying Practice' at AHRC *International Network on the Practice of International History in the 21st Century* (*PIH21*), Foreign and Commonwealth Office, London, 1 June 2017. https://www.gla.ac.uk/schools/humanities/research/historyresearch/researchprojects/thepracticeofinternationalhistoryinthe21stcenturynetwork/workshops/workshop4internationalhistoryandforeignpolicy/ [Accessed: 14 November 2018].

14 Peter Jackson, 'Pierre Bourdieu, the "Cultural Turn", and the Practice of International History', *Review of International Studies* 34 (2008), 155–81.

15 The Wolfson History Prize has been awarded annually since 1972. 'The roll call of winners – and the announcement of the Prize each year – is a public statement of the importance of historical writing within British cultural life.' http://www.wolfson.org.uk/history-prize/about-the-prize/history/ [Accessed: 14 November 2018].

16 David Reynolds, *In Command of History: Churchill Fighting and Writing the Second World War* (London: 2005), xxi–xxvi.

17 It was the opening line of L.P. Hartley's novel, *The Go-Between.* Hartley's theme was the difficulty that men in their 'fifties had in understanding their own, Edwardian, past'.

18 Simon Ball, *Alamein* (Oxford: 2016), 9–10. 'Shadows rather than substance' is derived from George Kennan.

19 Christopher Moran, *Classified: Secrecy and the State in Modern Britain* (Cambridge: 2013).

20 Sassmann and Schmitt, Report on 'Cultures of Intelligence', [footnote 12].

21 The first wave had comprised the release of the Cabinet Office official history, F.H. Hinsley *et al.*, *British Intelligence in the Second World War: Its Influence on Strategy and Operations* (5 volumes, London: 1979–1990) and the publication of the book with the most quoted title in intelligence studies, Christopher Andrew and David Dilks, eds., *The Missing Dimension* (London: 1984).

22 *British Security Coordination: The Secret History of British Intelligence in the Americas, 1940–1945*, introd. Nigel West (London: 1998); J.C. Curry, *The Security Service, 1908–1945: The Official History*, introd. Christopher Andrew (London: 1999); William Mackenzie, *The Secret History of SOE: Special Operations Executive, 1940–1945*, introd. M.R.D. Foot (London: 2000); *Camp 020: The Official History of MI5's Wartime Interrogation Centre*, ed. Oliver Hoare (London: 2000); David Garnett, *The Secret History of PWE: The Political Warfare Executive, 1939–1945*, introd. Andrew Roberts (London: 2002); Frank Birch, *The Official History of British SIGINT, 1914–1945*, ed. John Jackson (Milton Keynes: 2004 and 2007).

23 Richard Aldrich, 'Grow Your Own: Cold War Intelligence and History Supermarkets', *Intelligence and National Security* 17 (2002), 135–52.

24 J. Hanbury-Williams and E.W. Playfair, 'Report to the Minister of Economic Warfare on the Organisation of SOE', 18 June 1942, HS 8/1021, The National Archives (hereafter TNA), London.

25 Robert Benford and David Snow, 'Framing Processes and Social Movements: An Overview and Assessment', *Annual Review of Sociology* 26 (2000), 611–39.

26 'Professor Donald Cameron Watt', obituary, *Daily Telegraph*, 13 November 2014.

27 Donald Cameron Watt, 'Britain and the Historiography of the Yalta Conference and the Cold War', *Diplomatic History* 13 (1989), 67–98.

28 Michael Bentley, *Modernizing England's Past: English Historiography in the Age of Modernism, 1870 to 1970* (Cambridge: 2005), 13.

CHAPTER ONE

1 'History of Military SIGINT, 1914–1945', HW 3/92, TNA.

2 Note by Walter Long, 31 January 1919, WO 32/2180, TNA.

3 Victor Madeira, 'No Wishful Thinking Allowed: Secret Service Committee and Intelligence Reform in Great Britain, 1919–1923', *Intelligence and National Security* 18 (2003), 1–20.

4 Harris to Cunningham, 30 January 1919, KV 4/151 & Papers for Secret Service Committee (Reviewed by DMI, 7 April 1919), WO 32/21380, TNA.

5 Edward Troup to B.B. Cubitt, 2 May 1919, WO 32/21382, TNA.

6 Moran, *Classified*, 53.

7 Basil Thomson, 'Autobiography of a Spy', *Times Literary Supplement*, 11 April 1918.

8 J.E. Edmonds, 'Memoirs', Edmonds 3/5/1-33, Liddell Hart Centre for Military

Archives (LHCMA), King's College London. Edmonds discussed his role as an intelligence officer in the Boer War in a letter to *The Times* in May 1922.

9 Andrew Green, *Writing the Great War: Sir James Edmonds and the Official Histories, 1915–1948* (London: 2003). The first volume of the official history was published in 1925.

10 [Brigadier-General Sir James Edmonds], 'The German Press Bureau' [review of *Nachrichdienst: Presse und Volksstimmung im Weltkrieg*, by W. Nicolai], 8 July 1920, and 'Germany and Secret Service' [review of *Geheime Mächte, Internationale Spionage und ihre Bekämpfung im Weltkriege und Heute*, by W. Nicolai], *Times Literary Supplement*, 17 July 1924. Edmonds reviewed the German editions. W. Nicolai, *The German Secret Service*, translated by George Renwick of the *Daily Chronicle*, was published in English in November 1924.

11 Michael Rupp, 'Public Discourses on Intelligence in Great Britain, 1900–1927', Sassmann and Schmitt, Report on 'Cultures of Intelligence'.

12 Major-General W. Thwaites, DMI, 'Historical Sketch of the Directorate of Military Intelligence in the Great War', 6 May 1921, WO 32/10776, TNA.

13 J.T. More (MI6L) to Major Potts, 9 December 1919, WO 208/3106, TNA.

14 Keith Jeffery, *MI6: The History of the Secret Intelligence Service, 1909–1949* (London: 2010), 244; Emmanuel Debruyne, 'Intelligence in Occupied Belgium: The Business of Anglo-Belgian Espionage and Intelligence Co-operation during the Two World Wars', *Intelligence and National Security* 28 (2013), 313–36; Henry Landau, *Spreading the Spy Net* (London: 1938).

15 Jim Beach, *Haig's Intelligence: GHQ and the Germany Army, 1916–1918* (Cambridge: 2013).

16 R. Drake, 'History of I(b) GHQ, 1917–1918', 5 May 1919, WO 106/45, TNA. Beach, *Haig's Intelligence*, and others, regard the figure of six thousand as an overestimate.

17 'Some Intelligence "Bull's Eyes" Scored, 1914–1918', KV 4/183, TNA.

18 *Secret Supplement of the Manual of Military Intelligence in the Field*, 1923, WO 33/1024, TNA

19 Director of Military Intelligence to Director of Naval Intelligence, 14 November 1918, WO 32/21380, TNA.

20 Director of Military Intelligence to Director of Naval Intelligence, 28 November 1918, WO 32/21380, TNA.

21 Lord Drogheda to Lord Curzon, 30 January 1919, KV 4/151, TNA.

22 Lord Hardinge of Penshurst to DMI, 3 December 1918, WO 32/21380, TNA.

23 Lord Hardinge to DMI, 25 November 1918, WO 32/21380, TNA.

24 Admiral W.R. Hall (DNI) to General W. Thwaites (DMI), 26 November 1918, WO 32/21380; Minutes of Conference held at the Foreign Office to consider the question of the proposed new Code & Cypher Department, 1919, HW 3/34, TNA.

25 James Bruce, 'A Shadowy Entity: M.I.1 (b) and British Communications Intelligence, 1914–1922, *Intelligence and National Security* 32 (2017), 313–32.
26 [Colonel M.J. Ellingworth], 'The History of the War Office Y Group, 1926–1945', April 1948, HW 41/119, TNA.
27 [David Hogarth], 'Lawrence and the Arabs', *Times Literary Supplement*, 10 March 1927, 151.
28 Polly Mohs, *Military Intelligence and the Arab Revolt: The First Modern Intelligence War* (London: 2008).
29 John Ferris, 'The British Army and Signals Intelligence in the Field during the First World War', *Intelligence and National Security* 3 (1988), 23–48.
30 Douglas Haig, *War Diaries and Letters, 1914–1918*, edited by Gary Sheffield and John Bourne (London: 2005), 14 December 1917.
31 [James Edmonds], 'A Commentator at GHQ', *Times Literary Supplement*, 24 September 1931, 714.
32 Louis Halewood, '"A Matter of Opinion": British Attempts to Assess the Attrition of German Manpower, 1915–1917', *Intelligence and National Security* 32 (2017), 333–50.
33 J.E. Edmonds to Winston Churchill, 27 July 1926, CHAR 8/203, Churchill Archive Centre (CAC), Cambridge.
34 D Branch, MI5, 'Report on the Establishment of a Special Intelligence Service in the Colonies and the Overseas Dominions', 1921, KV 1/15, TNA.
35 Thwaites, DMI, 'Directorate of Military Intelligence in the Great War'.
36 Christopher Andrew, *Defence of the Realm: The Authorized History of MI5* (London: 2009) and Jeffery, *MI6*.
37 Lt. Col. William R.V. Isaac, 'The History of the Development of the Directorate of Military Intelligence, The War Office, 1855–1939', WO 106/6083; War Office, 'The Organisation of the Services of Military Secrecy, Security and Publicity', October 1917, KV 4/183, TNA.
38 'The British Secret Service: Great War Record', *The Times*, 2 January 1919, 4.
39 Greg Kennedy, 'Intelligence and the Blockade, 1914–1917: A Study in Administration, Friction, and Command', *Intelligence and National Security* 22 (2007), 699–721.
40 MI5, Chronological List of Staff taken to 31 December 1919, KV 1/59 and Central Special Intelligence Bureau (M.I. 5), I. P. Book 12, *Duties of H. Branch*, December 1917, KV 1/54, TNA.

Officers of MI5, 1909–1919

Late Officers	Serving Officers	Civilians in uniform	Civilians
14%	62%	9%	15%

'Late officers' had held a regular commission in the Army or Royal Navy but had resigned that commission. They were recalled to the Colours in 1914. Kell himself remained on the Active List until 1923. 'Serving officers' were serving officers in the Army or Royal Navy, with a regimental affiliation in the case of military officers. 'Civilians in uniform' were civilian officials specially commissioned by the Army in order that they might better carry out intelligence duties. Civilians were civilians.

41 Nicholas Hiley, 'Entering the Lists: MI5's Great Spy Round-up of August 1914', *Intelligence and National Security* 21 (2006), 46–76.

42 Record of a Meeting at the Admiralty to consider the question of Secret Service funding, 7 April 1919, WO 32/21381, TNA.

43 Hiley, 'Entering the Lists', 46–76.

44 'Rough Draft Summary of G Branch Report' [April 1921], KV 1/48, TNA.

45 Jules Gaspard, 'A Lesson Lived Is a Lesson Learned: A Critical Re-examination of the Origins of Preventative Counter-Espionage in Britain', *Journal of Intelligence History* 16 (2017), 150–71.

46 Lecture delivered by Mr Moresby, O.B.E, at Harrow [Intelligence Course], 1 June 1918, KV 4/159, TNA.

47 MI5, 'H Branch Report, Summary', KV 1/63, TNA.

48 G Branch Report.

49 H Branch Report.

50 G Branch Report.

51 J. Curry, 'The Security Service: Its Problems and Organisational Adjustments, 1908–1945', March 1946, KV 1/1, TNA.

52 Curry, 'The Security Service'.

53 G Branch Report.

54 Hiley, 'Entering the Lists'.

55 Wim Klinkert, 'A Spy's Paradise? German Espionage in the Netherlands, 1914–1918', *Journal of Intelligence History* 12 (2013), 21–35.

56 Markus Pöhlmann, 'German Intelligence at War, 1914–1918', *Journal of Intelligence History* 5 (2005), 25–54.

57 'Franz von Papen', KV 2/520, TNA.

58 Stephen Schwab, 'Sabotage at Black Tom Island: A Wake-up Call for America', *International Journal of Intelligence and CounterIntelligence* 25 (2012), 367–91.

59 Nicholas Hiley, 'Internal Security in Wartime: The Rise and Fall of P.M.S.2, 1915–1917', *Intelligence and National Security* 1 (1986), 395–415, and Nicholas Hiley and Julian Putkowski, 'A Postscript on P.M.S.2', *Intelligence and National Security* 3 (1988), 326–31.

60 Florian Altenhöner, 'Total War: Total Control? German Military Intelligence on the Home Front, 1914–1918', *Journal of Intelligence History* 5 (2005), 55–72.

61 Curry, 'The Security Service'.

62 Pöhlmann, 'German Intelligence at War, 1914–1918'.
63 G Branch Report.
64 H Branch Report. According to the authorized history of MI5, the moving force behind the attempted takeover of MI5 had been Colonel Drake, the historian of GHQIb.
65 G Branch Report.
66 Extract from a Memorandum by the Secretary of State for War, 19 March 1920, KV 4/159, TNA.
67 MI5, 'D Branch Report: The Establishment of a Special Intelligence Service in the Colonies and the Overseas Dominions', 1921, KV 1/15, TNA.
68 Holt-Wilson to Compton Mackenzie, 5 May 1931, and 'Greek Memories by Compton Mackenzie: Memorandum by Lt.-Col. Holt-Wilson', 28 October 1932, KV 2/1271, TNA.
69 '*Greek Memories* by Compton Mackenzie: Schedule of Objectionable Passages' KV 2/1271; Hector Bywater, 'Mystery Chief of the Secret Service', *Daily Telegraph*, 27 October 1932, KV 2/1271, TNA.
70 Redacted [SIS] to Sir Vernon Kell, 23 March 1940, KV 2/1272, TNA.
71 [Harry Pirie-Gordon], 'The RNVR in the Aegean', *Times Literary Supplement*, 18 November 1920, 747. Pirie-Gordon was head of EMSIB in Salonika. David Gill, 'Harry Pirie-Gordon, Historical Research, Journalism, and Intelligence-gathering in the Eastern Mediterranean, 1908–1918', *Intelligence and National Security* 21 (2006), 1045–59. Evidence of Mr X [Valentine Vivian], CRIM 1/630, TNA.
72 [Harry Pirie-Gordon], 'Hard Lying', *Times Literary Supplement*, 12 November 1925, 749.
73 [Harry Pirie-Gordon], 'The Allies and Greece', *Times Literary Supplement*, 23 April 1931, 1525.
74 Memorandum No. 1: 'Naval Intelligence Organisation Inside the Admiralty', [March 1922], ADM 1/8623/64, TNA.
75 Memorandum by the Director of Naval Intelligence, 1 September 1918, based on Vice Admiral H.H. Campbell, 'Imperial Intelligence and London Intelligence Centre: Organisation to Perpetuate Lessons in Intelligence Work Learned during the Great War', March 1918, ADM 1/8532/214, TNA.
76 Andrew McDonald, 'The Geddes Committee and the Formulation of Public Expenditure Policy, 1921–1922', *The Historical Journal* 32 (1989), 643–74.
77 J.R. Chancellor (Secretary to Mond Committee) to Lord Lee (First Lord of the Admiralty), 17 February 1922, ADM 1/8623/64, TNA.
78 M. Fitzmaurice (DNI) to Deputy Secretary, Mond Committee, 29 March 1922, ADM 1/8623/64, TNA.
79 'History for the Mond Committee', [March 1922], ADM 1/8623/64, TNA.

80 J. Goldrick and J.B. Hattendorf, eds., *Mahan Is Not Enough: The Proceedings of a Conference on the Works of Sir Julian Corbett and Admiral Sir Herbert Richmond* (Newport: 1993).

81 Sir Julian Corbett, *History of the Great War, Based on Official Documents: Naval Operations*, III, (London: 1923).

82 Roger Keyes to Winston Churchill, 2 November 1940, CHAR 20/5, CAC.

83 Archibald Hurd, 'The Battle of Jutland: The Official History', *Daily Telegraph*, 15 November 1923.

84 Oliver to Secretary of the Admiralty, 7 March 1919, quoted in Jason Hines, 'Sins of Omission and Commission: A Reassessment of the Role of Intelligence in the Battle of Jutland', *Journal of Military History* 72 (2008), 1117-54.

85 Lord Jellicoe, *The Grand Fleet* (1919), 187.

86 Nicholas Hiley, 'The Strategic Origins of Room 40', *Intelligence and National Security* 2 (1987), 245–73.

87 Calculation based on the catalogue of Churchill Papers.

88 Winston Churchill, *The World Crisis* (London: 1923), 505–21.

89 Andrew Lambert, 'Writing the Battle: Jutland in Sir Julian Corbett's Naval Operations', *The Mariner's Mirror* 103 (2017), 175–95.

90 Hurd, 'The Battle of Jutland'.

91 'A Contribution to the History of German Naval Warfare, 1914–18', 2 July 1920, HW 7/1 to HW 7/4, TNA.

92 Hilmar-Detlef Brückner, 'Germany's First Cryptanalysis on the Western Front: Decrypting British and French Naval Ciphers in World War I', *Cryptologia* 29 (2005), 1–22.

93 Frank Birch, 'British SIGINT, 1914–1942', HW 43/1, TNA.

94 40 O.B. to DNI, 4 March 1919, HW 3/34, TNA.

95 Admiral James to DNI, 4 December 1936 in John Godfrey, 'GC&CS', ADM 223/469, TNA.

96 Peter Freeman, 'MI1(b) and the Origins of British Diplomatic Cryptanalysis', *Intelligence and National Security* 22 (2007), 206–28.

97 Alfred Ewing, 'Some Special War Work: A Lecture to the Edinburgh Philosophical Institution, 13 December 1927', in R.V. Jones, 'Alfred Ewing and "Room 40"', *Notes and Records of the Royal Society of London* 34 (1979), 65–89. Geoff Sloan, 'Dartmouth, Sir Mansfield Cumming and the Origins of the British Intelligence Community', *Intelligence and National Security* 22 (2007), 298–305.

98 Rhodri Jeffreys-Jones, 'The Sensitivity of SIGINT: Sir Alfred Ewing's Lecture on Room 40 in 1927', *Journal of Intelligence History* 17 (2018): 18–29.

99 'Obituary of Sir Alfred Ewing: War Work in Room 40', *The Times*, 8 January 1935.

100 Hector Bywater and H.C. Ferraby, *Strange Intelligence* (London: 2015 [1931]).

101 'Secret Service', *The Saturday Review*, 7 November 1931, 598.
102 'Two Naval Books', *The Saturday Review*, 24 September 1932, 325.
103 'German Naval Officer and a War Book: Libel Action Settled', *The Times*, 27 October 1933, 4.
104 Charles Morgan, 'Naval Intelligence, 1939–1942', August 1944, ADM 223/464, TNA. Morgan tackled the lessons of the First World War in the autumn of 1943, but abandoned his original plan of writing a detailed history, opting instead for a summary of its 'ending effects' – which amounted to little more than an acknowledgement that cryptography was very important.
105 J.H. Godfrey, 'The Navy and Naval Intelligence, 1939–1942: Introduction', January 1947, with additional comments, May 1948, ADM 223/619, TNA.
106 Note by OAH [Jasper Harker] of a Meeting with the Attorney General, Director of Public Prosecutions and Major Vivian [SIS] at the House of Commons, 15 November 1938, KV 2/1271, TNA.
107 [Cyril Falls], 'Secret Service', *Times Literary Supplement*, 4 December 1930, 1025.
108 Review in *Times Literary Supplement*, April 1928.
109 'Secret Service', *The Saturday Review*.
110 Pirie-Gordon, 'The RNVR in the Aegean'.

CHAPTER TWO

1 David Walker, *Lunch with a Stranger* (London: 1957), 33.
2 For example: Ferdinand Tuohy, 'Spy Fever: The Growing Menace of Post-war Espionage' and 'Spy Fever: The Green Eyes of International Jealousy', *The Graphic*, 26 March, 484, and 2 April 1927, 14–15. Billed as serving in the Intelligence Corps and on 'special duties', Tuohy had published *The Secret Corps* with John Murray in July 1920 and went on to publish *The Battle of Brains* with Heinemann in April 1930.
3 Lord Drogheda to Lord Curzon, 30 January 1919, KV 4/151, TNA.
4 Christopher Andrew, *Secret Service: The Making of the British Intelligence Community* (London: 1985), 297–353.
5 William Wiseman, 'Intelligence and Propaganda Work in Russia, July to December 1917', 19 January 1918, reproduced in Robert Calder, *W. Somerset Maugham and the Quest for Freedom* (London: 1972), 286–7.
6 Comment by Sir Eric Drummond on notes for Maugham's meeting with the prime minister, October 1917. Calder, *Maugham*, 288.
7 W. Somerset Maugham, *Ashenden* (London: 2000 [1928]).
8 R.H. Bruce Lockhart, *Memoirs of a British Agent* (London: 1932).
9 Capt. G.A. Hill (4th Manchester Regiment and RAF) to DMI, 'Report on Work Done in Russia', 26 November 1918, FO 371/3350/203967, TNA.
10 George Hill, *Go Spy the Land* (London: 2014 [1932]).
11 Arthur Ransome, *Six Weeks in Russia, 1919* (London: 2012 [1919]).

12 Political Intelligence Department, Foreign Office, 'Conflicting Reports on Conditions in Soviet Russia', 16 October 1919, CAB 24/90, TNA.
13 Paul Dukes, 'Bolshevism at Close Quarters', *The Times*, 14 October 1919, 13.
14 Paul Dukes, Letter to the Editor, 29 April 1920, *The Times*, 30 April 1920, 10.
15 Hill, *Go Spy the Land*.
16 Wiseman to Sir Eric Drummond, 24 September 1917, reproduced in Appendix B, Calder, *Maugham*.
17 Leonid I. Strakhovsky, 'The Allies and the Supreme Administration of the Northern Region, August, 2–October 7, 1918: A Page in the History of Allied Intervention in North Russia', *The Slavonic Yearbook* 1 (1941), 102–23; Brock Millman, 'The Problem with Generals: Military Observers and the Origins of Intervention in Russia and Persia, 1917–1918', *Journal of Contemporary History* 33 (1998), 291–320; Geoffrey Swain, 'An Interesting and Plausible Proposal: Bruce Lockhart, Sidney Reilly, and the Latvian Riflemen, Russia 1919', *Intelligence and National Security* 14 (1999), 81–102.
18 Bruce Lockhart, *Memoirs of a British Agent*, 290.
19 Madeira, 'No Wishful Thinking Allowed'.
20 Secret Service Committee: Minutes of First Meeting, 3 February 1919, and Report of Secret Service Committee, 7 February 1919, and Secret Service Committee: Minutes of Third Meeting, 4 April 1919, KV 4/151, TNA.
21 Minutes of a Conference held at the Foreign Office to consider the question of the proposed new Code and Cypher Department, 29 April 1919, HW 3/34, TNA.
22 Record of a Meeting at the Admiralty to consider the question of Secret Service Expenditure, 7 April 1919, WO 32/21387, TNA.
23 Cabinet: Report of the Committee Appointed by the Cabinet on 22 March, 27 July 1921, KV 4/151, TNA.
24 Lord Curzon to Lord Lee, 25 April 1921, HW 3/38, TNA.
25 Cabinet: Report of Sir Warren Fisher's Committee on Secret Service, 4 April 1922, KV 4/151, TNA.
26 Draft Minutes of the 1st Meeting of the Secret Service Committee appointed by the Conference of Ministers held in Mr. Chamberlain's room at the House of Commons on Tuesday, November 8, 1921, 15 November 1921, KV 4/151, TNA.
27 Draft Minutes of the 1st Meeting of the Secret Service Committee appointed by the Conference of Ministers held in Mr. Chamberlain's room at the House of Commons on Tuesday, November 8, 1921, 15 November 1921, KV 4/151, TNA.
28 Prime Minister's Secret Service Committee, 1925: Minutes of 1st Meeting, 26 February 1925, FO 1093/68, TNA.
29 Prime Minister's Secret Service Committee, 1927: Minutes of 1st Meeting, 11 March 1927, FO 1093/71, TNA.
30 Note for the Record by the Secretary to the Secret Service Committee, 24 June 1931, FO 1093/74, TNA.

31 John Ainsworth, 'Sidney Reilly's Reports from South Russia, December 1918–March 1919', *Europe-Asia Studies* 50 (1998), 1447–70.

32 Richard Spence, 'Englishmen in New York: The SIS American Station, 1915–1921', *Intelligence and National Security* 19 (2004), 511–37.

33 Jeffery, *MI6*, 181.

34 'The "Daily Herald"', *The Times*, 19 August 1920, 10.

35 Victor Madeira, 'Because I Don't Trust Him, We Are Friends: Signals Intelligence and the Reluctant Anglo-Soviet Embrace, 1917–1924', *Intelligence and National Security* 19 (2004), 29–51.

36 'A Secret Service Man on His Work', *Manchester Guardian*, 8 February 1921, 7; Winston Churchill, 'The Secret Service', 24 December 1921, KV 4/151, TNA.

37 'Mr. Shortt on Fomenters of Revolution: Secret Service "Never More Efficient"', *Manchester Guardian*, 1 May 1922, 8.

38 Basil Thomson, *Odd People* (London: 2015 [1922 under original title, *Queer People*]).

39 [E.E. Mavrogordato], 'Queer People', *Times Literary Supplement*, 16 November 1922, 737.

40 Gill Bennett, 'The Zinoviev Letter of 1924: A Most Extraordinary and Mysterious Business', *FCO History Notes* 14 (February 1999); Wim Coudenys, 'A Life Between Fact and Fiction: The History of Vladimir G. Orlov', *Revolutionary Russia* 21 (2008), 179–202.

41 Arthur Ransome, 'The Lockhart Memoirs', *Manchester Guardian*, 2 November 1932, 5; [H.M. Stannard], 'Memories from Moscow', *Times Literary Supplement*, 10 November 1932, 823. Stannard was the MI5 officer who had drafted the history of G Branch, MI5, in 1918–1919.

42 Air Ministry Papers 71096 and War Office Jacket 258152/1 with Memorandum, 25 June 1931, KV 2/827, TNA.

43 Lord Hardinge to DMI, 3 December 1918, WO 32/21380, TNA.

44 Minutes of a Conference held at the Foreign Office to consider the question of the proposed new Code and Cypher Department, 29 April 1919, HW 3/34, TNA.

45 Note by Walter Long, 31 January 1919, WO 32/21380, TNA.

46 Ephraim Maisel, 'The Formation of the Department of Overseas Trade, 1919–1926', *Journal of Contemporary History* 24 (1989), 169–90.

47 Zara Steiner and Michael Dockrill, 'The Foreign Office Reforms, 1919–1921', *The Historical Journal* 17 (1974), 131–56.

48 Prime Minister's Secret Service Committee, 1925: Minutes of 2nd Meeting, 2 March 1925, FO 1093/68, TNA.

49 Victor Madeira, *Britannia and the Bear: The Anglo-Russian Intelligence Wars, 1917–1929* (Woodbridge: 2014), 92.

50 Cabinet: Report of the Committee appointed by the Cabinet on March 22nd, 27 July 1921, KV4/151, TNA.

51 John Ferris, 'Whitehall's Black Chamber: British Cryptology and the

Government Code and Cypher School, 1919–1929', *Intelligence and National Security* 2 (1987), 54–91.

52 Prime Minister's Secret Service Committee, 1925: Minutes of 1st Meeting, 26 February 1925, FO 1093/68, TNA.

53 Prime Minister's Secret Service Committee, 1925: Minutes of 2nd Meeting, 2 March 1925, FO 1093/68, TNA.

54 Edward Troup, 'The Home Office Secret Service: Historical Note', 28 November 1921, KV 4/151, TNA.

55 Prime Minister's Secret Service Committee, 1925: Minutes of 2nd Meeting, 2 March 1925, FO 1093/68, TNA.

56 Note for the Record by the Secretary to the Secret Service Committee, 24 June 1931, FO 1093/74, TNA.

57 Prime Minister's Secret Service Committee, 1925: Minutes of 2nd Meeting, 2 March 1925, FO 1093/68, TNA.

58 'The Secret Service Vote: A Cause of Labour Suspicion', *Manchester Guardian*, 17 December 1919, 9.

59 Prime Minister's Secret Service Committee, 1925: Minutes of 4th Meeting, 10 March 1925, FO 1093/68, TNA.

60 Ferdinand Tuohy, 'Spy Fever'.

61 Prime Minister's Secret Service Committee, 1925: Minutes of 2nd Meeting, 2 March 1925, FO 1093/68, TNA.

62 Cabinet: Report of the Committee appointed by the Cabinet on March 22nd, 27 July 1921, KV 4/151, TNA.

63 Record of a Meeting at the Admiralty to consider the question of Secret Service Expenditure, 7 April 1919, WO 32/21387, TNA.

64 'Revised Estimates: £200,000 More for Secret Service', *Manchester Guardian*, 9 December 1919, 10.

65 John Anderson to Mark Sturgis, 7 December 1920, quoted in Mark Sturgis, *The Last Days of Dublin Castle: The Mark Sturgis Diaries*, ed. Michael Hopkinson (Dublin: 1999), 250.

66 'A Record of the Rebellion in Ireland in 1920–21, and the Part Played by the Army in Dealing with It (Intelligence)', [1922], in *British Intelligence in Ireland, 1920–21: The Final Reports*, ed., Peter Hart (Cork: 2002).

67 Cabinet: Report of the Committee appointed by the Cabinet on March 22nd, 27 July 1921, KV 4/151, TNA.

68 Cabinet: Report of the Committee appointed by the Cabinet on March 22nd, 27 July 1921, ibid.

69 Cabinet. Report of Sir Warren Fisher's Committee on Secret Service, 4 April 1922, KV 4/151, TNA.

70 C [Hugh Sinclair] to [Sir Eyre] Crowe, 3 November 1923, FO 1093/66, TNA.

71 Jeffery, *MI6*, 154–5.

72 Madeira, *Britannia and the Bear*, 152.

73 *Army Estimates, 1922–23*, 8 March 1922, House of Commons, 1922–23, 38.

74 Timothy Phillips, *The Secret Twenties: British Intelligence, the Russians, and the Jazz Age* (London: 2017), Epilogue.

75 Madeira, *Britannia and the Bear*, 242.

76 Prime Minister's Secret Service Committee, 1925: Minutes of 10th Meeting, June 1925, FO 1093/68, TNA.

77 Hotham to Bland, 15 June 1925, FO 1093/67, TNA.

78 Prime Minister's Secret Service Committee, 1925: Minutes of 10th Meeting, June 1925.

79 Tuohy, 'Spy Fever'.

80 'French Air Espionage Charge: Arrested Man's Career', *The Times*, 30 December 1926, 9.

81 'Vivian Stranders Again', *The Times*, 10 July 1929, 15, and 'Vivian Stranders: Former British Official Becomes German Citizen', *Manchester Guardian*, 25 April 1933, 15.

82 Prime Minister's Secret Service Committee, 1927: Minutes of 1st Meeting, 11 March 1927, FO 1093/71, TNA.

83 Prime Minister's Secret Service Committee, 1927: Minutes of 2nd Meeting, 22 March 1927, FO 1093/71, TNA.

84 'Sir Basil Thomson', *The Times*, 17 December 1925, 16.

85 Prime Minister's Secret Service Committee, 1925: Minutes of 6th Meeting, 17 March 1925, FO 1093/68, TNA.

86 Winston Churchill, 'The Secret Service', 24 December 1921, KV 4/151, TNA.

87 Cabinet: Report of the Committee appointed by the Cabinet on March 22nd, 27 July 1921.

88 'Draft Minutes of the 1st Meeting of the Secret Service Committee appointed by the Conference of Ministers held in Mr. Chamberlain's room at the House of Commons on Tuesday, November 8, 1921, 15 November 1921, KV 4/151, TNA.

89 Report of Secret Service Committee, 1 December 1925, FO 1093/69, TNA.

90 Prime Minister's Secret Service Committee, 1925: Minutes of 2nd Meeting, 2 March 1925.

91 Prime Minister's Secret Service Committee, 1925: Minutes of 3rd Meeting, 5 March 1925, FO 1093/68, TNA.

92 Sir William Horwood to Nevile Bland, 29 March 1927, FO 1093/73, TNA.

93 C to Nevile Bland, 18 March 1925, FO 1093/67, TNA.

94 Prime Minister's Secret Service Committee, 1925: Minutes of 9th Meeting, 31 March 1925, FO 1093/68, TNA.

95 Ray Wilson and Ian Adams, *Special Branch: A History, 1883–2006* (London: 2015).

96 Prime Minister's Secret Service Committee, 1925: Minutes of 6th Meeting, 17 March 1925.

97 Reiner Tosstorff, *The Red International of Labour Unions (RILU), 1920–1937* (Leiden: 2016), 762.
98 Gregory Kealey, 'The Early Years of State Surveillance of Labour and the Left in Canada: The Institutional Framework of the Royal Canadian Mounted Police Security and Intelligence Apparatus, 1918–26', *Intelligence and National Security* 8 (1993), 129–48.
99 Prime Minister's Secret Service Committee, 1925: Minutes of 7th Meeting, 19 March 1925, FO 1093/68, TNA.
100 Prime Minister's Secret Service Committee, 1925: Minutes of 9th Meeting, 31 March 1925.
101 Prime Minister's Secret Service Committee, 1925: Minutes of 10th Meeting, June 1925, FO 1093/68, TNA.
102 Incomplete memorandum to Prime Minister, FO 1093/67, TNA.
103 Sir Russell Scott's Report on His Investigation of Scotland Yard, November 1925, FO 1093/67, TNA.
104 A.H. Bodkin [Director of Public Prosecutions] to Sir Douglas Hogg [Attorney-General], 30 December 1926, FO 1093/73, TNA.
105 Sir Maurice Hankey to Nevile Bland, 18 March 1927, FO 1093/73, TNA.
106 'Sir Wyndham Childs', *The Times*, 8 October 1928, 13.
107 'Sir Leo Money Fined', *The Times*, 12 September 1933, 6.
108 'Libel Actions by Late Police Commissioners [Childs and Horwood vs. *New Statesman*]', *The Times*, 16 April 1929, 5, and 'Ex-Police Chiefs' Libel Action', 19 April 1929, *Manchester Guardian*, 6.
109 'Police Inquiry', *The Times*, 16 October 1928, 8.
110 Note for the Record by the Secretary to the Secret Service Committee, 24 June 1931, FO 1093/74, TNA.
111 'Security Service: Staff and Distribution of Duties', October 1931, KV4/127, TNA.
112 R.H.B. Lockhart, 'Memorandum on the Internal Situation in Russia', 1 November 1918, sent under cover of Lockhart to Balfour, 7 November 1918, printed for War Cabinet, CAB 24/73, TNA.
113 Paul Dukes, 'Bolshevism at Close Quarters', *The Times*, 14 October 1919, 13.
114 PID, Foreign Office, 'Conflicting Reports on Conditions in Soviet Russia', 16 October 1919.
115 Madeira, 'Signals Intelligence and the Reluctant Anglo-Soviet Embrace, 1917–1924'.
116 C to Sir William Tyrrell, 26 May 1927, FO 1093/73, TNA.
117 Madeira, *Britannia and the Bear*, 155.
118 Paul Dukes, 'Lenin's World Aims', *The Times*, 14 and 15 January 1920.
119 Andrew Barros, 'A Window on the "Trust": The Case of Ado Birk,' *Intelligence and National Security* 10 (1995), 273–93; Vadim Birstein, 'Soviet Military

Counterintelligence from 1918 to 1939', *International Journal of Intelligence and CounterIntelligence* 25 (2012), 44–110.

120 Paul Dukes, *Red Dusk and the Morrow* (London, 1922; 2012 edition).

121 Prime Minister's Secret Service Committee, 1925: Minutes of 4th Meeting, 10 March 1925, FO 1093/68, TNA.

122 Ferris, 'Whitehall's Black Chamber'.

123 Jonathan Haslam, *Near and Distant Neighbours: A New History of Soviet Intelligence* (Oxford: 2015).

124 OAH [Harker] to Chief of Special Intelligence [Kell], 30 June 1927 KV 3/15, TNA.

125 P. Tomaselli, 'C's Moscow Station: The Anglo-Russian Trade Mission as Cover for SIS in the Early 1920s', *Intelligence and National Security* 17 (2002): 173–80.

126 Haslam, *Near and Distant Neighbours*.

127 Ibid.

128 'British Secret Service', *Manchester Guardian*, 12 September 1927, 12.

129 Sidney Reilly, *Adventures of a British Master Spy: The Memoirs of Sidney Reilly* (London: 2014 [1931].

130 'Spies Sentences to Stand', *Manchester Guardian*, 28 February 1928, 3; Madeira, *Britannia and the Bear*, 169.

131 Victor Madeira, 'Moscow's Interwar Infiltration of British Intelligence, 1919–1929', *The Historical Journal* 46 (2003), 915–33.

132 'History of a Section of the Russian Intelligence Service operating in this country under the management of William Norman Ewer, 1919–1929' [January 1930], quoted in John Callaghan and Mark Phythian, 'State Surveillance and Communist Lives: Rose Cohen and the Early British Communist Milieu', *Journal of Intelligence History* 12 (2013), 134–55.

133 Note for the Record by the Secretary to the Secret Service Committee, 24 June 1931, FO 1093/74, TNA.

134 Colonel W.H. Courtenay, ACMA, London District to General Staff (Intelligence), 8 April 1919, Sidney G. Reilly, 'Rutenberg', 11 September 1919, and O.A.H., 'Rutenberg', 29 May 1922, KV 2/827, TNA.

135 Bruce Lockhart, *Memoirs of a British Agent*, 322–3.

136 Andrew Thorpe, 'The Membership of the Communist Party, 1920–1945', *Historical Journal* 43 (2000), 777–800.

137 Prime Minister's Secret Service Committee, 1925: Minutes of 2nd Meeting, 2 March 1925.

138 Bruce Lockhart, *Memoirs of a British Agent*, 277.

CHAPTER THREE

1 'The Secret Services: Inquiry by the Minister without Portfolio, Second Report dealing with the Security Service (MI5)', 11 May 1940, CAB 127/383, TNA.

2 Lord Hankey to Winston Churchill, 11 May 1940, CAB 127/383, TNA.
3 Ball, *Alamein*, 68.
4 Hankey to Churchill, 24 May 1940, CAB 127/383; Hankey to Halifax, 24 May 1940, FO 1093/193, TNA.
5 Simon Ball, *The Bitter Sea: The Struggle for Mastery in the Mediterranean, 1935–1949* (London: 2009), 30–5.
6 Wesley Wark, 'Something Very Stern: British Political Intelligence, Moralism, and Grand Strategy in 1939', *Intelligence and National Security* 5 (1991), 150–70; Dawn Miller, 'Dark Waters: Britain and Italy's Invasion of Albania, 7 April 1939', *International Journal of Intelligence and Counterintelligence* 16 (2003), 290–323.
7 Simon Ball, *The Guardsmen* (London: 2004), 187–8.
8 For an example of the classified information and analysis Morton was leaking see, Desmond Morton to Winston Churchill, 30 September 1935, CHAR 2/244, CAC.
9 Note of a Meeting held at 10 Downing Street, 17 January 1940, FO 1093/208, TNA; Summary of Evidence Supplied to Lord Hankey in His Investigation of the Secret Intelligence Service: MEW [Ministry of Economic Warfare], Morton, 17 January 1940, FO 1093/193, TNA.
10 'The Secret Services: Inquiry by the Minister without Portfolio, First Report', 11 March 1940, CAB 127/376, TNA.
11 Horace Wilson to Alec Cadogan, 29 November 1939, FO 1093/127, TNA.
12 Note by Lord Halifax, 29 November 1939, FO 1093/127, TNA.
13 C to Jebb, 14 November 1939, FO 1093/127, TNA.
14 Jeffery, *MI6*, 328–31.
15 Inquiry into the Security Service: Minutes of meeting between Lord Hankey and Sir Vernon Kell, Brigadier Holt-Wilson, and Colonel Allen, 2 April 1940, CAB 127/383, TNA.
16 Hankey, First Report.
17 Hankey, Second Report.
18 Hankey, First Report.
19 Hankey to Neville Chamberlain, 11 March 1940, CAB 127/376, TNA.
20 Hankey, First Report.
21 Ralph Erskine, 'The Poles Reveal their Secrets: Alastair Denniston's Account of the July 1939 Meeting at Pyry', *Cryptologia* 30 (2006), 294–305. For a reconstruction of the meeting using French, Polish, and British sources, see, Peter Jackson, *La France et la Menace Nazi, 1933–1939* (Paris: 2017), 44–8.
22 Antony Best, 'Constructing an Image: British Intelligence and Whitehall's Perception of Japan, 1931–1939', *Intelligence and National Security* 11 (1996), 403–23.

23 Matthew Hefler, 'In the Way: Intelligence, Eden, and British Foreign Policy Towards Italy, 1937–38', *Intelligence and National Security* 33 (2018), 875–93.

24 John Ferris, 'From Broadway House to Bletchley Park: The Diary of Captain Malcolm D. Kennedy, 1934–1946', *Intelligence and National Security* 4 (1989), 421–50, 1 November 1937.

25 Antony Best, 'This Probably Over-Valued Military Power: British Intelligence and Whitehall's Perception of Japan, 1939–1941', *Intelligence and National Security* 12 (1997), 67–94.

26 Ralph Erskine and Peter Freeman, 'Brigadier John Tiltman: One of Britain's Finest Cryptologists', *Cryptologia* 27 (2003), 289–318.

27 Christopher Grey, 'The Making of Bletchley Park and Signals Intelligence, 1939–1942', *Intelligence and National Security* 28 (2013), 785–807.

28 Martin Alexander, 'Radio Intercepts, Reconnaissance, and Raids: French Operational Intelligence in 1940', *Intelligence and National Security* 28 (2013), 337–76.

29 Godfrey to Hankey, 2 February 1940, FO 1093/193, TNA.

30 Draft Minutes of the Co-ordination of Interception Committee Meeting, 28 April 1938, HW 42/1, TNA.

31 Godfrey to Hankey, 2 February 1940, FO 1093/193, TNA.

32 Co-ordination of Wireless Interception, Direction-Finding, Cryptography, and Allied Activities: Note by Minister without Portfolio, 22 February 1940. Appendix II to Hankey, First Report.

33 C to Jebb, 14 November 1939, FO 1093/127, TNA.

34 Summary of Evidence Supplied to Lord Hankey in His Investigation of the Secret Intelligence Service: DNI, Godfrey, [nd], FO 1093/193, TNA.

35 Adam Sisman, *Hugh Trevor-Roper: The Biography* (London: 2010), 75.

36 Lieutenant Commander L.A. Griffiths, RNVR, 'GC&CS Secret Service Sigint, Volume I: Organisation and Evolution of British Secret Service Sigint', HW 43/6, and History of the Postal and Telegraphic Censorship Department, 1938–1946, Volume I (1952), DEFE 1/333, TNA.

37 140/6/XI/39, Translation from German, ADM 1/23905, TNA.

38 Director of Intelligence [Buss] to DSR, 10 February 1939, AIR 2/3609; Summary of Evidence Supplied to Lord Hankey in His Investigation of the Secret Intelligence Service: DAI, Buss, 14 January 1940, FO 1093/193; Director of Intelligence to ACAS (O&I) [March 1940] and ACAS (O&I) to DCAS, 27 March 1940, AIR 2/5118, TNA.

39 'Jones Memorandum', 1953, AIR 40/2572, TNA.

40 Joe Maiolo, 'I Believe the Hun Is Cheating: British Admiralty Technical Intelligence and the German Navy, 1936–1939', *Intelligence and National Security* 11 (1996), 32–58, and J.P. Harris, 'British Military Intelligence and Rise of German

Mechanized Forces, 1929–1940', *Intelligence and National Security* 6 (1991), 395–417.

41 Summary of Evidence Supplied to Lord Hankey in His Investigation of the Secret Intelligence Service: DAI, Buss, 14 January 1940, FO 1093/193, TNA.

42 Summary of Evidence Supplied to Lord Hankey in His Investigation of the Secret Intelligence Service: MEW, Morton, 17 January 1940, FO 1093/193, TNA. Talbot Imlay, 'Allied Economic Intelligence and Strategy during the Phoney War', *Intelligence and National Security* 13 (1998), 107–32.

43 DNI to First Sea Lord, 12 November 1939, ADM 223/851, TNA.

44 DNI to DCNS, 'Control of Naval Secret Service', 30 November 1939, ADM 223/851, TNA.

45 DNI to Menzies, 18 November 1939, ADM 223/851, TNA.

46 DNI to DCNS, 'Control of Naval Secret Service', 30 November 1939, ADM 223/851, TNA.

47 Churchill to First Sea Lord [1939], ADM 223/851, TNA.

48 Ian Fleming, Minute, 9 April 1940, ADM 223/851, TNA.

49 DNI to First Sea Lord, 20 December 1939, ADM 223/851, TNA.

50 Winston Churchill to Alec Cadogan, 18 November 1939, FO 1093/127, TNA.

51 Summary of Evidence Supplied to Lord Hankey in His Investigation of the Secret Intelligence Service: DMI, Beaumont-Nesbitt, 8 January 1940, FO 1093/193, TNA.

52 War Diary DMI: Organisation and Establishments, WO 208/5568, TNA.

53 DDMI (O) to DMI, 4 January 1940, WO 208/5130, TNA.

54 Kent Fedorowich, 'Axis Prisoners of War as Sources for British Military Intelligence, 1939–1942', *Intelligence and National Security* 14 (1999), 156–78.

55 F.H.N. Davidson, Diary, Davidson 4/1, LHCMA.

56 Brian Bond, ed., *Chief of Staff: The Diaries of Lieutenant-General Sir Henry Pownall,* I: *1933–1940* (London: 1972), 18 September 1939.

57 John Ferris, 'The "Usual Source": Signals Intelligence and Planning for the Eighth Army Crusader Offensive, 1941', *Intelligence and National Security*, 14 (1999), 84–118.

58 Wesley Wark, 'Our Man in Riga: Reflections of the SIS Career and Writings of Leslie Nicholson', *Intelligence and National Security* 11 (1996), 625–44.

59 Sir Hugh Sinclair to F.B. Boyd, 7 October 1936, enclosing SIS report of 1 October 1937, FO 733/322/8, TNA.

60 Antony Best, 'British Intelligence and Whitehall's Perception of Japan, 1931–1939'.

61 H.M.G. Jebb, Minute, 2 December 1938, FO 1093/81, TNA.

62 Gladwyn Jebb, Brief on Draft Press Statement, 22 November 1939, FO 1093/200, TNA.

63 Tower [Intelligence Unit, Ministry of Information] to Peake, 22 November 1939, FO 1093/201, TNA.

64 Comment to Press, 22 November 1939, FO 1093/200, TNA.
65 Charles Peake to A. Cadogan, 23 November 1939, FO 1093/201, TNA.
66 Bland to Jebb, 22 December 1939, FO 1093/201, TNA.
67 Wesley Wark, 'Something Very Stern', 150–70.
68 Research to ADB 1, 8 January 1943, KV 4/170, TNA.
69 Memorandum by Sir Robert Vansittart, 15 November 1939, FO 1093/219, TNA.
70 Bob de Graaff, 'The Stranded Baron and the Upstart at the Crossroads: Wolfgang zu Putlitz and Otto John', *Intelligence and National Security* 6 (1991), 669–700.
71 C to Jebb, 14 November 1939, FO 1093/127, TNA.
72 SIS History of the Incident, Attached to C to Henry Hopkinson, 19 June 1941, FO 1093/202, TNA.
73 Hankey, First Report.
74 Stewart Menzies to Gladwyn Jebb, 14 February 1940, CAB 127/376, TNA.
75 Hankey, First Report: Appendix I: The Origins and Development of the SIS, 14 February 1940.
76 *Secret Supplement of the Manual of Military Intelligence in the Field*, 25 August 1939, WO 33/2721, TNA.
77 DNI to First Sea Lord, 20 December 1939, ADM 223/851, TNA.
78 Hankey, First Report: Appendix I.
79 C to Sir Ernle Chatfield, 9 October 1935, ADM 223/851, TNA.
80 'Future Organisation of the SIS' [The Bland Report], 12 October 1944, FO 1093/196, TNA.
81 Minutes of a meeting, 29 April 1940, CAB 127/383, TNA.
82 Eden to Churchill, 9 March 1943, HW 1/3789, TNA.
83 C to Jebb, 14 November 1939, FO 1093/127, TNA.
84 Halifax to Hankey, 26 March 1940, FO 1093/193, TNA.
85 Note by OAH [Harker], 15 November 1938, KV 2/1271, TNA.
86 [Vivian] to Kell, 23 March 1940, KV 2/1272, TNA.
87 'Explosives Seized in Stockholm', *The Times*, 3 May 1940; Hankey to Kell, 16 April 1940, CAB 127/383, TNA.
88 Jebb to Cadogan, 18 March 1940, and Hankey to Cadogan, 21 March 1940, FO 1093/232, TNA.
89 'History of Arrest', 8 May 1940, HS 2/264, TNA.
90 D/XE1 to D/G, 16 April 1940, HS 2/263, TNA.
91 R [Sutton-Pratt] [Military Attaché] to Ingram [Fraser] [SIS], 26 April 1940, HS 2/264, TNA.
92 A.F. Rickman (late D1 of SD, SIS), 'A Concise Report upon Operations in Sweden and Certain Deductions Therefrom', 11 July 1944, HS 2/268, TNA.
93 'The Scandinavian Invasion', 14 April 1940, PREM 1/435; Hankey to Anderson, 16 April 1940, and Minutes of a meeting, 22 April 1940, CAB 127/383, and Hankey to Horace Wilson, 29 April 1940, PREM 1/435, TNA.

94 DPP to Hankey, 11 April 1940, CAB 127/383, TNA.
95 Nigel West, ed., *The Guy Liddell Diaries,* Volume 1: *1940–1942: MI5's Director of Counter-Espionage in World War II* (London: 2005), 4 September 1939.
96 David Alvarez, 'Diplomatic Solutions: German Foreign Office Cryptanalysis, 1919–1945', *International Journal of Intelligence and CounterIntelligence* 9 (1996), 169–85.
97 Marcus Faulkner, 'The *Kriegsmarine*, Signals Intelligence and the Development of the *B-Dienst* before the Second World War', *Intelligence and National Security* 25 (2010), 521–46.
98 Horst Boog, 'German Air Intelligence in the Second World War', *Intelligence and National Security* 5 (1990), 350–424.
99 Robert Gerwarth, *Hitler's Hangman: The Life of Heydrich* (New Haven: 2011), 162.
100 Katrin Paehler, *The Third Reich's Intelligence Services: The Career of Walter Schellenberg* (Cambridge: 2017), 131–2.
101 Donald Watt, 'Francis Herbert King: A Soviet Source in the Foreign Office', *Intelligence and National Security* 3 (1988), 62–82.
102 *Guy Liddell Diaries*, I, 4 September 1939.
103 Beaumont-Nesbitt (DMI) to John Martin, 12 September 1940, PREM 3/418/2, TNA.
104 Boog, 'German Air Intelligence in the Second World War'.
105 B2 to B, 1 April 1940, CAB 127/383, TNA.
106 Hankey to Kell, 1 March 1940, CAB 127/383, TNA.
107 Minutes of meeting, 14 March 1940, CAB 127/383, TNA.
108 Minutes of meeting, 4 April 1940, CAB 127/383, TNA.
109 Minutes of meeting, 14 March 1940, CAB 127/383, TNA.
110 Inquiry into the Security Service: Minutes of a meeting between Lord Hankey and Rear-Admiral J.H. Godfrey (DNI), Major-General F.G. Beaumont-Nesbitt (DMI), and Air Commodore A.R. Boyle (DAI), CAB 127/383.
111 Inquiry into the Security Service: Minutes of meeting between Lord Hankey and Sir Vernon Kell, Brigadier Holt-Wilson, and Colonel Allen, 2 April 1940, CAB 127/383, TNA.
112 Inquiry into the Security Service: Minutes of meeting, 14 March 1940, CAB 127/383, TNA.
113 T.F. Turner, 'Internment of Enemy Aliens', 18 March 1940, CAB 127/383, TNA.
114 B2 to B, 1 April 1940, CAB 127/383, TNA.
115 C.A. Hankey to Gladwyn Jebb, 27 April 1940, CAB 127/383, TNA.
116 Hankey to Anderson and Anderson to Hankey, 16 April 1940, CAB 127/383, TNA.
117 'Inquiry into the Security Service': Minutes of a Meeting between Lord Hankey and Sir Alexander Maxwell and Mr Newsam', CAB 127/383, TNA.
118 Hankey, Second Report.

119 Eric Seal to Prime Minister, 25 July 1940, PREM 4/97/11, TNA.
120 WP (40) 172, 'War Cabinet. Home Defence (Security) Executive. Memorandum by the Lord President of the Council', 27 May 1940, PREM 3/418/1, TNA.
121 Hankey to Horace Wilson, 29 April 1940, PREM 1/435, TNA.
122 Davidson, Diary, 29 January 1941.
123 Davidson, Diary, 8 January 1941.
124 Colonel Butler to DDMI (O), 6 December 1940, WO 208/5130, TNA.
125 DMI to VCIGS, 31 August 1940, WO 208/4696, TNA.
126 Davidson, Diary, 10 January 1941.
127 Review of General Staff Organisation in the War Office, 1st Interim Report, 3 November 1940, WO 208/4696, TNA.
128 'Review of General Staff Organisation in the War Office'.
129 DMI to VCIGS, 31 August 1940, WO 208/4696, TNA.
130 COS (40) 932 (Final) Report on Provision of Intelligence, 14 November 1940, PREM 4/97/11, TNA.
131 Lord Privy Seal to Prime Minister, 28 November 1940, PREM 4/97/11, TNA.
132 Davidson, Diary, 17 April 1941.
133 Harold Nicolson, *Diaries and Letters, 1939–1945* (London: 1967), 4 and 13 April 1941.
134 Davidson, Diary, 25 April 1941.
135 Davidson, Diary, 16 April 1941.
136 Desmond Morton to Prime Minister, 20 January 1941, PREM 4/97/11, TNA.
137 DSR to ACAS (I), 12 May 1941, AIR 2/3609, TNA.
138 ADI (Science), 'The Intelligence Aspect of the Bruneval Raid', 4 March 1942, PREM 3/173, TNA.
139 Operations Recording Section, Combined Operations Headquarters, '*Biting*: Intelligence', July 1942, DEFE 2/100, TNA.
140 ADI (Science), 'The Intelligence Aspect of the Bruneval Raid', 4 March 1942, PREM 3/173, TNA.
141 D.A. Parry to Rowan, 6 March 1942, PREM 3/173, TNA.
142 ADI (Science), Air Scientific Report No. 15, 13 July 1942, AIR 20/1631, TNA.
143 Charles Morgan, 'Naval Intelligence, 1939–1942', August 1944, Preface to First Edition, 6 July 1942, ADM 223/464, TNA. The 1942 preface was carried over to 1944 version, but all copies of the 1942 text were ordered 'destroyed by fire': notes on 1969 re-issue in ADM 223/472.
144 C to DNI, 5 August 1941, ADM 223/851, TNA.
145 Diary of Captain Malcolm D. Kennedy, 4 March 1942.
146 Grey, 'The Making of Bletchley Park and Signals Intelligence', 785-807.
147 Stuart Ball, ed., *Parliament and Politics in the Age of Churchill and Attlee: The Headlam Diaries, 1934–1951* (Cambridge: 1999), 13 February 1942.
148 R.A. Ratcliff, 'Searching for Security: The German Investigations into Enigma's Security', *Intelligence and National Security* 14 (1999), 146–67.

149 Morgan, 'Naval Intelligence, 1939–1942'.
150 Kenneth Strong, *Intelligence at the Top* (London: 1968), 18.
151 NID 01114/39 approved by Winston Churchill, First Lord of the Admiralty, 14 September 1939, ADM 1/10224.
152 Donald McLachlan, *Room 39: Naval Intelligence in Action, 1939–45* (London: 1968).
153 Morgan, 'Naval Intelligence, 1939–1942'.
154 Memorandum by Phillips, 11 September 1939, ADM 1/10224, TNA.
155 Charles Morgan, 'The Information Section', ADM 223/464, TNA.
156 Morgan, 'Naval Intelligence, 1939–1942'.
157 J.H. Godfrey, DNI, 'Intelligence in the United States', 7 July 1941, Appendix to Bradley Smith, 'Admiral Godfrey's Mission to America, June/July 1941', *Intelligence and National Security* 1 (1986), 441–50.

CHAPTER FOUR

1 Liddell Diary, 23 October 1945, KV 4/466, TNA.
2 Liddell Diary, 4 September 1944, KV 4/195, TNA.
3 Liddell Diary, 16 July 1945, KV 4/466, TNA.
4 Major R. Moody, 'History of Communications Section (F Section)', 15 June 1945, AIR 34/84, TNA.
5 Michael Seibold, 'The Demise of an Industrious Intelligence Centre: The Re-organisation of Economic Intelligence at the End of the Second World War, 1943–1945', *Journal of Intelligence History* 12 (2013), 156–76. The German proverb was popularized by a nineteenth-century fairy tale; the English version is a line from *As You Like It*, as adapted for an English air.
6 Brett Lintott, 'Dudley Clarke's Official History of Military Deception, 1944–1945', *Intelligence and National Security* 32 (2017), 54–67.
7 Sir Norman Kendall [Metropolitan Police] to Sir Edward Bridges (secretary of the Cabinet), 27 July 1943, CAB 301/11, TNA.
8 [R.V. Jones], 'A Scientific Staff College', 8 November 1945, AIR 20/1713, TNA.
9 The Bland Report, 12 October 1944.
10 Bland to Jebb, 12 November 1939, Tel. 196, FO 1093/200, TNA.
11 Christopher Murphy, *Security and Special Operations: SOE and MI5 during the Second World War* (Basingstoke: 2006), 148–69.
12 [Ewen Montagu], 'The W. Board', KV 4/70, TNA.
13 Hanbury-Williams and Playfair, 'Report to the Minister of Economic Warfare on the Organisation of SOE'.
14 William Armstrong to Ronald Wells, 28 June 1945, CAB 21/3499, TNA.
15 'The Intelligence Machine: Report to the Joint Intelligence Sub-Committee' [The Capel-Dunn Report], 10 January 1945, ADM 223/472, TNA.
16 Eden to Herbert Morrison, 22 November 1944, FO 1093/197, TNA.

17 'Report on the Security Service by Sir Findlater Stewart', 27 November 1945, CAB 301/31, TNA.
18 Sir Alexander Cadogan to Sir Edward Bridges, 28 January 1945, CAB 301/11, TNA.
19 Draft: SIS and Connected Services and The Bland Report, 12 October 1944, FO 1093/196, TNA.
20 Churchill to Duff Cooper, 4 April 1943, FO 1093/194, TNA.
21 Richard Aldrich, 'Policing the Past: Official History, Secrecy, and British Intelligence since 1945', *The English Historical Review* 119 (2004), 922–53.
22 Strong to Secretary, Joint Chiefs of Staff, 12 June 1944, WO 193/432, and Director-General to Major-General K.W.D. Strong, 22 December 1944, Draft letter (not sent), KV 4/100, and J.C. Masterman, B1A, 'The Double-Cross System in the War of 1939 to 1945', [1945], KV 4/5, TNA.
23 Sir Edward Bridges, 'Ministerial Responsibility for the Security Service', 22 December 1943, 'Note for the Record', 29 December 1943, and 'Note for the Record', 5 January 1944, CAB 21/3499, TNA; Peter Davies, 'Geoffrey Vickers and Lessons from the Ministry of Economic Warfare for Cold War Defence Intelligence', *Intelligence and National Security* 31 (2016), 810–28; COS (45) 504 (O) [Cavendish-Bentinck Report], 31 July 1945, FO 1093/198.
24 Victor Cavendish-Bentinck, 7 October 1944, FO 1093/195, and Denis Capel-Dunn to Cavendish-Bentinck, 2 April 1945, FO 1093/196, TNA.
25 Memorandum on 'French Secret Services', 26 April 1944, FO 660/383, TNA.
26 Victor Cavendish-Bentinck, 7 October 1944.
27 Draft: SIS and Connected Services.
28 Arnold-Forster to DNI, 8 December 1943, ADM 223/851; E. Beddington, DDMI (F) to DMI, via C, 10 May 1944, FO 1093/195, TNA.
29 Boyle to Loxley, 'Some Reflections on the Future Organisation of SIS', 22 March 1944, and 'Note from a member of C', filed by Loxley on 19 April 1944, FO 1093/194, TNA. Despite the billing, the context suggests that Loxley's Eton friend was Peter Fleming, a military intelligence officer rather than a member of SIS.
30 Memorandum by P.N. Loxley, 7 April 1944 (based Woollcombe to Loxley, 3 April 1944), FO 1093/194, TNA.
31 Draft: SIS and Connected Services.
32 Note to Loxley, 'Estimated Post-Hostilities Effect of the Proposals at HQ and Abroad', 6 April 1944, FO 1093/194, TNA.
33 CPA to CSS, 25 September 1944, HW 3/169, TNA.
34 C to Peter Loxley, 24 April 1944, FO 1093/195, TNA.
35 Ibid.
36 Cadogan to Eden, 9 November 1944, and Minute from Cadogan to Eden, 10 November 1944, FO 1093/197, TNA.

37 Note by Victor Cavendish-Bentinck, 28 July 1944, FO 1093/195, TNA.
38 The Findlater Stewart Report, 27 November 1945, CAB 301/31, TNA.
39 Note by Victor Cavendish-Bentinck, 7 October 1944, FO 1093/195, TNA.
40 Richard Davenport-Hines, ed., *Hugh Trevor-Roper: The Wartime Journals* (London: 2012), August 1943, 170, and January 1945, 214.
41 Victor Cavendish-Bentinck, 11 October 1944, FO 1093/195, TNA.
42 A2/2519, 3 February 1945, HW 16/62, TNA. Named as 'Tim' in Liddell Diary, 30 December 1944, KV 4/195, TNA.
43 [Victor Cavendish-Bentinck], 'The Secret Services', [November] 1944, CAB 301/11, TNA.
44 C to Cadogan, 2 November 1944, FO 1093/196, TNA.
45 [Henry Hopkinson], 'The German Generals' [June 1941], FO 1093/201, TNA.
46 SIS History of the Incident, 19 June 1941.
47 Camp 020, Report of the Case of Alfred Naujocks, KV 2/279, TNA.
48 The Bland Report, 12 October 1944.
49 Nevile Bland to Alec Cadogan, 13 October 1944, FO 1093/195, TNA.
50 Liddell Diary, 31 December 1945, KV 4/467, TNA.
51 Nevile Bland to Alec Cadogan, 13 October 1944, FO 1093/195, TNA.
52 Nigel West, ed. *The Guy Liddell Diaries*, Volume 2: *1942–1945: MI5's Director of Counter-Espionage in World War II* (London: 2005), 24 October 1944.
53 The morphology of the internal history of Bletchley Park is tabulated in Christopher Grey, *Decoding Organization: Bletchley Park, Codebreaking, and Organization Studies* (Cambridge: 2012), Table 1: *Summary of frequently cited documents*, 25.
54 E.W. Travis to CSS, 7 September 1943, HW 14/87, TNA.
55 Brief for Travis, 16 December 1944, HW 62/15, TNA.
56 Section II (c) to CSS, 2 December 1944, HW 62/15, TNA.
57 Richard Aldrich, *GCHQ* (London: 2010), 62–4.
58 Telford Taylor to Director-General, GC&CS, 27 January 1945, HW 62/16, TNA.
59 'Writing of Japanese SIGINT History in Washington', 29 August 1945, HW 14/134, TNA.
60 Director's Order, No. 76, 'Historical Committee', 20 September 1945, HW 62/16, TNA.
61 Director's Order No. 71, 28 August 1945, HW 16/62, TNA.
62 DD (NS), Note No. 131: Conversion of Naval Section to Historical Tasks Organisation, 12 October 1945, HW 3/22, TNA.
63 Director's Order 88, 6 January 1946, HW 14/164, TNA.
64 Victor Cavendish-Bentinck, 7 October 1944, FO 1093/195, TNA.
65 A.G. Denniston to Director-General, 11 October 1944, HW 3/169, TNA. John Croft, 'A Note on Diplomatic Intercepts in England during World War II', *Journal of Intelligence History* 13 (2014), 91–3.
66 Minute by A.G. Denniston, 31 October 1944, HW 3/32, TNA.

67 A.G. Denniston to Director-General, GC&CS (copy to DD (NS)), 18 November 1944 with Traffic Supplement, 2 December 1944, HW 3/32, TNA.

68 Gordon Welchman, 'Ultra Revisited: A Tale of Two Contributors', *Intelligence and National Security* 32 (2017), 244–55.

69 AD (Mch), 'Revised Report to Sub-Committee B on the Place of Cryptography and Traffic Analysis in Signal Intelligence', 1 January 1945, HW 3/169, TNA.

70 Edward Crankshaw, Harry Hinsley, and Gordon Welchman to Sir Edward Travis, 'A Note on Intelligence and Security by Three Temporary Members of GC&CS', 17 September 1944, HW 3/169, TNA.

71 Preliminary Draft Memorandum, HW 3/169, TNA.

72 Nigel de Grey to Captain H.F. Layman, DDSDY, 22 April 1945, HW 62/16, TNA.

73 'The Making of Bletchley Park and Signals Intelligence, 1939–42', 785–807.

74 Frank Birch, 'A History of British Sigint, 1914-1945. Vol. 2: British Sigint, 1942–1945', HW 43/1, TNA.

75 Sigint Centre: Conditions of Service, 7 September 1945, HW 62/16, TNA.

76 C to Director, GC&CS, 'Post-War Organisation of GC&CS', 15 September 1944, HW 3/169, TNA.

77 Third Meeting of the Committee, Bletchley Park, 13 October 1944, HW 14/161, TNA.

78 Crankshaw, Hinsley, and Welchman, 'A Note on Intelligence and Security', 17 September 1944.

79 Fifth Meeting of the Committee, Bletchley Park, 21 October 1944, HW 14/161, TNA.

80 Rodney Brunt, 'Special Documentation Systems at the Government Code and Cypher School, Bletchley Park, during the Second World War, *Intelligence and National Security* 21 (2006), 129–48.

81 E.R. Vincent, Final Report of Sub-committee B, 1 February 1945, HW 14/161, TNA.

82 Sixth Meeting of the Committee, Bletchley Park, 28 October 1944, HW 14/161, TNA.

83 Lieutenant-Colonel J.C. Blair-Cunynghame, 'Post European War Signals Problem', 5 August 1944, HW 62/15, TNA.

84 Director's Order, No. 79, 31 October 1945, HW 62/16, TNA.

85 'Post-War Organisation of SIGINT Services', 28 April 1945 (Final Version), HW 62/16, TNA.

86 Nigel de Grey to Frank Birch, 12 June 1945, HW 62/16, TNA.

87 Head, Air Section [Brownall] to DDAS, 'Post-war History Writing about the GAF', 23 April 1945, HW 62/16, TNA.

88 Central Office Note No. 195: Ultra, 27 April 1945, HW 3/29, TNA. The copy in the National Archives has the comment 'A very stupid memo' scrawled across it.

89 Frank Birch, Notes on folder of Charles Morgan, NID 17, 24 November 1948, ADM 223/463, TNA.

90 Y Committees, Y Board, and SIGINT Board: Organisation and Origins, 1924–1945, HW 42/30, TNA.

91 Director's Order No. 51, 5 May 1945, HW 16/62, and 'Outline History of SLU', 21 May 1945, HW49/5, TNA.

92 [Group Captain Humphrey], 'The Use of "U" in the Mediterranean and Northwest African Theatres', October 1945', HW 3/174, and 'History of the Italian Military Section of the Combined Bureau Middle East', HW 51/14, TNA.

93 Liddell Diary, 4 July 1945, KV 4/466, TNA.

94 Head of S Department, GCHQ to HHS, Queensgate (Mr Griffiths) enclosing rough notes on RSS by F. Stowe, HW 34/1, TNA.

95 Lt-Col. Gore Brown, 'Special Liaison Units', 6 June 1945, HW 49/6 and [Commander G.A. Titterton], 'Synopsis for a History of Naval Sigint in the Mediterranean', 11 December 1945, HW 50/39, TNA.

96 Commander G.E. Hughes, RNVR (Sp), 'The Naval Y Service in Wartime, 1939–1945', 28 November 1945, HW 8/98, TNA.

97 NID 12, Report on Special Intelligence Summaries, July to December 1943, 10 September 1945, ADM 223/792, TNA.

98 NID 12, 'History of NID 12, Volume 1: History, Organisation, and Material', 30 September 1945, ADM 223/792, TNA.

99 Hughes 'The Naval Y Service in Wartime, 1939–1945'.

100 Ibid.

101 Captain (RN) D.A. Wilson to Director, GC&CS, Sub-Committee G Report, 6 May 1945, HW 14/161, TNA.

102 Charles Morgan, NID 9 [nd], with note on the folder by FB [Frank Birch], 24 November 1948, ADM 223/463, TNA.

103 R.T. Barrett, 'German Success against British Codes and Cyphers', ADM 223/469, TNA.

104 *Cmd.* 6351, *The Organisation for Joint Planning* (London, 1942), cited in Michael Goodman, *The Official History of the Joint Intelligence Committee. Volume 1: From the Approach of the Second World War to the Suez Crisis* (London: 2014), 121.

105 Michael Herman, 'The Postwar Organization of Intelligence: The January 1945 Report to the Joint Intelligence Committee on "The Intelligence Machine"', Dover and Goodman, *Learning from the Secret Past.*

106 The Intelligence Machine, 10 January 1945.

107 Ibid.

108 Goodman, *The Official History of the Joint Intelligence Committee.*

109 Secretary, JIC to DNI, 13 August 1942, ADM 223/465, TNA.

110 Capel-Dunn to Morgan, 4 March 1944, ADM 223/465, TNA.

111 Lieutenant-Commander Lord Dunwich to DNI, 29 September 1943, ADM 223/465, TNA.
112 Captain Drake, 'The JIC at Work, 1941 to 1945, and JIS', ADM 223/465, TNA.
113 Charles Morgan, 'Joint Intelligence Committee and Offshoots', ADM 223/465, TNA.
114 Major-General F.H.N. Davidson, DMI, to Secretary, JIC, 24 October 1943, FO 1093/194, TNA.
115 Brigadier C.S. Vale, DDMI (O), to Colonel J.H. Tiltman, Commandant, Military Component, GC&CS, c/o MI6, 30 June 1943, HW 62/15, TNA.
116 Vale to Tiltman, 15 February 1944, HW 62/15, TNA.
117 Lintott, 'Dudley Clarke's Official History of Military Deception'.
118 Liddell Diary, 14 August 1945, KV 4/466, TNA.
119 'Mediterranean Theatre, 1940–45: "A" Force Narrative War Diary', WO 169/2487, 2488 and 2489, TNA.
120 Huw Dylan, 'Thinking about Defence Intelligence: Victor Cavendish-Bentinck, Denis Capel-Dunn, Kenneth Strong, and the Joint Intelligence Bureau as Foundation for the Defence Intelligence Staff', *Intelligence and National Security* 31 (2016), 829–43.
121 Air Vice-Marshal Elmhirst, ACAS (I), to Chairman of SIGINT Board, 23 August 1945, HW 14/134, TNA.
122 S.D. Felkin to Director of Intelligence (Operations), 'Short History of ADI (k)', 24 March 1944, with Appendix, August 1944, AIR 2/4591, TNA.
123 [Group Captain S.D. Felkin], 'Intelligence from Interrogation: A Study of the Work of ADI (k) during the War of 1939–1945', 31 December 1945, AIR 40/1177, TNA.
124 'The History of CSDIC (UK)', [1945], WO 208/4970, TNA.
125 'The Story of MI19', [1945], WO 208/4970, TNA.
126 Stephen McGinty, *Camp Z: How British Intelligence Broke Hitler's Deputy* (London: 2012), 11.
127 Liddell Diary, 23 September 1948, KV 4/470, TNA.
128 Falko Bell, '*Die Deutsche Spionage ist auf Zack*: German Soldiers Speak about Intelligence Services, 1939–1945', *Journal of Intelligence History* 12 (2013), 49–59.
129 JIC/183/45, Report by Chairman on Personnel for the Combined Services Detailed Interrogation Centre, 11 February 1945, WO 208/3451, TNA; Falko Bell, 'One of our Most Valuable Sources of Intelligence: British Intelligence and the Prisoner of War System in 1944', *Intelligence and National Security* 31 (2016), 556–78.
130 AI (k) to DDI (Org), 14 April 1943, AIR 2/4591, TNA.
131 Felkin, 'Intelligence from Interrogation', 31 December 1945.
132 ADI (k) State, 20 February 1945, AIR 2/4591, TNA.
133 AVM Inglis to Victor Cavendish-Bentinck, 27 April 1944, FO 1093/195, TNA.

134 Orme Sargent, Minute, 14 July 1944, FO 1093/195, TNA.
135 The Intelligence Machine, 10 January 1945.
136 Liddell Diary, 31 August 1945, KV4/466, TNA.
137 Drake, 'The JIC at Work, 1941 to 1945, and JIS', and Dylan, 'Thinking about Defence Intelligence'.
138 Liddell Diary, 8 August 1945, KV4/466, TNA.
139 Davies, 'Geoffrey Vickers and Lessons from the Ministry of Economic Warfare'.
140 Liddell Diary, 7 July 1945, KV4/466, TNA.
141 Hanbury-Williams and Playfair, 'Report to the Minister of Economic Warfare', 18 June 1942.
142 Brigadier Williams to Cavendish-Bentinck, 21 June 1945 and COS (45) 698 (O), 24 December 1945, FO 1093/198, TNA.
143 Brigadier C.M. Keble (MO4) to Secretary of the Defence Committee, GHQ, MEF, 8 April 1943, HS 5/307, TNA.
144 Hanbury-Williams and Playfair, 'Report to the Minister of Economic Warfare', 18 June 1942.
145 Hugh Dalton to Prime Minister, 28 March 1941, and 'Report by Colonel George Taylor and Mr T.S. Masterson on certain SO2 Activities in Yugoslavia', HS 5/928, TNA.
146 Brigadier E.C.W. Myers, 'Inside Greece: A Review', [25 August 1943], HS 7/152, TNA.
147 Lord Selborne to Lord Cherwell, 4 April 1944, CAB 126/171, TNA.
148 'SOE and Heavy Water', [April 1944], CAB 126/171, TNA.
149 E.D. Masterman, 'Secret Army Fought Nazi Atom Bomb', *Daily Express*, 21 May 1945, HS 2/189, TNA.
150 'Spies, RAF, Commandos in Battle of Wits', *Daily Mail*, 7 August 1945, 1.
151 Sporborg to Rickett [Cabinet Office], 27 August 1945, CAB 126/171, and 'Norwegian "Heavy Water" Operations', [July 1945], HS 2/189, TNA.
152 Rickett to Perrin [Directorate of Tube Alloys], with marginal note by Eric Welsh, 28 August 1945, CAB 126/171, TNA.
153 [Lionel Hale], 'SOE in Europe, 1938–1945', HS 7/1, TNA.
154 H.N. Sporborg to Cavendish-Bentinck, 23 June 1945, FO 1093/198.
155 Peter Loxley to Rex Leeper, 27 June 1944, FO 1093/195, TNA.
156 Selborne to Prime Minister, 4 November 1943, HS 5/310, and John Harvey, ed., *The War Diaries of Oliver Harvey* (London: 1978), 7 November 1943.
157 Cavendish-Bentinck to Sir Orme Sargent, 25 May 1945, FO 1093/198.
158 Note by Victor Cavendish-Bentinck, 25 June 1945, and Cavendish-Bentinck Report on SOE, 31 July 1945, FO 1093/198, TNA.
159 Liddell Diary, 29 October 1945, KV 4/466, TNA.
160 Hale, 'SOE in Europe, 1938–1945'.
161 SIS, VCSS's Lectures (copy to Mr Lionel Hale), 16 May 1946, HS 7/1, TNA.

162 C to Cadogan, 2 November 1944, FO 1093/196, TNA.
163 Sir David Petrie to Sir Anthony Eden, 26 June 1944, KV 4/87, TNA.
164 Murphy, *Security and Special Operations*, 3–4.
165 Major-General K.W.D. Strong to Sir David Petrie, 10 November 1944, KV 4/100, TNA.
166 SHAEF G-2 Counter-Intelligence War Room: Statement of Agreement between Director of the War Room and the Heads of the Special Services, [20] February 1945, KV 4/100, TNA.
167 T.A. Robertson (Director, War Room) to Bird, 30 August 1945, KV 4/100, TNA.
168 'History of the Counter-Intelligence War Room, March 1–November 1, 1945', KV 4/100, TNA.
169 Liddell Diary, 25 August 1945, KV 4/466, TNA.
170 G. Sampson, 'Report on Camp 020', 20 September 1945, KV 4/8; Lt-Col. Baxter, 'History of the London Reception Centre, 1940 to 1945', [July 1945], KV 4/7, TNA.
171 Liddell Diary, 29 October 1945, KV 4/466, TNA.
172 Liddell Diary, 8 August 1945, KV 4/466, TNA.
173 Liddell Diary, 13 September 1945, KV 4/466, TNA.
174 *Liddell Diaries, 1942–1945*, 27 January 1945.
175 Murphy, *Security and Special Operations*, 148-69.
176 *Liddell Diaries, 1942–1945*, 20 December 1944.
177 *Liddell Diaries, 1942–1945*, 10 February 1944.
178 *Liddell Diaries, 1942–1945*, 7, 10 and 12 February 1945.
179 Liddell Diary, 28 June 1945, KV 4/466, TNA.
180 Ben Wheatley, 'Revisited: The Security Service's Investigation of the British *Abwehr/SD* Agent Ronald Sydney Seth', *Journal of Intelligence History* 16 (2017), 116–49.
181 Liddell Diary, 29 October 1945, KV 4/466, TNA.
182 Wilson (B1W) to Colonel Stephens (Camp 020), 24 May 1945, KV 2/961; 'Translation from the Dutch [of the interrogation of Protze], HQ Netherlands Security Service, 3 April to 1 May 1946', and Protze, 'Home-Work', [April 1946], KV 2/1740, TNA.
183 Liddell Diary, 27 July 1945, KV 4/466, TNA.
184 Liddell Diary, 18 June 1945, KV 4/466, TNA.
185 Liddell Diary, 8 August 1945, KV 4/466, TNA.
186 Liddell Diary, 24 September 1945, KV 4/466, TNA.
187 Camp 020, 'Meisner/Ludwig/Giskes', 21 August 1945, KV 2/963, TNA.
188 Masterman, 'The Double-Cross System in the War of 1939 to 1945'.
189 T. Harris, 'Summary of the GARBO Case, 1941–1945', 21 November 1945, in *GARBO: The Spy Who Saved D-Day*, ed. Mark Seaman (London: 2000).
190 Masterman, 'The Double-Cross System in the War of 1939 to 1945'.

191 Liddell Diary, 29 October 1945, KV 4/466, and Montagu, 'The W. Board'.
192 Masterman, 'The Double-Cross System in the War of 1939 to 1945'.
193 W. Board, Minutes of Meeting, 10 May 1945, in Montagu, 'The W. Board'.
194 Masterman, 'The Double-Cross System in the War of 1939 to 1945'.
195 Montagu, 'The W. Board'.
196 Baxter, 'History of the London Reception Centre, 1940 to 1945'.
197 Sir John Dashwood, 'Alleged Leakage at Ankara', 9 August 1945, FO 370/2930, TNA.
198 Masterman, 'The Double-Cross System in the War of 1939 to 1945'.
199 Ibid.
200 Ibid.
201 Liddell Diary, 29 October 1945, KV 4/466, TNA.
202 Harris, 'Summary of the GARBO Case, 1941–1945', 21 November 1945.
203 W Board, Minutes of Meeting, 13 July 1941, in Montagu, 'The W. Board'.
204 W Board, Minutes of Meeting, 28 March 1942, in Montagu, 'The W. Board'.
205 W Board, Minutes of Meeting, 10 May 1945, in Montagu, 'The W. Board'.
206 Liddell Diary, 23 October 1945, KV 4/466, TNA.
207 Cooper to Churchill, FO 1093/194, TNA.
208 Duff Cooper to Sir David Petrie, 5 April 1943, KV 4/448, TNA.
209 Eden to Herbert Morrison, 22 November 1944, FO 1093/197, TNA.
210 Sir Edward Bridges to Peter Loxley, 13 June 1944, CAB 21/3499; Loxley to Cadogan, 18 December 1944, and Sir Alexander Maxwell to Sir Edward Bridges, 29 January 1945, FO 1093/197, TNA.
211 Sir Herbert Creedy, 'The Future of the Security Executive', March 1945, CAB 21/3499, TNA.
212 Peter Loxley to Sir Alec Cadogan, 7 June 1944, FO 1093/197.
213 Sir David Petrie, 'Draft. Re-adjustments in the Functions of MI5 and MI6', January 1945, CAB 301/11, and Liddell Diary, 6 July 1945, KV 4/466, TNA.
214 Liddell Diary, 12 October 1945, KV 4/466, TNA.
215 Liddell Diary, 22 and 25 June 1945, KV 4/466, TNA.
216 J.P. de C. Day, B.1.B, to ADB 1, 26 April 1943, KV 4/115, TNA.
217 Findlater Stewart Report, 27 November 1945, and Daniel Lomas, 'The Defence of the Realm and Nothing Else: Sir Findlater Stewart, Labour Ministers, and the Security Service', *Intelligence and National Security* 30 (2015), 793–816.

CHAPTER FIVE

1 JIC (49) 123rd Meeting, 25 November 1949, FO 1093/388, TNA. The proposal before the JIC on this occasion was for a book on resistance movements written by the former head of SOE, Colin Gubbins.
2 Liddell Diary, 16 January 1946, KV 4/467, TNA.
3 Liddell Diary, 7 February 1946, KV 4/467, TNA.

4 Desmond Morton to R.C.S. Stevenson (FO), 14 January 1941, PREM 7/6, TNA, and Prime Minister to Sir Donald Somervell (Attorney-General), 25 March 1941, CHAR 20/21, CAC.
5 Liddell Diary, 7 May 1946, KV 4/467, TNA.
6 Extract from Best to Menzies, 15 January 1946, FO 1093/339, TNA.
7 Captain S. Payne Best, *The Venlo Incident* (London: 1950).
8 C to Harold Caccia, 9 February 1946, FO 1093/339, TNA.
9 Colonel R. Stephens to Brigadier O.A. Harker, 28 March 1946, KV 4/8, TNA.
10 O.A. Harker to Colonel R. Stephens, HQ CSDIC (WEA), BAOR, KV 4/8, TNA.
11 [R. Stephens and R. Short], 'A Digest of Ham, 1940–47', Hoare, *Camp 020*.
12 [R. Stephens], 'Editor's Note' for 'A Digest of Ham, 1940–47'.
13 [R. Stephens], 'A Digest of Ham, Volume One: A Digest of Ham on the Interrogation of Spies, 1940–47', 117–18.
14 Liddell Diary, 28 June 1947, KV 4/469, TNA.
15 Liddell Diary, 1 August 1946, KV 4/467, TNA.
16 Liddell Diary, 28 June 1947, KV 4/469, TNA.
17 Liddell Diary, 28 June 1947, KV 4/469, TNA.
18 Liddell Diary, 28 June 1947, KV 4/469, TNA.
19 [R. Stephens], 'A Digest of Ham, Volume One: A Digest of Ham on the Interrogation of Spies, 1940–47', 103.
20 'The History of PWIS (H), [1945], and 'The History of CSDIC (UK), [1945], WO 208/4970, TNA.
21 A.P. Scotland, 'The London Cage' (1954), WO 208/5381, TNA, and Helen Fry, *The London Cage: The Secret History of Britain's World War II Interrogation Centre* (London: 2017), Chapters 11 and 13.
22 Liddell Diary, 19 July 1948, KV 4/470, TNA.
23 Liddell Diary, 24 April 1948, KV 4/470, TNA.
24 Liddell Diary, 27 April 1948, KV 4/470, TNA.
25 Liddell Diary, 18 December 1947, KV 4/469, TNA.
26 Daniel Lomas, *Intelligence, Security, and the Attlee Governments, 1945–1951: An Uneasy Relationship?* (Manchester: 2016).
27 Liddell Diary, 24 March 1948, KV 4/470, TNA.
28 Liddell Diary, 22 April 1949, KV 4/471, TNA.
29 Liddell Diary, 16 April 1948, KV 4/470, TNA.
30 Liddell Diary, 24 March 1948, KV 4/470, TNA.
31 JIC (45) 255 (O), 'Release of Captured Documents', 17 August 1945, HW 14/134, TNA.
32 Christopher Moran, *Classified*, 101.
33 '£52,000,000 Secrets', *Daily Mail*, 2 May 1946, 3.
34 Montague Smith, 'That's the Way the Money Goes, Pop Goes the Budget,' *Daily Mail*, 9 April 1946, 2. Real price calculation by the present author.

35 Professor R.V. Jones, 'Scientific Intelligence', *Journal of the Royal United Service Institution* 92 (1947), 352–69.
36 Major-General Sir Colin Gubbins, K.C.M.G., D.S.O., M.C., 'Resistance Movements in the War', *Royal United Service Institution Journal* 93 (1948), 210–23.
37 Sir Robert H. Bruce Lockhart, 'Political Warfare', *Journal of the Royal United Service Institution* 95 (1950), 193–206.
38 J.R.M. Butler, 'The British Official Military History of the Second World War', *Military Affairs* 22 (1958), 149–51, and Robin Higham, ed., *Official Military Historical Offices and Sources: Europe, Africa, the Middle East, and India* (Westport: 2000).
39 JIC (51) 124, 'Official History of British War Production by Professor H.M. Postan', 14 December 1951, CAB 158/13, TNA.
40 Brook to Hubback, 28 January 1948, CAB 104/282, TNA.
41 Liddell Diary, 4 February 1948, KV 4/470, TNA.
42 E.G. Hastings, for Director, LSIC to CSS, 3 February 1948, CAB 104/282, TNA.
43 Minute for Sir Norman Brook, CAB 103/595, TNA.
44 Peter Beck, 'Locked in a Dusty Cupboard'.
45 'The Security Executive: An Outline of Its Course and Functions', February 1946, CAB 21/3498, and 'History of the Postal and Telegraphic Censorship Department, 1938–1946'.
46 Liddell Diary, 15 January 1946, KV 4/467, TNA.
47 Liddell Diary, 22 July 1946, KV 4/467, TNA.
48 JIC (49) 125th Meeting, 2 December 1949, FO 1093/388, TNA.
49 [Colpoys], 'The Use of Special' with additional comments by R.T. Barrett, ADM 223/469, TNA.
50 William Mackenzie, *The Secret History of SOE*.
51 'A Short Note on the Security Service and Its Responsibilities', October 1946, KV 4/158, TNA.
52 Liddell Diary, 22 July 1946, KV 4/467, TNA.
53 Liddell Diary, 22 February 1946, KV 4/467, TNA.
54 Minutes of an Ad Hoc Meeting of Ministers on 7 March 1946, 11 March 1946, CAB 301/31, TNA.
55 Directive to the Director-General, Security Service, 17 April 1946, CAB 301/30.
56 Liddell Diary, 22 July 1946, KV 4/467, TNA.
57 Liddell Diary, 18 June 1946, KV 4/467, TNA.
58 [Ellingworth], 'The History of the War Office Y Group, 1926–1945', April 1948.
59 'History of Military SIGINT', February 1950.
60 'History of Military SIGINT'.
61 Liddell Diary, 23 September 1948, KV 4/470, TNA.
62 Head of S Department, GCHQ to HHS, Queensgate (Mr Griffiths) n.d., HW 34/1, TNA.

63 Memorandum by Mr de Grey on Lessons of 1939–45 War for Future War, 17 August 1949, HW 14/145, TNA.
64 Griffiths, 'Secret Service Sigint'.
65 SIS, VCSS's Lectures, 16 May 1946, HS 7/1, TNA.
66 Liddell Diary, 2 January 1946, KV 4/467, and 25 June 1947, KV 4/469, TNA.
67 Andrew Defty, *Britain, America, and Anti-Communist Propaganda: The Information Research Department, 1945–1953* (Abingdon: 2004), 27.
68 Garnett, *The Secret History of PWE*, 'Introduction', February 1947.
69 COS (48) 36th, Confidential Annex, 10 March 1948, FO 1093/375, TNA.
70 Sir Orme Sargent to Secretary of State, 30 March 1948, with Bevin's comment, FO 1093/375, TNA.
71 COS (48) 36th, Confidential Annex, 10 March 1948, FO 1093/375, TNA.
72 Norman Brook to William Hayter, 'Anti-Communist Propaganda: Note by the Secretary of the Cabinet', 23 March 1948, FO 1093/375, TNA.
73 Garnett, *The Secret History of PWE*, 'Introduction', February 1947.
74 COS (48) 36th, 10 March 1948.
75 'DMI War Diary, 1939–1945' and 'The Story of MI19'.
76 Brigadier E.E. Mockler-Ferryman, 'Military Intelligence Organisation', 1952, WO 33/2723, TNA.
77 MI4/14, 'Use of ULTRA by MI14', 21 December 1945, HW 3/173, TNA.
78 Major O'Donovan (MI14) to Major Bennett [Bletchley], 4 January 1946, HW 3/173, TNA.
79 Brigadier Williams, 'The Use of Ultra', 5 October 1945, WO 208/3575, TNA.
80 MI4/14, 'Use of ULTRA by MI14', 21 December 1945.
81 Hirsch (DDMI) to Bennett, 14 January 1946, HW 3/72, TNA.
82 Technical Sub-Committee on Axis Oil, AO (46) 1, 'Oil as a Factor in the German War Effort, 1933–1945, Annex A: The Intelligence Assessment of the German Oil Position', 8 March 1946, CAB 81/133, TNA.
83 John Godfrey, 'Joint Intelligence Committee (JIC) and Joint Intelligence Staff (JIS)', 2 May 1947, ADM 223/851, TNA.
84 Williams, 'The Use of Ultra', 5 October 1945.
85 [Lt-Col. L. Kirwan and Major G. Waterfield], 'Use of Ultra by JIS (Military)', annotated by [Brigadier] Hirsch, 26 February 1946, HW 3/172, TNA.
86 JIC (46) 33 (Final), 'Some Weaknesses in German Strategy and Organisation, 1933–1945', 20 October 1946, CAB 81/132, TNA. Widely circulated.
87 [Ronald Wingate], 'Historical Record of Deception in the War against Germany and Italy', [1945–46], CAB 154/100 and 101, TNA.
88 Liddell Diary, 14 January 1946 and 20 May 1946, KV 4/467, TNA.
89 Roger Hesketh, 'A History of Strategic Deception in North Western Europe, April 1943 to May 1945', [1949 and 1976], eventually published as Roger Hesketh, *Fortitude: The D-Day Deception Campaign*, ed. Nigel West (Woodstock, 2002).

90 JIC (46) 33 (Final), 'Some Weaknesses in German Strategy and Organisation, 1933–1945', 20 October 1946.

91 Liddell Diary, 4 October 1948, KV 4/470, TNA.

92 LCS (48) 3, 'Russian Knowledge of Deception', 27 July 1948, FO 1093/380, TNA.

93 Liddell Diary, 25 October 1949, KV 4/471, TNA.

94 Liddell Diary, 27 April 1946, KV 4/467, TNA.

95 Liddell Diary, 10 October 1946, KV 4/468, TNA.

96 Liddell Diary, 14 October 1946, KV 4/468, TNA.

97 Liddell Diary, 10 March 1948, KV 4/470, TNA.

98 Misc/P (47) 31, 'Review of Intelligence Organisations, 1947: Report by Air Chief Marshal Sir Douglas Evill', 6 November 1947, CAB 163/7, TNA.

99 The Evill Report, 6 November 1947.

100 Group-Captain P.J.A. Riddell, 'Photographic Reconnaissance and Intelligence', Lecture to Royal United Service Institution, 22 November 1944, published in *Journal of the Royal United Service Institution* [RUSI], 90 (1945), 79–92; AHB (1), 'RAF Narrative: Photographic Reconnaissance', [1945], AIR 41/6 and AHB (1), 'RAF Narrative: Photographic Reconnaissance', [1948], AIR 41/7, TNA.

101 The Evill Report, 6 November 1947.

102 JIC/1185/49, 'Review of Evill Report by John Gardiner, Secretary of JIC', 4 July 1949, FO 1093/387, TNA.

103 Minutes of a Meeting on the Organisation of JIC and JIS, 3 December 1948, CAB 163/6, TNA.

104 John Godfrey, Introduction to Monograph 1, January 1947, ADM 223/466, TNA.

105 Liddell Diary, 21 June 1947, KV 4/469, and John Godfrey, 'Truth, Reality, and Publicity', November 1947, ADM 223/466, TNA.

106 Godfrey to DNI [Vice-Admiral Edward Parry], 1 March 1947, ADM 223/469, TNA.

107 John Godfrey, 'History of the Measures Taken in the Admiralty to Safeguard the Security of Special Intelligence', 7 May 1947, ADM 223/469, TNA.

108 Godfrey, 'Truth, Reality, and Publicity', November 1947.

109 J.H. Godfrey, 'The Navy and Naval Intelligence, 1939–1942: Afterthoughts', 4 November 1950, ADM 223/619, TNA.

110 John Godfrey, Comments on Charles Morgan, 'Problem of Relations between NID and C', ADM 223/851, TNA.

111 Later marginal note on F.W. Birch, 'A Contribution to the History of German Naval Warfare, 1914–1918, Volume 1: The Fleet in Action', 2 July 1920, HW 7/1, TNA.

112 [Colpoys], 'The Use of Special'.

113 'Note by NID9 Officer, 1939–45', ADM 223/469, TNA.

114 De Grey, 'Lessons of 1939–45', 17 August 1949.

115 Nigel de Grey to Eric Jones, 7 August 1949, HW 14/145, TNA.
116 De Grey, 'Lessons of 1939–45', 17 August 1949.
117 There were indoctrinated women: the teleprinters in the Operational Intelligence Centre (NID 8) in the Admiralty, receiving decrypts from Bletchley Park, for instance, were run by female staff. The indoctrinated female intelligence officer, as opposed to ancillary staff member, was vanishingly rare. Jane Archer of MI5 and SIS was the case cited in the MI5 history. The histories of the 1940s devoted space to female staff as support workers, usually in 'women's sections'. See Paddy Hayes, *Queen of Spies: Daphne Park, Britain's Cold War Spy Master* (London: 2015) for an account of a woman who wanted to be an intelligence officer.
118 Rory Cormac, *Disrupt and Deny: Spies, Special Forces, and the Secret Pursuit of British Foreign Policy* (Oxford: 2018), 3 and *passim.*
119 Roger Arditti, 'Security Intelligence in the Middle East (SIME): Joint Security Intelligence Operations in the Middle East, 1939–1958', *Intelligence and National Security* 31 (2016), 369–96.
120 Sir Gerald Templer, 'Report on Colonial Security', 23 April 1955, CAB 129/76, TNA; David French, *The British Way in Counter-Insurgency, 1945–1967* (Oxford: 2011), 19–41; and Rory Cormac, *Confronting the Colonies: British Intelligence and Counterinsurgency* (Oxford: 2013), Chapters 2 and 3.

CHAPTER SIX

1 C to Cadogan, 20 September 1945, FO 1093/199, TNA.
2 C to Sargent, 25 June 1948, FO 1093/447, TNA.
3 Gill Bennett, *The Zinoviev Letter: The Conspiracy that Never Dies* (Oxford: 2018).
4 'Sir Joseph Jonas fined £2,000', *The Times*, 30 July 1918.
5 J.C. Curry, 'The Security Service: Its Problems and Organisational Adjustments, 1908–1945', March 1946.
6 Eric Ambler, *The Dark Frontier* (1936) and *Cause for Alarm* (1938).
7 'German Long Range Weapons', [November 1944], AIR 20/2364; 'Crossbow Draft History, November 1944, WO 106/5182, [The Black History]; ACIU, 'Crossbow: History of the PI Investigation, 1943–1945', September 1945, AIR 34/80; Air Defence Division, SHAEF, 'An Account of the Continental Crossbow Operation, 1944–1945', AIR 37/999, TNA.
8 Liddell Diary, 17 October 1945, KV 4/466, TNA.
9 Joan Paine to H.A.R. Philby, 18 November 1946, KV 2/1740, TNA.
10 Translation from the Dutch, HQ Netherlands Security Service, 3 April to 1 May 1946, KV 2/1740.
11 Protze, 'Home-Work', [April 1946], KV 2/1740, TNA.
12 Liddell Diary, 28 November 1949, KV 4/471, TNA.

13 Sir William Strang, Letter to Missions Overseas, 20 June 1952, CAB 21/3878, TNA.
14 Liddell Diary, 16 October 1947, KV 4/469, TNA.
15 Liddell Diary, 19 February 1951, KV 4/473, and 5 January 1953, KV 4/475, TNA.
16 Liddell Diary, 4, 5, 6 July 1951, KV 4/473, TNA.
17 Liddell Diary, 1, 7, 8, 28 February 1952, KV 4/474, TNA.
18 Norman Brook, Note for the Record, 28 April 1950, CAB 301/18, TNA.
19 Liddell Diary, 1 February 1950, KV 4/472, TNA.
20 Liddell Diary, 4 March 1950, KV 4/472, TNA.
21 Norman Brook, Note for the Record, 28 April 1950, CAB 301/18, TNA.
22 Edward Bridges to Norman Brook, 25 May 1950, CAB 301/18, TNA.
23 Liddell Diary, 24 January 1950, KV 4/472, TNA.
24 Liddell Diary, 1 March 1950, KV 4/472, TNA.
25 John Prebble, 'A War Spy in the British Embassy', *Daily Express*, 15 January 1950, KV 6/8, TNA.
26 Liddell Diary, 21 October 1950, KV 4/472, TNA.
27 Liddell Diary, 31 May 1950, KV 4/472, and Edward Bridges to William Strang, 31 May 1950, CAB 301/18 TNA.
28 Christian Schlaepfer, 'Signals Intelligence and British Counter-subversion in the Early Cold War', *Intelligence and National Security* 29 (2014), 82–98.
29 Attlee to Sillitoe and Menzies, 6 June 1950, CAB 301/18, TNA.
30 Liddell Diary, 14 November 1945, KV 4/467, TNA.
31 Liddell to Cadogan, 24 September 1945, FO 1093/538, TNA.
32 'Soviet Espionage Organisation in Canada', 19 March 1946, FO 1093/540, TNA.
33 Guy Liddell to Harold Caccia, 2 August 1946, FO 1093/541, TNA.
34 Liddell Diary, 25 November 1947, KV 4/469, TNA.
35 Liddell Diary, 9 August 1949, KV 4/471, TNA.
36 Liddell Diary, 20 September 1949, KV 4/471, TNA.
37 Liddell Diary, 5 December 1949, KV 4/471, TNA.
38 British-US Communication Intelligence Agreement, 5 March 1946, HW 80/4, TNA.
39 Liddell Diary, 19 December 1949, KV 4/471, TNA.
40 Liddell Diary, 17 March 1950, KV 4/472, TNA.
41 Liddell Diary, 30 December 1949, KV 4/471, TNA.
42 Liddell Diary, 17 March 1950, KV 4/472, TNA.
43 Liddell Diary, 31 May 1950, KV 4/472, and Edward Bridges to William Strang, 31 May 1950, CAB 301/18 TNA.
44 Edward Bridges to Prime Minister, CAB 301/18, TNA.
45 Liddell Diary, 27 July 1950, KV 4/472, TNA.
46 Rodney Lowe, *The Official History of the British Civil Service: Reforming the British Civil Service: The Fulton Years, 1966–1981* (Abingdon: 2011), 54–5.

47 Norman Brook to Prime Minister, 25 October 1950, PREM 8/1527, TNA.
48 Ibid.
49 'The Secret Intelligence and Security Services: Report of Enquiry by Sir Norman Brook' [The Brook Report], March 1951, CAB 301/17, TNA.
50 Emanuel Shinwell to Prime Minister, 13 October 1950, PREM 8/1527, TNA.
51 The Secret Intelligence and Security Services: Note of a Meeting held in the Prime Minister's Room, House of Commons, on Tuesday, 5th June, 1951, at 5.30 pm, 11 June 1951, CAB 301/18, TNA.
52 Liddell Diary, 16 June 1950, KV 4/472, TNA.
53 E. Compton to Sir Norman Brook, 'Cost of the Secret Service', 16 June 1950, CAB 301/19, TNA.
54 SIS Expenditure [June 1950] and Sillitoe to Brook, 21 June 1950, CAB 301/20, TNA.
55 The Brook Report, March 1951.
56 Ibid.
57 John Godfrey to DNI, 'Security of Naval Intelligence', 1 March 1947, ADM 223/469; Liddell Diary, 28 October 1949, KV 4/471 and 17 October 1950, KV 4/472, TNA.
58 Drew to Cliffe, 12 January 1951, CAB 301/19, TNA.
59 Norman Brook, 'Value of SIS Intelligence', 5 June 1951, CAB 301/18, TNA.
60 Norman Brook, 'Value of SIS Intelligence'.
61 Norman Brook to Prime Minister, 25 October 1950, PREM 8/1527, TNA.
62 Sir William Elliott to Minister of Defence, 21 June 1951, CAB 301/120, TNA.
63 Norman Brook, Interviews at Leconfield House, 7 July 1950, CAB 301/20, TNA.
64 Liddell Diary, 1 November 1950, KV 4/472, TNA.
65 Liddell Diary, 5 July 1950, KV 4/472, TNA.
66 Counter Espionage: Some Statistics of Work Done since Autumn 1945, [July 1950], CAB 301/20, TNA.
67 Subversive Movements: Some Statistics of Work Done since Autumn 1945, [July 1950], CAB 301/20, TNA.
68 Liddell Diary, 2 June 1950, KV 4/472, TNA.
69 Norman Brook, Interviews at Leconfield House, 12 July 1950, CAB 301/20, TNA.
70 'B Division', [July 1950], CAB 301/20, TNA.
71 Norman Brook, Interviews at Leconfield House, 7 July 1950.
72 Norman Brook, Interviews at Leconfield House, 12 July 1950.
73 Ibid.
74 Liddell Diary, 27 July 1950, KV 4/472, TNA.
75 Norman Brook, Interviews at Leconfield House, 7 July 1950.
76 The Brook Report, March 1951.
77 Bridges, Note for the Record, 11 April 1951, CAB 301/18, TNA.
78 Norman Brook, Interviews at Leconfield House, 7 July 1950.

79 Norman Brook, Interviews at Leconfield House, 14 July 1950.
80 Liddell Diary, 1 May 1951, KV 4/473, TNA.
81 Liddell Diary, 21 and 23 October 1950, KV 4/472, TNA.
82 The Brook Report, March 1951.
83 Brook, 'Value of SIS Intelligence', 5 June 1951.
84 The Brook Report, March 1951.
85 C to Strang, 16 April 1951, CAB 301/18, TNA.
86 Jeffery, *MI6*, 669–71.
87 Kristie Macrakis, 'Can a Tunnel Become a Double Agent – for the Soviets?' *International Journal of Intelligence and CounterIntelligence* 31 (2018), 374–86.
88 'Relations between the Secret Service (SIS) and the Security Service', 29 April 1949, FO 1093/380, TNA.
89 Liddell Diary, 30 March 1949, KV 4/471, TNA.
90 Ibid.
91 Memorandum of Agreement between Heads of Services, July 1949, FO 1093/380, TNA.
92 Norman Brook to Prime Minister, 25 October 1950, PREM 8/1527, TNA.
93 Liddell Diary, 2 March 1949, KV 4/471, TNA.
94 'CE Activities of SIS in Relation to those of the Security Service', [June 1950], CAB 301/21, TNA.
95 C.A.L. Cliffe to Norman Brook, 28 November 1950, CAB 301/18, TNA.
96 Norman Brook, Note for the Record, 5 December 1950, CAB 301/18, TNA.
97 'Organisation', 20 June 1950, CAB 301/21, TNA.
98 R. Gambier-Parry to John Drew, 25 September 1950, CAB 301/18, TNA.
99 The Brook Report, March 1951.
100 SIS Expenditure [June 1950], CAB 301/19, TNA.
101 Report of Committee of Enquiry [Cadogan Report], 1 November 1951, CAB 301/120, TNA; Michael Hughes and Douglas Platt, 'Far Apart but Close Together: A Quantitative and Qualitative Analysis of the Career Structure and Organisational Culture of the Post-War British Diplomatic Service', *Diplomacy and Statecraft* 26 (2015), 266–93.
102 'The SIS Cover Problem', [April 1951], CAB 301/21, TNA.
103 GEN. 374/1st Meeting, 11 July 1951, CAB 301/23, TNA.
104 ACORN Brief [October 1950], CAB 301/18, TNA.
105 C.A.L. Cliffe to Sir Norman Brook, [July 1951], CAB 301/22, TNA.
106 Vice-Admiral P.W. Brooking (Retrd.), Report on Noise Listening, [July 1951], CAB 301/22, TNA.
107 Liddell Diary, 13 June 1951, KV 4/473, TNA.
108 Liddell Diary, 7 July 1951, KV 4/473, TNA.
109 The Cadogan Report, 1 November 1951.
110 Unless otherwise noted, the account of Soviet intelligence is based on Haslam, *Near and Distant Neighbours*.

111 Richard Thurlow, 'Soviet Spies and British Counter-Intelligence in the 1930s: Espionage in the Woolwich Arsenal and the Foreign Office Communications Department', *Intelligence and National Security* 19 (2004), 610–31.
112 Zdzisław Kapera, 'Summary Report of the State of the Soviet Military Sigint in November 1942 Noticing "ENIGMA"', *Cryptologia* 35 (2011), 247–56.
113 [C.A.L. Cliffe], 'Survey of Russian Espionage in Britain, 1935–1955', [May 1956], KV 3/417, TNA.
114 Liddell, *Diaries*, 14 August 1941.
115 Robert Pringle, 'SMERSH: Military Counterintelligence and Stalin's Control of the USSR', *International Journal of Intelligence and CounterIntelligence* 21 (2008), 122–34.
116 Liddell Diary, 19 January 1948, KV 4/470, TNA.
117 Liddell Diary, 9 August 1949, KV 4/471, TNA.
118 Leslie Hollis to William Hayter, 15 July 1948, FO 1093/380, TNA.
119 R.H. Hillenkoeter [Director of Central Intelligence] to Stewart Menzies, 20 June 1949, FO 1093/563, TNA.
120 Cormac, *Disrupt and Deny*, 38–56.
121 Christopher Andrew and Vasili Mitrokhin, *The Mitrokhin Archive: The KGB in Europe and the West* (London: 2000), 185–6.
122 Liddell Diary, 14 March 1952, KV 4/474, TNA.
123 The Cadogan Report, 1 November 1951.
124 Liddell Diary, 7 July 1951, KV 4/473, TNA.
125 Liddell Diary, 1 October 1951, KV 4/473, TNA.
126 Liddell Diary, 22 October 1951, KV 4/473, TNA.
127 Liddell Diary, 7 December 1951, KV 4/473, TNA.
128 Liddell Diary, 21 December 1951, KV 4/473, TNA.
129 Ben Macintyre, *A Spy Among Friends: Philby and the Great Betrayal* (London: 2014), 171–7.
130 Cliffe, 'Survey of Russian Espionage in Britain, 1935–1955', [May 1956].
131 Liddell Diary, 3 October, KV 4/474, TNA.
132 *The Times*, 26 October 1955, 4.
133 Burgess and Maclean: Notes for Speech in Reply to the Address, [February 1956], CAB 21/3878, TNA.
134 A.J. de la Mare to Sir Frank Newsam, 6 November 1955, CAB 21/3878, TNA.
135 C.A.L. Cliffe (D1B) to D1 (Courtnay Young), 16 April 1956, KV 3/417, TNA.
136 Cliffe, 'Russian Espionage in Britain, 1935-1955'.
137 Ibid.
138 Ibid.
139 Ibid.
140 Ibid.
141 Liddell Diary, 19 April 1951, KV 4/473, TNA.
142 Cliffe, 'Russian Espionage in Britain, 1935–1955'.

143 Richard Aldrich, 'Soviet Intelligence, British Security, and the End of the Red Orchestra: The Fate of Alexander Rado', *Intelligence and National Security* 6 (1991), 196–217.
144 Liddell Diary, 28 January 1949, KV 4/471, TNA.
145 Cliffe, 'Russian Espionage in Britain, 1935–1955'.
146 Ibid.
147 William Tyrer, 'The Unresolved Mystery of ELLI', *International Journal of Intelligence and CounterIntelligence* 29 (2016), 785–808.
148 Liddell Diary, 24 October 1945, KV 4/466, TNA.
149 Cliffe, 'Russian Espionage in Britain, 1935–1955'.
150 Ibid.
151 Ibid.
152 *Liddell Diaries, 1942–1945*, 7 February 1945.
153 Cliffe, 'Russian Espionage in Britain, 1935–1955'.
154 Ibid.
155 Liddell Diary, 1 January 1953, KV 4/475, TNA.
156 Liddell Diary, 5 September 1952, KV 4/474, TNA.
157 Isaac, 'The History of the Development of the Directorate of Military Intelligence'.
158 Liddell Diary, 28 October 1949, KV 4/471; 17 October 1950, 9 November 1950, 16 November 1950, KV 4/472; 7 April 1951, 5 May 1951, KV 4/473; 5 January 1953, 14 January 1953, 23 February 1953, KV 4/475, TNA.
159 Ewen Montagu, *The Man Who Never Was* (London: 2003 [1953]).
160 Ian Fleming, *Casino Royale* (London: 2012 [1953]) and *From Russia with Love* (London: 2004 [1957]).

CONCLUSION

1 Sassmann and Schmitt, Report on 'Cultures of Intelligence'.
2 R. Gerald Hughes, Philip Murphy, and Philip Davies, 'The British Secret Intelligence Service, 1909–1949', *Intelligence and National Security* 26 (2011), 701–29.
3 Thomas F. Troy, 'The "Correct" Definition of Intelligence', *International Journal of Intelligence and CounterIntelligence* 5 (1991), 433–54.
4 Morgan, 'Naval Intelligence, 1939–1942'.

Index

Please note that page numbers in *italics* denote images.